Veröffentlichungen zum Verfahrensrecht
Band 45

herausgegeben von
Rolf Stürner und Gerhard Walter

Christoph Kern

Justice between Simplification and Formalism

A Discussion and Critique of the World Bank Sponsored Lex Mundi Project on Efficiency of Civil Procedure

Mohr Siebeck

Christoph Alexander Kern, born 1975; studied law in Goettingen, Geneva (Switzerland) and Freiburg i.Br.; 2004 Doctoral degree (Ph.D.) in law; 2006 LL.M. (Harvard); Research Assistant at Freiburg University.

ISBN 978-3-16-149247-1
ISSN 0722-7574 (Veröffentlichungen zum Verfahrensrecht)

The Deutsche Nationalbibliothek lists this publication in the Deutsche Nationalbibliographie; detailed bibliographic data is available in the Internet at *http://dnb.d-nb.de.*

The book was printed by Gulde-Druck in Tübingen on non-aging paper and bound by Buchbinderei Held in Rottenburg.

Printed in Germany.

Preface

Civil procedure is often regarded as a complicated and merely technical matter, as a field of law where small mistakes as to the form of a procedural act may be decisive for winning or losing in court. It cannot surprise that a field of law with such a reputation comes under scrutiny in today's world, where it seems that in all economically relevant areas liberalization and deregulation is king.

In 2003, four well-known economists – Simeon Djankov, Rafael La Porta, Florencio Lopez-de-Silanes and Andrei Shleifer – have published in the Quarterly Journal of Economics a study on procedural formalism and judicial quality in 109 countries. This study, funded by the World Bank and Yale School of Management, is based on data collected from lawyers about the civil procedural law in their respective country, and on other available sources. The authors combine the data using statistical methods and provide an interpretation of their findings.

The present small book offers a first analysis of this study from the perspective of a legal scholar who had the pleasure of following closely the recent developments in comparative civil procedure at an institute dedicated to research in the field of civil procedural law. It is the amended version of an LL.M. paper which has been written in conjunction with Professor Peter L. Murray's seminar *Comparative Law: European and American Civil Justice* at Harvard Law School in fall 2005.

The author would like to express his deepest appreciation and gratitude to Peter L. Murray, Edward L. Johnston Lecturer on Law and Robert Braucher Visiting Professor of Law from Practice, Harvard Law School, and to Rolf Stürner, professor of law at the University of Freiburg, Germany and a judge on the State Court of Appeals of Karlsruhe, Germany. He is also indebted to Nicole Binder, Research Assistant in the Department of Empirical Economic Research and Econometrics at the University of Freiburg, for considerable input on an earlier draft of this paper. Thanks are due as well to Marietta Auer, assistant professor (Wissenschaftliche Assistentin), University of Munich, Germany, and S.J.D. Candidate at Harvard Law School, to Holger Spamann, Terence M. Cosidine Fellow and S.J.D. Candidate at Harvard Law School, and to the author's LL.M. colleagues and friends Silvana Schenone de Kavanagh, Jeanette Aliaga, Ephyro Amatong, Gabriel Ejgenberg, Freddy Escobar, Haim Machluf and Pablo Marquez as well as to the staff of Harvard Law School's graduate program. Last but not least, he gratefully acknowledges the German law firm Gleiss Lutz and the German Academic Exchange Service (Deutscher Akademischer Austauschdienst, DAAD) for their financial support of his LL.M. studies at Harvard Law School (Alfred-Gleiss-Fellowship 2005).

Freiburg im Breisgau, September 2006 *Christoph Kern*

Table of Contents

Part I

Introduction

Economics scholars are celebrating the revival in recent years of Comparative Economics.[1] Indeed, this discipline, whose main interest historically was a comparison between capitalism and socialism,[2] and which obviously lost much of its appeal with the collapse of socialism in Eastern Europe and the Soviet Union,[3] has discovered that there exist considerable differences among those economic systems we generally regard as capitalist economies. Consequently, Comparative Economics scholars have started to focus on comparing capitalist economies. To date, such comparisons cover various special aspects, as, for example, private credit,[4] the regulation of labor[5] and the regulation and supervision of banks,[6] media ownership,[7] and the regulation of entry of start-up firms.[8]

---

[1] Simeon Djankov, Edward L. Glaeser, Rafael La Porta, Florencio Lopez-de-Silanes & Andrei Shleifer, *The New Comparative Economics*, 31 JOURNAL OF COMPARATIVE ECONOMICS 595 (2003), first published as NBER Working Paper 9608 (2003), p. II, <http://papers.nber.org/papers/w9608.pdf> (last visited July 17, 2006).

[2] *See, e.g.,* Andrew Zimbalist, *The State of the Art of Comparative Economics*, 31 COMPARATIVE ECONOMIC STUDIES 6–15 (1989); Josef C. Brada, *What Is Comparative Economics, and What Ought It Be?*, 31 COMPARATIVE ECONOMIC STUDIES 16, 18 (1989).

[3] Djankov et al., *supra* note 1, at 596.

[4] Simeon Djankov, Caralee McLiesh & Andrei Shleifer, *Private Credit in 129 Countries*, NBER Working Paper 11078 (2005), <http://papers.nber.org/papers/w11078.pdf> (last visited July 17, 2006).

[5] Juan Botero, Simeon Djankov, Rafael La Porta, Florencio Lopez-de-Silanes & Andrei Shleifer, *The Regulation of Labor*, 119 THE QUARTERLY JOURNAL OF ECONOMICS 1339–1382 (2004), first published as NBER Working Paper 9756 (2003), <http://papers.nber.org/papers/w9756.pdf> (last visited July 17, 2006).

[6] James R. Barth, Gerard Caprio Jr. & Ross Levine, *Bank Regulation and Supervision: What Works Best?*, 13 JOURNAL OF FINANCIAL INTERMEDIATION 205–248 (2004).

[7] Simeon Djankov, Caralee McLiesh, Tatiana Nenova & Andrei Shleifer, *Who Owns the Media?*, 46 JOURNAL OF LAW AND ECONOMICS 341–381 (2003), first published as NBER Working Paper 8288 (2001), <http://papers.nber.org/papers/w8288.pdf> (last visited July 17, 2006).

[8] Simeon Djankov, Rafael La Porta, Florencio Lopez-de-Silanes & Andrei Shleifer, *The Regulation of Entry*, 117 QUARTERLY JOURNAL OF ECONOMICS 1–37 (2002), first published as NBER Working Paper 7892 (2001), <http://papers.nber.org/papers/w7892.pdf> (last visited July 17, 2006).

Lately, comparative economists have found a new object for their studies: civil procedure. This is by no means surprising. Undoubtedly, courts as the institutions securing property and enforcing contracts fulfill a very important economic function.[9] It was therefore a mere matter of time until the new comparative economists addressed the topic of courts and the rules for their functioning. In April 2002, World Bank financial economist Simeon Djankov, together with Rafael La Porta, then associate professor at Harvard University's Department of Economics, Florencio Lopez-de-Silanes, then professor at Yale School of Management, and Andrei Shleifer, professor at Harvard University's Department of Economics, released in the National Bureau of Economic Research (NBER)'s Working Paper 8890 a study entitled "Courts: The Lex Mundi Project",[10] republished in May 2003 in the Quarterly Journal of Economics under the title "Courts".[11] The Study undertakes to construct an index of procedural formalism of dispute resolution for 109 countries, and to analyze the relationship between procedural formalism and certain aspects of quality of the judicial systems, such as duration and fairness. Based on consultations with Lex Mundi[12] member law firms in more than 100 countries, this study aggregates a considerable amount of empirical data. It certainly provides the most comprehensive up-to-date field research on civil procedure sys-

---

[9] *See, e.g.*, Ronald H. Coase, *The Problem of Social Cost*, 3 JOURNAL OF LAW AND ECONOMICS 1, 19 (1960); STEVEN SHAVELL, FOUNDATIONS OF ECONOMIC ANALYSIS OF LAW 294 (2004) (listing four general functions of courts in the field of contracts).

[10] NBER Working Paper 8890 (2002), <http://papers.nber.org/papers/w8890.pdf> (last visited July 17, 2006).

[11] 118 QUARTERLY JOURNAL OF ECONOMICS 453–517 (2003). Hereinafter, I will reference to this study as the "Lex Mundi Study" or simply the "Study". Unfortunately, the complete data used in the Study are not included in the Study's publication in the Quarterly Journal of Economics. Moreover, they are no longer available at the URL indicated in this publication's first footnote. However, the complete data are available in Excel format for download on the co-author Andrei Shleifer's website at the Harvard University Department of Economics at <http://www.andrei-shleifer.com/data.html> and on the co-author Rafael La Porta's website at the Tuck School of Business at Dartmouth, <http://mba.tuck.dartmouth.edu/pages/faculty/rafael.laporta/publications/LaPorta%20PDF%20Papers-ALL/Courts-LexMundiProject-All/Courts-LuxMundi.xls> (last visited July 17, 2006); there is no indication that these data are not the data actually used. Hereinafter, I will reference to the dataset as the "Dataset".

[12] On its website's statement of purpose, Lex Mundi describes itself as "an organization of independent law firms providing for the exchange of professional information about the local and global practice and development of law, facilitating and disseminating communications among its members and improving the members' abilities to serve the needs of their respective clients." *See* Lex Mundi, *Statement of Purpose*, <http://www.lexmundi.com/lexmundi/Statement_of_Purpose.asp?SnID=1281338160> (last visited July 17, 2006).

tems. For that reason alone, it deserves the attention not only of economists, but also of the legal community.

Actually, to the legal scholar and the well-informed lawyer, comparisons of different procedural systems are nothing new.[13] In the last decades a constantly increasing number of monographs and law journal articles dealing with nearly any aspect of comparative civil procedural law has been published around the world.[14] Entire journals are dedicated to comparative, foreign and international civil procedure.[15] Articles and textbooks

---

[13] Things have changed considerably since Mauro Cappelletti's *[An] Open Letter to Professor Hans Schima about the Need, Difficulties and Purposes of Comparative Civil Procedure*, *in* FESTSCHRIFT FÜR HANS SCHIMA ZUM 75. GEBURTSTAG 125–131 (Hans W. Fasching & Winfried Kralik, eds., 1969). *But see also* John H. Langbein, *The Influence of Comparative Procedure in the United States*, 43 AM. J. COMP. L. 545–554 (1993); Rolf Stürner, *Der deutsche Prozeßrechtslehrer am Ende des 20. Jahrhunderts*, *in* FESTSCHRIFT FÜR GERHRAD LÜKE ZUM 70. GEBURTSTAG 829, 833–834 (Hanns Prütting & Helmut Rüssmann, eds., 1997). That scholarly activities in the field of comparative civil procedure are all but new is illustrated inter alia by the fourth conference of the *Vereinigung der Zivilprozessrechtslehrer* in Munich in 1925, where appeals procedures in Germany, England, Austria, Switzerland and Scandinavia, and Italy have been discussed and scholars from Hungary, Sweden, Italy, the U.S. (Edwin M. Borchard from Yale) and Denmark have been elected correspondent members of the association. *See* Wolfram Henckel, *Zur Geschichte der Zivilprozeßrechtslehrervereinigung 1920–1933*, *in* FESTSCHRIFT FÜR HANS W. FASCHING ZUM 65. GEBURTSTAG 213, 218–219 (Richard Holzhammer, Wolfgang Jelinek & Peter Böhm, eds., 1988).

[14] Without any claim to comprehensiveness, *see, e.g.*, MIRJAN R. DAMAŠKA, THE FACES OF JUSTICE AND STATE AUTHORITY: A COMPARATIVE APPROACH TO THE LEGAL PROCESS (1986); ROBERT A. KAGAN, ADVERSARIAL LEGALISM: THE AMERICAN WAY OF LAW (2001); OSKAR HARTWIEG, DIE KUNST DES SACHVORTRAGS IM ZIVILPROZESS (1988); MARIUS KOHLER, DIE ENTWICKLUNG DES SCHWEDISCHEN ZIVILPROZESSRECHTS (2002); Konstantinos D. Kerameus, *A Civilian Lawyer Looks at Common Law Procedure*, 47 LA. L. REV. 493 (1987); *see also* the controversy sparked by the article of John H. Langbein, *The German Advantage in Civil Procedure*, 52 U. CHI. L. REV. 823 (1985): Ronald J. Allen, Stefan Köck, Kurt Riecherberg & D. Toby Rosen, *The German Advantage in Civil Procedure: A Plea for More Details and Fewer Generalities in Comparative Scholarship*, 82 NW. U. L. REV. 705 (1988); John H. Langbein, *Trashing the German Advantage*, 82 NW. U. L. REV. 763 (1988); Ronald J. Allen, *Idealization and Caricature in Comparative Scholarship*, 82 NW. U. L. REV. 785 (1988); John C. Reitz, *Grundlegende Unterschiede zwischen dem deutschen und dem U.S.-amerikanischen Zivilprozeßrecht: Vorzüge, die sich ausschließen?*, 104 ZEITSCHRIFT FÜR ZIVILPROZESS [ZZP] 381 (1991); Bradley Bryan, *Justice and Advantage in Civil Procedure: Langbein's Conception of Comparative Law and Procedural Justice in Question*, 11 TULSA J. COMP. & INT'L L. 521 (2004) and references in n. 8; for an excellent overview, see Peter Gottwald, *Zum Stand der Zivilprozessrechtsvergleichung*, *in* FESTSCHRIFT FÜR PETER SCHLOSSER ZUM 70. GEBURTSTAG 227–245 (Birgit Bachmann, Stephan Breidenbach, Dagmar Coester-Waltjen, Burkhard Heß, Andreas Nelle & Christian Wolf, eds., 2005).

[15] A decade ago, the first volume of the Zeitschrift für Zivilprozess International (ZZPInt), edited by Dieter Leipold and Rolf Stürner in collaboration with the Wissen-

about foreign countries' civil procedure have been published in other countries and easily accessible languages.[16] Conferences organized by renowned associations and institutes for civil procedure have brought together lawyers from different countries and different legal systems.[17] Such conferences provide excellent opportunities for an exchange of ideas, for a discussion of different legal approaches and their cultural, historical and sociological background.[18] As a consequence of the globalization of the economy and the unprecedented mobility of private persons, more and more courts and practitioners are faced with cases involving foreign court proceedings and questions of foreign procedural law. Cooperation may sometimes still prove difficult. The times of more open conflicts, however, seem to be overcome, giving way to the honest desire of better understanding.[19] Probably the most prominent illustration of this development are the

---

schaftliche Vereinigung für Internationales Verfahrensrecht e.V., appeared in the Carl Heymanns Verlag, Cologne.

[16] *See, e.g.,* ELIO FAZZALARI & PIERRE FORTIN (EDS.), CIVIL JUSTICE IN THE COUNTRIES OF THE EUROPEAN UNION (1998); MAURO CAPPELLETTI & JOSEPH M. PERILLO, CIVIL PROCEDURE IN ITALY (1965); JOSEPH W.S. DAVIS, DISPUTE RESOLUTION IN JAPAN (1996); CARL F. GOODMAN, JUSTICE AND CIVIL PROCEDURE IN JAPAN (2004); TAKAAKI HATTORI & DAN FENNO HENDERSON, CIVIL PROCEDURE IN JAPAN (2nd ed., loose-leaf, release 2, December 2004); CHRISTOPHER HEATH & ANJA PETERSEN (EDS.), DAS JAPANISCHE ZIVILPROZESSRECHT (2002); HARALD KOCH & FRANK DIEDRICH, CIVIL PROCEDURE IN GERMANY (1998); STEFAN LEIBLE, PROCESO CIVIL ALEMÁN (2nd ed., 2000); BENGT LINDELL, CIVIL PROCEDURE IN SWEDEN (2004); PETER L. MURRAY & ROLF STÜRNER, GERMAN CIVIL JUSTICE (2004); NICOLA PICARDI ET AL., IL PROCESSO CIVILE CINESE (Nicola Picardi & Allesandro Giuliani, eds., 1998); HAIMO SCHACK, EINFÜHRUNG IN DAS US-AMERIKANISCHE ZIVILPROZESSRECHT (3rd ed., 2003); ULRIKE BÖHM, AMERIKANISCHES ZIVILPROZESSRECHT (2005); Vincenzo Varano, *Civil Procedure Reform in Italy*, 45 AM. J. COMP. L. 657–674 (1997); Takeshi Kojima, *Japanese Civil Procedure in Comparative Law Perspective*, 46 U. KAN. L. REV. 687–726 (1998); Yasuhei Taniguchi, *The 1996 Code of Civil Procedure of Japan – A Procedure for the Coming Century?*, 45 AM. J. COMP. L. 767–791 (1997).

[17] *See* among many others the impressive list of world conferences on procedural law in Florence 1950, Vienna 1953, Venice 1962, Athens 1967, Mexico City 1972, Ghent 1977, Würzburg 1983, Utrecht 1987, Coimbra/Lisbon 1991, Taormina 1995, Vienna 1999, Mexico City 2003.

[18] *See, e.g.,* Rolf Stürner, *Procedural Law and Legal Cultures, in* PROZESSRECHT UND RECHTSKULTUREN/PROCEDURAL LAW AND LEGAL CULTURES 9 (Peter Gilles & Thomas Pfeiffer, eds., 2004) (Inaugural speech to the XIIth World Congress on Procedural Law 2003 in Mexico City, organized by the International Association of Procedural Law).

[19] *See, e.g.,* Rolf Stürner, *Why Are Europeans Afraid to Litigate in the United States?*, 45 REVIEW OF THE CENTRO DI STUDI E RICERCHE DI DIRITTO COMPARATO E STRANIERO 1–23 (2001), *available at* <http://w3.uniroma1.it/idc/centro/publications/45sturner.pdf> (last visited July 17, 2006); Peter L. Murray, *Taking Evidence Abroad – Understanding American Exceptionalism*, 10 ZZPINT 343, 344, 354–357 (2005). On the so-called "jurisdiction conflict" resulting from the extraterritorial application of U.S. procedural law,

Principles of Transnational Civil Procedure, prepared by a joint American Law Institute/UNIDROIT Study Group and adopted and promulgated by ALI and the Governing Council of UNIDROIT in April and May 2004.[20]

In the meantime, some members of the legal community called for more empirical data.[21] Thanks to the Lex Mundi Study, such data are now available. And indeed, we are witnessing the first articles, written by legal scholars, which make use of these data.[22]

---

see, e.g., the contributions of Rolf Stürner, Dieter G. Lange & Yasuhei Taniguchi *in* DER JUSTIZKONFLIKT MIT DEN VEREINIGTEN STAATEN VON AMERIKA/THE JURISDICTION CONFLICT WITH THE UNITED STATES OF AMERICA (Edgar Habscheid, ed., 1986); PETER SCHLOSSER, DER JUSTIZKONFLIKT ZWISCHEN DEN USA UND EUROPA (1985); Hanns Prütting, *Ein neues Kapitel im Justizkonflikt USA–Deutschland, in* 1 FESTSCHRIFT FÜR ERIK JAYME 709–718 (Heinz-Peter Mansel, Thomas Pfeiffer, Herbert Kronke, Christian Kohler & Rainer Hausmann, eds., 2003); Rolf A. Schütze, *Zum Stand des deutsch-amerikanischen Justizkonfliktes*, 50 Recht der Internationalen Wirtschaft [RIW] 162–167 (2004); Rolf A. Schütze, *Conceptual Differences and Areas of Potential Collision between United States and "Civil Law" Procedure from the German Perspective, in* LITIGATION OF BUSINESS MATTERS IN THE UNITED STATES AND INTERNATIONAL LEGAL ASSISTANCE 21–41 (Roger Zäch, ed., 1984); Burkhard Hess, *Aktuelle Brennpunkte des transatlantischen Justizkonflikts*, 50 DIE AKTIENGESELLSCHAFT (AG) 897–905 (2005).

[20] ALI/UNIDROIT, PRINCIPLES OF TRANSNATIONAL CIVIL PROCEDURE (2006); IX UNIF. L. REV. NS 749–809 (2004-4) (hereinafter: ALI/UNIDRPOIT Principles), English version *available at* <http://www.unidroit.org/english/principles/civilprocedure/ali-unidroitprinciples-e.pdf> (last visited July 17, 2006). On the final version of the ALI/UNIDROIT Principles, see the articles in the 2004-4 UNIF. L. REV. volume and Rolf Stürner, *The Principles of Transnational Civil Procedure. An Introduction to Their Basic Conceptions*, 69 RABELS ZEITSCHRIFT FÜR AUSLÄNDISCHES UND INTERNATIONALES PRIVATRECHT [RABELSZ] 201–254, 341–350 (2005). For a discussion of earlier drafts, see the contributions in VERS UN PROCÈS CIVIL UNIVERSEL? LES RÈGLES TRANSNATIONALES DE PROCÉDURE DE L'AMERICAN LAW INSTITUTE (Philippe Fouchard, ed., 2001), THE FUTURE OF TRANSNATIONAL CIVIL LITIGATION (Mads Andenas, Neil Andrews & Renato Nazzini, eds., 2004) and LA PROCÉDURE CIVILE MONDIALE MODÉLISÉE (Frédérique Ferrand, ed., 2004).

[21] Allen et al., *supra* note 14.

[22] *See, e.g.,* Herbert M. Kritzer, *American Adversarialism*, 38 LAW & SOC'Y REV. 349, 367 (2004) (book review); Robert E. Scott & Paul B. Stephan, *Self-Enforcing International Agreements and the Limits of Coercion*, 2004 WISCONSIN L. REV. 551, 571 (not referring to the data, but to the authors' general statements about the judge as disinterested referee); Amir N. Licht, *Legal Plug-Ins: Cultural distance, Cross Listing, and Corporate Governance Reform*, 22 BERKELEY J. INT'L L. 195, 230 (2004) (mentioning the Study as an example for a study showing interrelations between cultural aspects and legal rules); Robert Kossick, *The Rule of Law and Development in Mexico*, 21 ARIZ. J. INT'L & COMP. L. 715, 814 (2004) (using the Study's data on duration and the formalism index for both the check collection and the eviction case in a table about legal sector performance indicators for Mexico, Argentina, Brazil, and Chile [talking of "enforcement of contract" instead of "check collection"]); Frank B. Cross, *America the Adversarial*, 89 VA. L. REV. 189, 197 (2003) (book review); Hiram E. Chodosh, *Emergence from the*

But the Lex Mundi Study is much more than a mere collection of data. It also does not limit itself to making comparative statements about the different levels of formalism in the reviewed countries' civil procedure systems. In addition to all this, the Study suggests a strong relationship between formalism and the "quality of dispute resolution" and concludes with a recommendation for reform. It is this messianic tendency, backed by an amount of data which seems to be a guarantee for the Study's universal validity, in conjunction with the support of the World Bank which makes the Lex Mundi Study so important.

Surprisingly enough, however, legal and economics scholars apparently have not yet thoroughly reviewed and discussed the Study and the conclusions its authors draw from the collected data.[23]

The present small book attempts to provide a first critical approach to the Lex Mundi Study. After a short presentation of the Study (sub II.), it starts with a discussion of what can be called the "input" to the Study (sub III.-VI.). Although being convinced that much could be said about the correctness of the Lex Mundi lawyers' individual statements on the applicable law in each of the covered legal systems,[24] the book does not focus on this aspect. In other words, this publication does not suggest a "re-coding" of the formalism index. What deserves at least as much attention is the theoretical framework and method on which the Study is based. Therefore, the third part of the book will address the variables based on the questionnaire that was used to collect the data from the Lex Mundi member firms. It provides a discussion of the Study's two model cases and a review of the indi-

---

Dilemmas of Justice Reform, 38 TEX. INT'L L.J. 587, 605 (2003) and *Reforming Judicial Reform Inspired by U.S. Models*, 52 DEPAUL L. REV. 351, 361 (2002) (mentioning the Study as a quantitative analysis which is "deficient in qualitative assessment of what value the judicial system should produce and at what cost of time or money", and noting that the Study implicitly treats efficiency as the absence of delay).

[23] *But see* Kevin E. Davis, *What Can the Rule of Law Variable Tell Us About Rule of Law Reforms?*, 26 MICH. J. INT'L L. 141, 145, 159, 161 (2004) (according to whom "these data ought to be eminently useful to would-be legal reformers", but noting that "despite claims to the contrary by the designers of the Lex Mundi study and others who have subsequently used the study for the purposes of testing the relationship between law and development, it is misleading to characterize data derived from this study as an overall measure of the enforceability of contracts in any given jurisdiction.").

[24] In particular, we have severe doubts as to whether attorneys in large firms really have sufficient experience with check collection and eviction cases, as the Study claims to have "discovered" (Djankov et al, *supra* note 11, at 460 note 4). Above all, it is hard to believe that many large firms work for their clients on normal eviction cases. It would be very naive to believe that one can rely on sufficient familiarity with the model cases because of the questionnaire's procedural safeguards described by Djankov et al., *id.*, at 461, and a plausibility check on the basis of the answers and the legal texts furnished by the participating attorneys.

vidual variables and their definitions. In the fourth part, the book will focus on how the answers were classified, evaluating first the "neighbor model" which constitutes the basis for the Study's classifications and then turning to the individual variables. What is being analyzed here is not how the Study classifies individual countries, but rather the relevance of this or that answer for an index measuring formalism. Part V shall be dedicated to the Study's aggregation of the different results. It follows the schema of the two preceding parts in that it begins with general comments on the Study's approach and then assesses critically different aspects of the weighting the Study undertakes. The sixth part reviews the "external sources", that is the data from other surveys and publications, used by the Study to link formalism to the quality of the judicial system, to determine the countries' legal origin and to control for the results.

Following this extensive discussion of the "input", part VII of the book turns to the way the Study combines the data and, in particular, how it interprets the results. Part VIII contains some brief thoughts about the implication of the Study's conclusion, in particular its recommendation, and is followed by some more general comments about the Study in part IX. Part X addresses some objections to our criticism that might have come into the readers mind. Part XI concludes.

This publication's larger ambition, it should be noted at the outset, is by no means to discredit the Study or its authors, but to provide insights that may help the reader to evaluate the Study and to use it in a responsible way.

Part II

The Study in Brief

The Study assembles data on procedural formalism, the incentives of the parties, and duration of the proceedings in practice. It supplements these self-collected data with data and information from other sources on what it calls "other judicial quality measures" (e.g., cost, fairness, and corruption, as perceived by people in the respective country) and "other variables" (e.g., income, legal origin, and education). On the resulting dataset, the Study applies statistical methods.

Insofar as it measures procedural formalism, incentives and duration, the Study is based on data derived from a questionnaire which was answered by cooperating attorneys in 109 countries. The questionnaire asked the attorneys to describe the exact procedures used by litigants and courts in two hypothetical settings: the eviction of a residential tenant for non-payment of rent and the collection of a bounced check. The hypothetical forum was to be a local court in the country's largest city. The hypothetical cases were presented with significant detail in order to avoid the problem that different procedures might arise in different circumstances. Aspects of the procedure covered by the questionnaire were (1) step-by-step description of the procedure, (2) estimates of the actual duration at each stage, (3) indication of whether written submissions were required at each stage, (4) indication of specific laws applicable at each stage, (5) indication of mandatory time limits at each stage, (6) indication of the form of the appeal, and (7) the existence of alternative administrative procedures. In addition, the participating law firms were asked questions about the incentives of judges, attorneys, and the litigants.[25]

In order to determine the degree of formalism of a country's civil procedure system, the authors compare certain features of that country's civil procedural law to what they call the "neighbor model". In brief, this "neighbor model" is the way disputes, in the eyes of the authors, would most probably be resolved among neighbors in the absence of courts.[26]

The Study is not merely interested in describing the phenomenon of formalism, but aims at clarifying the "crucial question" whether formalism

---

[25] Djankov et al., *supra* note 11, at 459–461.
[26] *Id.*, at 455–456 and 461–476.

secures justice.[27] It is for this purpose that the questionnaire also collects data about duration, assuming that the faster a dispute is resolved, the higher the quality of the civil procedure system is. In addition to these data, the Study uses information from existing surveys, mostly on the quality of the legal system. Moreover, the authors assemble some data on incentives for judges, attorneys, and litigants, namely whether judges face mandatory time deadlines, whether lawyers may charge contingency fees, and whether losers in civil disputes must pay the winners' legal fees. They also consult data on 1999 per capita income in each country, the average years of schooling, and ethno-linguistic fractionalization. The authors want to use their data to examine alternative hypotheses concerning determinants of judicial quality.[28]

Their conclusion, put in a few words, is that procedural formalism is highest in countries with socialist and French legal origin and lowest in countries with English legal origin, that a higher level of formalism is accompanied by a lower quality of adjudication, and that therefore formalism should be reduced.

[27] *Id.*, at 477 and 506.
[28] *Id.*, at 456 and 476–477.

Part III

The Questionnaire

A study which is mainly based on the answers of practicioners to specific questions can only then claim to be of any significance and to permit generalizing conclusions if the questionnaire used to collect the data is based on correct assumptions and asks the right questions, and that in the right way. This part of the book first comments on the two hypothetical cases – eviction and check collection – and then scrutinizes the individual variables, that is, the questions posed to the attorneys of the different countries.[29]

A. The Two Hypothetical Cases

1. General Remarks

Without any doubt, it is a good idea in a comparative survey using a questionnaire to choose hypothetical cases. This method is probably the only way to obtain more or less comparable results. The more vividly the cases are described, i.e., the more details are furnished by the researchers collecting the data, the less likely it is that differences in the answers result merely from different understandings of the underlying facts and not from actual differences in the law itself. This is even more true for a comparison in the field of civil procedural law. It has been noted that for this field of the law, "the difference between law in action and law in the books is more significant than in substantive law", as "[t]he atmosphere of a trial is nothing that could be found in law books."[30]

---

[29] References to "questions" and the "questionnaire" shall mean the data collected by the Study itself, as opposed to data from external sources. The questionnaire actually sent to the Lex Mundi member law firms may have looked differently, the more so as there was an "additional round of questions" in most cases (Djankov et al., *supra* note 11, at 461).

[30] Rolf Stürner & Astrid Stadler, *Eigenarten der Prozeßrechtsvergleichung – Special features of comparative procedural law –, in* TRANSNATIONALES PROZESSRECHT – TRANSNATIONAL ASPECTS OF PROCEDURAL LAW, GERMAN REPORTS FOR THE WORLD CONFERENCE ON PROCEDURAL LAW IN TAORMINA, SICILY, 1995, 263, 281–282, 291 (Peter Gilles, ed., 1996). *See also* Peter Gilles, *Prozessrechtsvergleichung – Comparative*

However, one should not oversee that this method also has a conceptual and a practical downside: From a conceptual point of view, the more concrete and detailed the hypothetical cases are presented, the more weight must be assigned to the inquiry of whether the results can be generalized. From a practical point of view, it is difficult to invent realistic hypothetical scenarios which could actually occur in each of the many countries under examination. Taking into account the considerable differences in economic circumstances, lifestyle and culture among the world's countries, it seems obvious that only a limited number of settings are suited for the purpose of a comparative survey which aims at embracing the whole world. This, in turn, raises once more the issue of whether the data relying on only a few hypothetical cases, selected from the already restricted number of qualifying scenarios, are eligible for a generalization.

Finally, the number and type of model cases should be determined in a way which takes into consideration the object of the study. As for the number of cases, the minimum necessary to temper accidental differences certainly is two. However, with only two cases, it is impossible to find out, in the event of remarkable differences, whether one or the other of the two cases involves a situation which should not constitute the basis for a generalization. Three or more cases, in turn, would not only provide a more reliable basis, but such higher number of cases would also allow the researchers to verify the selection of the model cases and, if necessary, to eliminate one case for the ultimate interpretation.

With regard to the type of cases, it is of course crucial that the model cases are characteristic in the sense that they stand for a considerable quantity of cases and do not leave uncovered an important field of court activity. Moreover, in a study comparing civil procedure systems it would seem desirable to choose cases which are tried in the ordinary procedural order and which do not involve special procedural features, unless the study's object is limited respectively.

2. The Eviction Case

The eviction of a residential tenant for nonpayment of rent indeed "represents [a] typical situation of default on an everyday contract in virtually every country".[31] It can also be assumed that such cases appear in great numbers all over the world. However, one could have some doubts as to whether such scenario actually constitutes an adequate model case.[32] In many countries, the rules governing the eviction of a residential tenant are

---

Procedural Law, in TRANSNATIONAL ASPECTS OF PROCEDURAL LAW 967, 1031–1036 (Int'l Ass'n of Procedural Law, ed., 1998); Gottwald, *supra* note 14, at 231, 234–235.

[31] Djankov et al., *supra* note 11, at 460.

[32] *See also* Davis, *supra* note 23, at 159.

extensive and numerous, complex, and subject to frequent amendments. This is true for substantive law as well as for procedural law.[33] The reason for this phenomenon is the intention of courts and the legislature in many countries to protect the tenant, for whom the eviction from his dwelling may have disastrous effects, without totally depriving the owner or lessor from his or her better right. Balancing these conflicting interests is difficult, and the level of tenant protection deemed just and adequate by a nation's society changes from time to time, entailing the respective changes in that nation's law.

The authors of the Study do not completely neglect this feature. In a footnote, they mention the possible concern that rules governing eviction are shaped by what they somewhat depreciatively call "a nation's 'socialist' sentiments". However, according to them "[t]he fact that the structures of dispute resolution for eviction and check collection are so similar is inconsistent with the view that socialism drives the results".[34]

It is not at all clear, though, what the authors mean with the "structures of dispute resolution". To demonstrate this, let us have a look at the Study's data concerning duration. Referring to duration seems justified, for nobody would reasonably argue that striking differences in the expected duration have nothing to do with what is the "structure of dispute resolution", however defined. Now, from the Study's own data, it follows that the average "duration of trial" in an eviction case is 23.4% higher than in a check collection case.[35] Although the average "duration until completion of service of process" and the average "duration of enforcement" in a check collection case are slightly higher than in an eviction case,[36] the average total duration in an eviction case still exceeds the average total duration of a check collection case by 8.5%.[37] These findings alone cast doubt in the authors' statement that "the structures of dispute resolution for eviction and check collection are so similar".

One could still disregard the longer duration in eviction cases if it occurred throughout all the countries, thus having no influence on the ultimate comparison and the conclusions drawn from the results. However, as

[33] For an illustration, see *infra* notes 39 to 43 and accompanying text.

[34] Djankov et al., *supra* note 11, at 460 in footnote 3.

[35] According to the Dataset, the aggregated duration of trial in an eviction case is 16456 days with the average duration being 151.0, in a check collection case 13334 days with the average duration being 122.3 days. *See* Djankov et al., *supra* note 11, at 499.

[36] The aggregated duration until completion of service of process in an eviction case is 3116.5 days, in a check collection case 3403.5 days; the aggregated duration of enforcement in an eviction case is 8085.5 days, in a check collection case 8717 days.

[37] According to the Dataset, the aggregated total duration in an eviction case is 27659 days (average 253.8), in a check collection case 25513.5 days (average 234.1). *See* Djankov et al., *supra* note 11, at 499.

one might expect taking into account the importance of policy issues in eviction cases mentioned above, it follows from the Study's data that this is definitely not the case. For example, in Australia – a country nobody would say to be completely irrelevant – the total duration of an eviction case equals 44 days, whereas the total duration of a check collection case equals 320 days, which is approximately eight times as long. Even more striking is the result for Canada with 43 and 421 days respectively, whereas the United Kingdom (115/101 days), the U.S. (49/54 days) and Italy (630/645 days) do not show any significant difference between the two scenarios. Germany (331/154 days), Austria (547/434 days) and Denmark (225/83 days) in turn are clearly in line with the general trend.[38] Many other examples could be cited here, but these may suffice to show that the postulated similarity of eviction and check collection cases does not find support in the Study's own data. Rather, it must be suspected that the authors only looked to the legal systems with which they were familiar – the U.S. and maybe also the United Kingdom – when drafting the footnote, a typical pitfall in comparative law.

As stated in the general remarks, it would seem desirable that a model case for a general comparison of formalism in civil procedure be tried in the ordinary procedural order and do not involve any special procedural features. However, for the policy reasons described above, this is often not true with the eviction of a residential tenant. In Germany, for example, such cases are assigned by statute to the *Amtsgericht* (local court) as first instance court without regard to the amount of the claim,[39] which entails a simplified procedure.[40] In addition, there are special rules for the court's decision[41] and the enforcement of a judgment ordering eviction.[42] Special rules for eviction cases can also be found in many other legal systems.[43]

---

[38] At a later point, the Study even mentions that in German legal origin countries, eviction cases take more time than check collection cases (Djankov, *supra* note 11, at 501). However, it frames this in a terminology of "efficiency" and does not make any reference to what it earlier called "a nation's 'socialist' sentiment". *See also infra* sub VII.B.3.

[39] § 23 no. 2 lit. a Gerichtsverfassungsgesetz (GVG); *see* Murray & Stürner, *supra* note16, at 133. For Austria (*Bezirksgericht*), see § 49(2) no. 5 Jurisdiktionsnorm (JN).

[40] §§ 495–510b Zivilprozessordnung (ZPO); for Austria cf. §§ 431–447 ZPO.

[41] § 257 ZPO: no judgment ordering the dispossession of the residential living space at a certain day in the future (what is possible for land or rooms not serving as living space); § 308a ZPO: if the court finds that the lessor's claim for eviction is not legally founded, it is under certain circumstances entitled to determine in the judgment for how long and under which circumstances the lease shall be continued even without an application to this end by the lessee; § 721 ZPO: if the court finds that the lessor's claim for eviction is legally founded, it is entitled to grant the lessee an adequate period of time until eviction must be completed even without a application to this end by the lessee. Similarly in Austria § 34 Mietrechtsgesetz (MRG).

It follows that, contrary to what the authors of the Lex Mundi Study claim, in cases involving the eviction of a residential tenant, procedural particularities *are* significant. Moreover, as the law in this field is frequently reformed and adapted to the current view of a society about how the interests of lessor and lessee should be balanced, the state of the law in a country at one particular moment does not say too much about the procedural system as a whole. Consequently, the eviction case, albeit having the advantage of being familiar to attorneys all over the world, does not constitute a perfect model case, for it can only with great caution, if at all, be used to support general statements.

3. The Check Collection Case

According to the Study, the collection of a check returned for nonpayment is another scenario with which attorneys in all countries are familiar. This sounds plausible, although one should mention that, whereas in some countries the use of checks is very widespread,[44] in others the check is rarely used or has lost much of its former importance.[45]

In contrast to eviction cases, equity-oriented policy issues which might throw doubt on generalizations of the collected data regularly do not occur in check collection cases. However, in some countries like Germany[46] or Austria[47] claims aimed at the collection of a check returned for nonpayment can be, but need not be pursued in special proceedings. This causes two problems. First, it does not follow clearly from the Study and its data whether the attorneys in countries with such special proceedings did or did not assume these to be chosen. Second, even if the description of the

---

[42] § 765a ZPO: Court is entitled to forbid or suspend the enforcement of the judgment on application of the debtor if, in the presence of special circumstances and after having taken into account the just interest of the creditor, it finds that enforcement would constitute an unacceptable hardship for the debtor. Similarly in Austria § 35 MRG.

[43] *See, e.g.,* Switzerland: Art. 274–274g Obligationenrecht (OR), §§ 14–18 Gerichtsverfassungsgesetz Zurich; *see also* Art. 235–241 Vorentwurf (expert draft of June 2003) of the future Swiss Civil Procedure Code; France: Art. 62 Loi 91-650 portant réforme des procédures d'exécution, Art. L 613-1 et seq. Code de la Construction et de l'Habitation; Belgium: Art. 1344 quater Code judiciaire and GEORGES DE LEVAL, ÉLÉMENTS DE PROCÉDURE CIVILE 250, ¶ 180 n. 162 (2003); Greece: Art. 647–662H Code of Civil Procedure, *see* Konstantinos D. Kerameus, *Greece*, *in* Fazzalari & Fortin (*supra* note 16), at 189, 209.

[44] For France, see, *e.g.,* PHILIPPE DELEBECQUE & MICHEL GERMAIN, 2 TRAITÉ DE DROIT COMMERCIAL ¶ 2156 (17th ed., 2004).

[45] For Germany, see, *e.g.,* Gerd Nobbe, *Scheckverkehr, in* BANKRECHTS-HANDBUCH § 60 ¶ 19 (Herbert Schimansky, Hermann-Josef Bunte & Hans-Jürgen Lwowski, eds., 2nd ed., 2001). *See also* Davis, *supra* note 23, at 159.

[46] §§ 605a, 703a ZPO.

[47] § 59a Scheckgesetz (ScheckG) and §§ 556 et seq. ZPO.

model case wanted the answering attorneys to assume that the case not be pursued in special proceedings, the mere existence of such proceedings may have consequences for the data on cases tried in the normal procedural order.[48] It follows that here, too, some doubts remain as to the comparability of the answers. In addition, in some countries check collection cases may be tried initially or on motion of at least one of the parties before special courts or specialized divisions within a court.[49] All this again raises the question to what extent general statements can be built upon a model case involving such important particularities.

4. Are These Two Cases Characteristic?

It seems justified to assume that cases concerning the eviction of a residential tenant for nonpayment and the collection of a returned check are relatively frequent all over the world. They therefore fulfill the first, positive requirement for cases to be characteristic. The second, negative requirement is that the selected cases do not leave uncovered an important field of court activity. Unfortunately, the two model cases on which the Study is based fall short of meeting this second requirement.

As the Study correctly states, both cases are situations of default on everyday contracts, illustrating the enforcement of property rights (in a broader sense) and private contracts in a given legal environment.[50] Very surprisingly, though, the Study does not even mention that, besides the important field of contract cases, there exists, among others, the equally important field of tort cases.[51] But – a commonplace amongst legal schol-

---

[48] For example, if standard check collection cases are usually tried in the special proceedings, lawyers may have difficulty in answering questions about duration of a case tried in the ordinary proceedings for lack of experience with such ordinary proceedings.

[49] *See, e.g.,* Austria (Vienna): *Bezirksgericht für Handelssachen* or *Handelsgericht*, §§ 51(1) no. 8, 52 JN; Germany: *Kammer für Handelssachen* on motion of one of the parties, §§ 95(1) no. 3, 96, 98 GVG.

[50] Djankov et al., *supra* note 11, at 460.

[51] *See only* Kagan, *supra* note 14, at 126–155 (devoting a whole chapter to tort law because it is "the most controversial form of civil justice in the United States." *Id.*, at 100); Richard A. Posner, *A Theory of Negligence*, 1 JOURNAL OF LEGAL STUDIES 29 (1972) (stating that accident cases constitute the largest item of business of the civil side of the U.S.'s trial courts); Marc Galanter, *Reading the Landscape of Disputes: What We Know and Don't Know (and Think We Know) about Our Allegedly Contentious and Litigious Society*, 31 UCLA L. REV. 4, 42 (1983) (noting that "[o]n the civil side, there has been a shift from cases involving market transactions (contract, property, and debt collection) to family and tort cases."); *see also* Marc Galanter, *The Hundred-year Decline of Trials and the Thirty Years War*, 2005 STAN. L. REV. 1255 (noting that despite a decline in the number of trials, "the image of law in public consciousness is centered on the trial."). Even if the number of tort cases has declined in the last years, nobody would doubt that the number of tort cases remains important. For absolute numbers in the Fed-

ars interested in comparative civil procedure – it is just the rules for handling tort cases where striking – if not the most striking differences exist.[52] On the one hand, we have the U.S. with their civil procedure rules shaped by the idea of the jury trial even in cases which are not tried before a jury. On the other hand, we have more or less the rest of the world – including England[53] – where there is no jury trial at all, or at least not (or no longer) such a dominant influence of the jury trial on the appearance of the procedural rules.[54] Extensive, costly and time-consuming pre-trial discovery,[55]

---

eral Courts, see Department of Justice, *Number of Federal Tort Trials Fell by Almost 80 Percent from 1985 through 2003*, *available at* <http://www.ojp.usdoj.gov/newsroom/2005/fttv03pr.htm> (last visited July 17, 2006) (noting that in 2003, there were 49,166 tort cases completed in federal district courts).

[52] *Cf. only* Takeshi Kojima, *Legal Families in Procedural Law Revisited*, *in* TRANSNATIONAL ASPECTS OF PROCEDURAL LAW 1093, 1117–1118, 1131 (Int'l Ass'n of Procedural Law, ed., 1998) (mentioning in the second page of the General Report the unique power of U.S. juries to award large damages including punitive damages as one important difference, although not limiting this statement to torts).

[53] NEIL ANDREWS, ENGLISH CIVIL PROCEDURE ¶¶ 31.01, 34.08–34.09 (2003).

[54] *See, e.g.*, Peter L. Murray & John C. Sheldon, *Should the Rules of Evidence Be Modified for Civil Non-Jury Trials?*, 17 ME. B.J. 30, 30–32 (2002) (quoting Dean Charles McCormick's words that the rules of evidence "are absurdly inappropriate to any tribunal or proceeding where there is no jury" *in* 5 Encyclopedia of Social Sciences 637, 644 (1931). *Id.*, at 30); Geoffrey C. Hazard, Jr., *Discovery and the Role of the Judge in Civil Law Jurisdictions*, 73 NOTRE DAME L. REV. 1017, 1020 (1998) (observing that most common law countries other than the United States no longer use juries very much, but noting that nevertheless, they adhere to the tradition of concentrated trial procedure, and, by the same token, they adhere more or less to the need for pretrial discovery); John H. Langbein, *Historical Foundations of the Law of Evidence: A View from the Ryder Sources*, 96 COLUM. L. REV. 1168, 1168 (1998) (noting that "[a]lthough many cases fall outside the jury entitlement, and in many others the parties waive it, jury trial remains the presumptive norm in American civil and criminal procedure."); Stephen Goldstein, *On Comparing and Unifying Civil Procedural Systems*, *in* PROCESS AND SUBSTANCE, BUTTERWORTH LECTURES 1994, 1, 19–23 (Roger Cotterrell, ed., 1995); Andrews, *supra* note 53, at ¶¶ 34.06–34.07; Rolf Stürner, *Some European Remarks on a New Joint Project of the American Law Institute and UNIDROIT*, 34 INT. LAW. 1071, 1074 (2000) (noting the important consequences of the right to a jury trial for the structure of civil procedure and the law of evidence); Murray & Stürner, *supra* note 16, at 596; Kerameus, *supra* note 14, at 500–503, 508.

[55] Hazard, *supra* note 54, at 1018–1020 (noting that "[the] system of pretrial discovery is unique to the United States", and describing the need for a pretrial phase in an adjudicative system based on jury trial); JACK H. FRIEDENTHAL, MARY KAY KANE & ARTHUR R. MILLER, CIVIL PROCEDURE 398 (4th ed., 2005) (explaining that "discovery, as practiced in American litigation, is not available in most civil-law countries and is available in only a limited way in other common-law countries"); Kagan, *supra* note 14, at 107–109; Murray, *supra* note 19, at 347–348 and Murray & Stürner, *supra* note 16, at 603 (observing that "the effect of privatizing the presentation of evidence means that the evidence must be received twice in American proceedings, once when the lawyers elicit

jury selection and *voir dire*,[56] detailed rules on the admissibility of evidence, and extremely strict requirements as to the correctness of the judge's instruction of the jury[57] – they all play their perhaps most important role in tort cases.[58] To say that unlike the protection of property and the enforcement of contracts (for which the eviction case and the check collection case stand),[59] the adjudication of torts does not matter, would seem flawed under any relevant aspect – perception of the quality of the judicial system, protection of individual rights, and economic factors like investment environment, trade, and economic growth. These few keywords and the thousands of pages which have been written about procedural differences in tort cases suggest that the Study should have included a tort case. And it would not have been that difficult to invent an everyday tort case – what for example about a traffic accident?[60]

5. *Conclusion*

As we have seen, neither the eviction case nor the check collection case is as such a perfect model case: both describe situations that may involve special procedural features in at least some of the countries examined. For lack of more than these two cases, it is not clear whether such particularities are sufficiently tempered in the ultimate results. Even more important, the use of two contract cases in combination with the total omission of tort cases in the questionnaire casts serious doubt whether the Study can be

---

the evidence in discovery and witness preparation, and then all over again when the evidence is presented by one party of the other to the court"); Reitz, *supra* note 14, at 383–384; *see also* Stephen N. Subrin, *Discovery in Global Perspective: Are We Nuts?*, 52 DEPAUL L. REV. 299 (2002) (noting that from a comparative law perspective, the U.S. are really different in their approach to discovery).

[56] For an excellent overview, see Paul D. Carrington, *The Seventh Amendment: Some Bicentennial Reflections*, 1990 U. CHI. L. F. 33, 57–62; for an illustration, see DONALD P. LAY, LAW: A HUMAN PROCESS 150–156 (1996).

[57] *See, e.g.*, Mark Cammack, *Evidence Rules and the Ritual Functions of Trials: "Saying Something of Something"*, 25 LOY. L.A. L. REV. 783, 788–792 (1992) (describing these and other features of the jury trial as "ritual"); FLEMING JAMES, JR., GEOFFREY C. HAZARD, JR. & JOHN LEUBSDORF, CIVIL PROCEDURE § 7.22, 451–457 (5th ed., 2001).

[58] *Cf.* Paul D. Carrington, *The Civil Jury and American Democracy*, 13 DUKE J. COMP. & INT'L L. 79, 92 (2003).

[59] Djankov et al., *supra* note 11, at 460.

[60] *Cf.* Peter L. Murray, *A Comparative Law Experiment*, 8 IND. INT'L & COMP. L. REV. 231, 232 et seq. (1998) (describing how students tried the same simulated automobile accident case according to the procedures of a common law and a civil law system). The fact that the Study completely ignores tort cases is the more surprising as its authors not only have published many articles about legal issues, but also have received the advice of very distinguished law professors mentioned in the star footnote. It is hard to believe that the ignorance of tort cases is just an accidental lapse.

regarded as representative for "courts" and civil procedure in general. This does not mean that the whole questionnaire, and with it the whole study, was useless. Yet it suggests that one should be careful when generalizing the results, and even more careful when drawing conclusions used for an evaluation of entire civil procedure systems.

B. The Variables Which Are the Basis for the Formalism Index

1. General Remarks

In order to evaluate the reliability of the formalism index, we first must have a closer look at the individual variables on which it is based. The Study's authors collected data from the participating law firms' attorneys for 42 individual variables. 31 of these 42 variables constitute the basis for the calculation of the Study's formalism index, with the other variables concerning the incentives of the parties (eight) and the duration in practice (three).

The Study classes these 31 variables for the formalism index under seven categories: (1) Professionals versus laymen, (2) written versus oral, (3) legal justification, (4) statutory regulation of evidence, (5) control of superior review, (6) engagement formalities, and (7) independent procedural actions. From the variables of each of these seven categories, the Study calculates a sub-index. The following discussion of the variables maintains the order of the sub-indices.

2. Professionals versus Laymen

The first variable in the category "Professionals versus laymen" is entitled "General jurisdiction court". The authors of the Study want to know here "whether a court of general or of limited jurisdiction would be chosen or assigned to hear the case"[61]. In principle, there is nothing to criticize about that question. As we have seen, there are some countries in which one or both model cases are assigned to courts of limited jurisdiction. Also, as far as only this single point is concerned, the fact that both cases may not be representative for the whole system and therefore may not be generalized, is not per se detrimental, for it will always be special cases which are tried before specialized courts. One could even argue that as far as this variable is concerned, one should chose cases which really lend themselves to be assigned to special courts, like bankruptcy cases or labor law cases. Yet

---

[61] Djankov et al., *supra* note 11, at 463.

pursuant to this logic, the Study's inquiry should have covered all cases for which a specialized court might have jurisdiction, in order to find out how important a role courts of limited jurisdiction play in each of the countries. Picking out only eviction and check collection cases from all the cases which potentially fall under the jurisdiction of specialized courts will lead to skewed results.

Apart from that point, the significance of this variable is very limited. If one includes small-claims courts in the definition of "courts of limited jurisdiction", as the Study does, the actual amount of specialization can be very low. This is because still, theoretically, all kinds of litigation could end up before the small claims court. There is only some indirect specialization as to the type of cases due to the fact that some scenarios, like non-payment of consumer goods purchased online, will typically involve small claims, whereas others like medical malpractice or house construction defects will typically involve claims above the particular threshold.

In addition, the definition of the variable does not make clear whether a specialization within one and the same court also is to be qualified as a "court of limited jurisdiction". If a court assigns a certain type of cases always to particular judges or panels of judges, these judges will necessarily develop special skills and expertise in that very field of the law. Various degrees of such "internal" specialization are conceivable and can indeed be observed.[62] Whether the Study expressly wanted to exclude all forms of "internal" specialization because of the difficulty in deciding when it ought to be equated with a "court of limited jurisdiction", or

---

[62] *Cf.* Andrews, *supra* note 53, at ¶ 8.14 (mentioning informal listing arrangements within the Court of Appeal and the House of Lords); Stephen Goldstein, *The Utility of the Comparative Perspective in Understanding, Analyzing and Reforming Procedural Law*, 5 ZZPINT 375, 382–383 (2000) (noting that "the common law system allows the case allocator [...] to take into account such factors as the experience and capabilities of the different judges..." and that under the traditional continental system, the use of panels of judges helps "dealing with the problem of less experienced or less capable judges."); Sarang Vijay Damle, *Specialize the Judge, Not the Court: A Lesson From the German Constitutional Court*, 91 VA. L. REV. 1267, 1272 (2005) (noting that one of three solutions to specialization is the "manner in which cases are staffed", and describing this criterion as a "spectrum [] from those courts that staff cases exclusively with specialist judges, through those that employ some mix of expert and non-expert judges, to those that assign judges without regard to specialization"). *See*, as an example, the above mentioned *Kammer für Handelssachen* (*supra* note 49). The issue is further complicated if, as is the case in Germany, at each court a committee of judges (*Präsidium*) and, within the boundaries of the committee's decision, the majority of the professional judges in a panel of judges may decide that incoming cases are distributed within the court or the panel according to the type of dispute, but may also choose other criteria that satisfy certain requirements. §§ 21e, 21g GVG; OTTO RUDOLF KISSEL & HERBERT MAYER, GVG 579 (§ 21e ¶ 152), 598 (§ 21g ¶ 37) (4th ed., 2005).

whether the Study has simply overlooked this problem because "internal" specialization plays no role in the U.S., is an open question.

The second variable in the category "Professionals versus laymen", "Professional versus nonprofessional judge," is quite straightforward.[63] The third variable, "Legal representation is mandatory," proves to be problematic at least in connection with the check collection case. In many countries, the question whether representation of the party by a licensed attorney is mandatory typically depends on the amount of the claim in dispute. If this is the law, should the variable then be "one" for the answer "yes" because there are cases in which legal representation is required, "zero" for "no" because there are cases which can litigated without an attorney, "0.5" for "depends", or maybe a number reflecting the statistical repartition between cases where legal representation was mandatory and where it was not mandatory? Shall it make a difference if the amount in the model case, converted into national currency, is above or below the respective threshold? Need the conversion take into account different levels of income? Whatever the answers to these questions are, the explanatory power of this variable is limited.

3. Written versus Oral[64]

The questions concerning complaint and opposition are poorly defined: On the one hand, attorneys would have to answer with "one" if the complaint or opposition is *normally* or *should* be submitted in writing. On the other hand, the answer would have to be "zero" if complaint or opposition *can* or *may* be presented orally. This is logically inconsistent, because the two situations described do not exclude each other. In practice, oral declarations will be the exception, even if allowed by the law. One can wonder whether the mere possibility of oral presentation, even if almost never used, is characteristic for a country's law of civil procedure.

The variable "Evidence" is also unclear. The Study describes it in the following way: "Equals one if evidence is mostly submitted to the court in written form, in the form of attachments, affidavits, or otherwise, and zero if most of the evidence, including documentary evidence, is presented at

---

[63] Note, however, that it is not clear how the division of the judicial function into a laymen jury as fact finder and a professional judge as umpire for procedural issues would be categorized. Equally doubtful is the categorization of a panel consisting of laymen and a professional judge, in particular if the laymen hold the majority (as is the case for the *Kammer für Handelssachen*, § 105(1), (2) GVG).

[64] Some of the following observations have first been made by Holger Spamann in an unpublished draft paper reviewing the questions and answers for New York and Germany.

oral hearings before the judge."[65] Typically, evidence needs to be introduced at the oral hearings.[66] This does not exclude that parties announce or are required to announce evidence in written form prior to oral hearings, what can occasionally make redundant a formal taking of evidence in the oral hearings.

Devoting a separate question to "final arguments" is obviously informed by U.S. common law proceedings, where – once more as a consequence of the jury model – this moment is particularly important for the lawyers to influence the jurors' or judge's decision.[67] No doubt, lawyers also seek to convince the judge elsewhere. But in other countries' everyday court practice in civil (as opposed to criminal) cases, explicit final arguments may be rather the exception than the rule.[68] Does this suggest a formalistic system, because the judge probably relies most on written statements, or should this be regarded as less formalistic, because there is no need for final arguments as a separate step of the proceedings? The definition of the variable presupposes a notion of final arguments and gives no answer to this question.

By no means unambiguous are the variables "Judgment" and "Notification of judgment". One would assume that if the decision is issued "orally in a hearing attended by the parties" (equals "zero" for the variable "Judgment"), it should also be true that "the parties receive their *first notice* in an open court hearing attended by them" (equals "zero" for the variable

[65] Djankov et al., *supra* note 11, at 464.

[66] Today, completely written proceedings are the exception. The word "mostly" in the definition suggests that more than completely written proceedings can also result in the variable equaling "one".

[67] Friedenthal et al., *supra* note 55, at 495; James et al., *supra* note 57, at 393–394; Dennis J. Horan, Thomas L. Browne & George W. Spellmire, *Practical Tips in Handling a Legal Malpractice Case: Complaint Through Trial*, 9 AM. J. TRIAL ADVOC. 381, 408–409 (1986) (noting that "[n]o trial lawyer doubts the importance of final argument in determining the result in the case" and that "[i]n a close case, the final argument will make the difference."); Stephen D. Easton, *Cashing in Your Credibility During Final Argument*, 46-APR FED. LAW. 30 (1999); Peder B. Hong, *A Theory of Final Argument in Civil Trials*, 21 HAMLINE L. REV. 31, 53 et seq. (1997); for an illustration, see Lay, *supra* note 56, at 164–165.

[68] *See, e.g.,* Murray & Stürner, *supra* note 16, at 256–259 (describing the adversarial argument in German civil procedure as "[i]n a sense [...] part of a continuum of adversarial argument which starts with the complaint, and continues both orally and in writing at all stages of the proceeding until the last appellate decision has been rendered."). For an illustration, see Peter L. Murray, *A morning at the German* Amtsgericht*: German Civil Justice in Practice*, *in* LAW AND JUSTICE IN A MULTISTATE WORLD, ESSAYS IN HONOR OF ARTHUR T. VON MEHREN 779, 781–788 (James A.R. Nafziger & Symeon C. Symeonides, eds., 2002).

"Notification of judgment"; emphasis added).[69] Surprisingly, though, there are a few countries for which the answer is "zero" for "Judgment" and "one" for "Notification of judgment".[70] How can the judgment be issued orally in a hearing attended by the parties, but the parties receive their first notice of *the decision* in a written form, if "decision" means a valid and binding court opinion? Actually, both definitions do not make clear what they consider to be a final, i.e. valid and binding, decision and what they consider to be a (final) draft. It seems that by "previously made written decision", what is meant is not a decision that has been *made* but only a draft, for if the decision is *issued* in a hearing, probably it becomes valid only then. This would mean that a previous notice is impossible, because there is nothing the parties can be noticed of, apart from a draft which may be revised. Apparently, whoever drafted these definitions had not heard or thought about the importance of exactly defining from which moment there is a valid decision.

Another, but maybe less important, question is whether "decision" is just the decision or also a legal justification, if any. The tenor of the decision itself may be announced earlier and in a different way than the full opinion. Again, the definitions leave room for divergent interpretations. Due to these uncertainties in the definitions, the data collected by these two variables can hardly be seen as reliable.

The variable "Enforcement of judgment" is defined in a somewhat awkward way. According to the definition,[71] it "[e]quals one if the enforcement procedure is mostly carried out through the written court orders or written acts by the enforcement authority, and zero otherwise." But what does "mostly" mean? Obviously, a court order or other written act is not sufficient to make the defendant leave the apartment she occupies, and any judgment ordering payment can only be enforced solely by written acts if there is a bank account or other monetary claim like wages that can be garnished; if some tangible property needs to be seized and foreclosed, written acts alone hardly play the decisive role. Nevertheless, some act in writing seems to be indispensable before the application of more coercive means. It remains obscure what idea the authors of the Study have of the reality of enforcement of judgments. Except for St. Vincent, all attorneys

---

[69] Djankov et al., *supra* note 11, at 464. If – what sounds abnormal – the parties are first informed in writing but still have to attend an oral hearing, it is unclear whether according to the definition there would only be a valid decision in this oral hearing ("… issues …"). Note also that the opposite needs not be true under the Study's definition, according to which the "Judgment" variable equals "one" if the judge reads out a previously made decision.

[70] Cayman, Côte d'Ivoire and Gibraltar (check collection and eviction); Hong Kong and Senegal (only check collection).

[71] Djankov et al., *supra* note 11, at 464.

answered with "one" for both the eviction and the check collection case. It would be interesting to learn more about how judgments are enforced in St. Vincent... Most probably, it is not that different from the rest of the world, but the "zero" is the result of the strange way of asking or of another misunderstanding.

4. Legal Justification

Under this headline, the Study first wants to know whether the complaint must be legally justified. Here again, the definition allows for different interpretations: It asks whether the complaint is required, by law or court regulation, to include references to the applicable laws, legal reasoning, or formalities that would normally require legal training.[72] But what are formalities which require legal training? Is this already the case if the complaint must contain the identification of the parties and the court, the specification of the object of the lawsuit and a precise claim?[73] A complaint which does not allow the court and the defendant to get these fundamental pieces of information is hardly conceivable. Therefore, it would seem preferable not to see in the existence of such basic requirements a formality which normally requires legal training. Yet we can only guess how the answering attorneys in this or that country interpreted this variable. Furthermore, one can wonder why, with regard to this variable, only a *law* or *court regulation* requiring references to the law or legal reasoning should matter, and not what a complaint *normally* looks like – the standard employed by other variables. If even in the absence of such textual provision lawyers almost always include such references and reasoning in the com-

---

[72] Djankov et al., *supra* note 11, at 465.

[73] Apparently, this is what the *German* attorneys answering the questionnaire assumed, as they answered for both cases with "one" (*cf.* § 253(1) ZPO Germany). For apart from such rather simple formal issues, German law *requires* no legal justification of the complaint (*see* Murray & Stürner, *supra* note 16, at 194–195). The same is true for *Belgium*: The Dataset exhibits the value "one" for both model cases, what means that the complaint requires legal justification, but Belgian law makes no higher demands than German law, *cf.* Leval, *supra* note 43, at 32–37. Note also that in *France*, the requirement of a legal justification in Art. 56(2) Nouveau Code de Procédure Civile (NCPC) is relatively new and therefore can hardly be seen as representative for French legal origin; Philippe Hoonaker, *Comment introduire l'instance*, *in* DROIT ET PRATIQUE DE LA PROCÉDURE CIVILE ¶ 1732, p. 378 (Serge Guinchard, ed., 2002). Regarding the *United Kingdom*, the values in the Dataset are "zero" in both the check collection and the eviction case. However, it does not seem that the old Rules of the Supreme Court in Order 6, rule 2 or the new Civil Procedure Rules (CPR) in Rules 7.4 (Particulars of claim), 16.2 (Contents of the claim form), 16.4 (Contents of the particulars of claim) or 8.2 and the relevant Practice Directions require(d) less from the claimant for a "writ" or "claim form".

plaint, a comparison looking to the law in action should not make a distinction.

The next variable is whether the judgment must be legally justified. This can also be interpreted differently. The definition[74] – must the judgment expressly state the legal justification (articles of the law or case-law)? – presumably has not been made by a legal scholar. A legal scholar would have known that, contrary to what the general public mostly assumes, cases cannot always be decided solely by having a look to the articles of a code or to the relevant precedents. Rather, sometimes the judge can give no immediate justification from one article of the law or one precedent, but has to refer to the underlying principles or policies. In any legal system, there necessarily are cases in which for the *ratio decidendi* a legal justification in this strict sense is simply not possible. Therefore, a law according to which "the judgment must expressly state the legal justification (articles of the law or case-law) for the decision" would require something that is impossible to be complied with in some cases. Moreover, even if there is no statutory provision or precedent that immediately resolves the case, the judgment will still be based on legal and, as the case may be, policy arguments. Except for jury awards and some special types of judgments, court decisions normally have to contain a justification. It is not clear why it should make a difference whether this justification cites statutory provisions or case-law or does not do so, because there are none from which the decision could be directly derived, but contains ample and elaborate judicial reasoning.

Finally, as a third variable the Study wants to know whether the "judgment must be on law (not on equity)".[75] This is a very problematic question. If "equity" were to be understood in its technical sense, the question would only be pertinent with regard to common law countries, but not civil law countries.[76] If, what is more plausible, "equity" were to mean that the court is authorized to take into account whether a certain result is just and equitable, other problems arise.

Note first that unlike the other variables, this question concerns primarily a matter of substantive law as opposed to procedural law: The justification of the decision as regards its content, not the procedural way how the decision has been reached.[77] No doubt, resort to "equity" can have implica-

[74] Djankov et al., *supra* note 11, at 465.

[75] Djankov et al., *supra* note 11, at 465.

[76] With civil law countries like Belgium, Italy and Luxemburg answering at least once that the judgment may be based on equity grounds, apparently the attorneys of these countries have interpreted "equity" in a broader sense.

[77] Note that the question of "*procedural* equity" is also a very interesting object of study and comparison. *See generally* Fritz Baur, *Richtermacht und Formalismus im Verfahrensrecht*, *in* SUMMUM IUS SUMA INIURIA 97, 112–116 (1963) = FRITZ BAUR, BEITRÄ-

tions for the court's work. But these implications depend on how the court may use "equity". A court that is allowed to decide exclusively on the basis of "equity" without regard to "the law" in statutes or precedents needs not invest time and effort in finding out what the law is and applying it to the case at issue. On the other hand, a court that is required to first find and apply the law, and only then is obliged to verify whether the result is just and equitable (and, as the case may be, will correct that result respectively before rendering the judgment), has, from a methodological point of view, an additional burden: applying the law *and* confronting the potential outcome of the case with equitable principles. The Study's definition is ambiguous: The first sentence, asking "whether the judgment may be motivated on general equity grounds", suggests the first understanding, the second sentence, assigning to the variable the value "one" "when [the] judgment must be on law *only*"[78] appears to endorse the second understanding.

Besides this, the equity-variable raises other questions. One could ask, for example, whether the judgment is "on equity" as soon as the court bases its decision on policy considerations. Another question would be whether the existence of a broad provision[79] or an unwritten principle permitting courts to take into account fundamental principles of justice, human or civic rights, or constitutional values is already sufficient to say that the judgment may be based on equity. But even then, the answer is not clear. The definition does not tell whether the variable concerns the general possibility of courts to base the judgment on equity in *any* case, the possibility to base it on equity in *any eviction and check collection case*, or the specific analysis that the court would have based its judgment on equity in the precise setting of the respective *model case*.[80]

5. Statutory Regulation of Evidence

The first variable of this sub-index is whether the judge can freely request or take evidence that has not been requested, offered, or introduced by the

GE ZUR GERICHTSVERFASSUNG UND ZUM ZIVILPROZESSRECHT 115, 130–134 (1983), Italian translation 19 RIVISTA TRIMESTRALE DI DIRITTO E PROCEDURA CIVILE 1683, 1700–1704 (1965). That the variable does not concern procedural equity follows from the definition, which asks on what the judgment is "motivated" or "founded".

[78] Djankov et al., *supra* note 11, at 465 (emphasis added).

[79] *See, e.g.*, § 242 of the German Civil Code (Bürgerliches Gesetzbuch, BGB) in its interpretation by the courts, *cf.* Carl Baudenbacher, *Some Remarks on the Method of Civil Law*, 34 TEX. INT'L L.J. 333, 340–342 (1999). However, the answer that has been given by the Lex Mundi lawyers for Germany is that the judgment must be founded on law only.

[80] At least the attorneys of those 13 countries which show different answers for the two cases have not interpreted the question in the first, the broadest, sense.

parties.[81] This characteristic feature[82] has typically not been seen as an aspect of formalism but as part of the more general question of the active or passive role of the judge[83] or the distinction between "adversarial" and "inquisitorial" civil-justice systems.[84] Drawing the line for the purposes of a numerical analysis is of course difficult. Should the notion of "offering evidence" be understood in a broad sense so that it includes any reference to a document, a potential witness? Moreover, it deserves to be mentioned that in some legal systems, the answer is not either "yes" or "no", but rather "it depends", for the power of the judge to introduce evidence exists only under certain circumstances.[85] In such a case, it may be difficult to

---

[81] Djankov et al., *supra* note 11, at 465.

[82] *See, e.g.*, Rolf Stürner, *Parteidisposition über Tatsachen und Beweismittel im Prozess ausgewählter europäischer Staaten*, *in* RECHT UND RISIKO. FESTSCHRIFT FÜR HELMUT KOLLHOSSER ZUM 70. GEBURTSTAG 727, 728–731 (Reinhard Bork, Thomas Hoeren & Petra Pohlmann, eds., 2004).

[83] *See only* Oscar G. Chase, *Legal Processes and National Culture*, 5 CARDOZO J. INT'L & COMP. L. 1, 3–7, 17–19 (1997); J.A. Jolowicz, *Adversarial and Inquisitorial Models of Civil Procedure*, 52 ICLQ 281–295 (2003); Hazard, *supra* note 54; Friedenthal et al., *supra* note 55, at 2; Peter Gottwald, *Aktive Richter – Managerial Judges*, *in* LAW IN EAST AND WEST 705–718 (Institute of Comparative Law, Waseda University, ed., 1988);); Michele Taruffo, *Legal Cultures and Models of Civil Justice*, *in* FESTSCHRIFT FÜR HIDEO NAKAMURA ZUM 70. GEBURTSTAG 621, 624–629 (1996); Langbein, articles *supra* note 14; from a U.S.-centered point of view Judith Resnik, *Managerial Judges*, 96 HARV. L. REV. 374–448 (1982). For an interesting analysis of the (common law) argument that judges and jurors who are not merely passive would be biased, see Burkhard Schafer & Olav K. Wiegand, *Incompetent, Prejudiced and Lawless? A Gestalt-Psychological Perspective on Fact Finding in Law as Learning*, 3 LAW, PROBABILITY AND RISK 93–108 (2004). *But see also* John D. Jackson, *Playing the Culture Card in Resisting Cross-Jurisdictional Transplants: A Comment on "Legal Processes and National Culture"*, 5 CARDOZO J. INT'L & COMP. L. 51, 61 (1997) (noting that "there may not be as much difference in the role judges play vis-à-vis the parties as is sometimes thought.").

[84] *See* the references in the preceding note. It cannot be stressed often enough that describing civil law systems as "inquisitorial" is very problematic. As Judge Friendly of the U.S. Court of Appeals for the Second Circuit put it in testimony before Congress: "Whoever first characterized the continental European system as 'inquisitorial' did a profound disservice to constructive legal thought. Substitute 'inquiring' and the bad becomes the good. The adversary system is not the only way to the truth; indeed, it has too often been a game in which both sides vie in their efforts to obscure the truth. Hopefully, by the year 2000, we will have learned where to preserve the adversary system and where to substitute something else." Hearings before Commission on Revision of the Federal Court Appellate System, second phase, vol. I, at 205 (1974) (quoted from Friedenthal et al., *supra* note 55, at 2 n. 5).

[85] *See, e.g.*, for *France* Art. 10 NCPC (Judge has the authority to order *sua sponte* any legally appropriate investigation measures) and Art. 143 et seq., but also Art. 11 (Judge can order a party to produce a piece of evidence only upon the petition of the other party;

evaluate whether these particular situations are important enough to classify the whole system as one where the judge can introduce evidence.

The second variable concerns the judge's power to reject irrelevant evidence – an interesting feature also related to the role of the judge and closely connected with the preceding variable. However, the significance of answers to the so defined question is limited, because the importance of this power depends very much on what is seen as irrelevant as well as on how thoroughly the judge controls the proceedings at each stage. For example, in a system where after filing of the claim, it is up to the parties to discover the facts, a judge necessarily is not familiar with the case. Such a judge will not be able to avoid discovery measures regarding issues which, to an informed observer, would appear to be irrelevant.

The questions for the third variable, which concerns the hearsay-rule, the fourth variable, which is about mandatory pre-qualification of questions, the fifth variable, asking whether witnesses can be orally interrogated only by the judge or by the parties as well, and the sixth variable regarding the admissibility of documents which are not originals or certified copies seem quite straightforward. Note, however, that on a closer look, the fifth variable concerning who is permitted to question live witnesses and parties is very problematic. First, the definition[86] does not distinguish between the interrogation of parties and the interrogation of witnesses. Indeed, some legal systems have abandoned this distinction –

---

as to documents held by third parties, petition of one of the parties is necessary) and Art. 138–142. For the *juge d'instruction*, see Art. 771 no. 5.

For *Germany*, see § 143 (Court can order that the parties submit any relevant file they have in their possession), § 144 (Court can order the consultation of an expert and the inspection of objects or real property), § 273(2) no. 2 (Court can require public authorities to submit documents or to provide information), § 448 ZPO (Court can take the deposition of a party if the evidence presented so far shows a certain probability, but is not yet sufficient to decide the case on preponderance of evidence); for an excellent overview on German law before and after the 2001 reform, see Astrid Stadler, *The Multiple Roles of Judges and Attorneys in Modern Civil Litigation*, 27 HASTINGS INT'L & COMP. L. REV. 55, 64–68 (2003); Peter Gottwald, *Civil Procedure in Germany after the Reform Act of 2001*, 23 C.J.Q. 338 (2004).

According to the Study's Dataset, the French judge can freely introduce evidence, the German judge cannot. This interpretation seems doubtful even before the 2001 reform in Germany. For a comparison of the role of the judge in French and German civil procedure and ALI/UNIDROIT Principle 22, see Rolf Stürner, *Quelques remarques sur l'image actuelle de la procédure allemande et sa relation avec la procédure française et les tendances internationales*, *in* DE LA COMMÉMORATION D'UN CODE À L'AUTRE: 200 ANS DE PROCÉDURE CIVILE EN FRANCE 329, 331–332 (Loïc Cadiet & Guy Canivet, eds., 2006).

[86] Djankov et al., *supra* note 11, at 466.

among them Austrian and English law,[87] what may explain why the authors of the Study have neglected it. Concededly, the distinction is not necessarily connected with the question of who is permitted to question parties. However, the variable and its definition hint at a lack of experience in comparative procedural law on the part of the researchers.

Second, the definition does not distinguish between the interrogation by parties and by counsel,[88] although a limitation on party activity would, under the Study's concept of formalism, be considered as formalistic.

Third, it is doubtful whether this variable catches the crucial features. This may be illustrated comparing the data for France, Germany, the U.S. and the United Kingdom: In the Dataset, we find the value "one" for France, meaning that in France parties and witnesses can only be interrogated by the judge, and "zero" for Germany, the U.S. and the United Kingdom, meaning that in these countries witnesses and parties may be interrogated by the judge and the opposing party. It is true that in Germany, witnesses can generally be and sometimes are interrogated by counsel,[89] while in France this is only the case in rare circumstances.[90] Yet it seems incorrect to draw the line here. In reality, interrogation by counsel or the opposing party does not play as important a role in Germany as this is the case for the U.S. and the United Kingdom. In Germany, counsel for the parties may question live witnesses after the judge's initial questioning. But this initial questioning usually covers all the facts that the judge thinks are relevant to the case and need clarification. Therefore, in a good number of cases there may be no need for further questioning by counsel.[91] In contrast, in other countries (particularly the U.S.), counsel's performance of

[87] For a comparative analysis, see Rolf Stürner, *Die Partei als Beweismittel im europäischen Zivilprozeß*, *in* FESTSCHRIFT FÜR AKIRA ISHIKAWA ZUM 70. GEBURTSTAG 529, 535–536 (Gerhard Lüke, Takehiko Mikami & Hanns Prütting, eds., 2001). Even legal systems without a general distinction know at least some special rules for party examination; *see, e.g.,* Federal Rules of Evidence Rule 611(c) last sentence (leading questions permitted when adverse party is interrogated).

[88] *See, e.g.,* for Germany § 397(2) ZPO, distinguishing between the party (judge *can* allow questions) and her attorney (judge *must* allow questions).

[89] § 397 ZPO; Murray & Stürner, *supra* note 16, at 15.

[90] *See* Art. 214 NCPC: "Les parties ne doivent ni interrompre ni interpeller ni chercher à influencer les témoins qui déposent, ni s'adresser directement à eux, à peine d'exclusion. Le juge pose, s'il l'estime nécessaire, les questions que les parties lui soumettent après l'interrogation du témoin." Jacques Borel & Stephen M. Boyd, *Opportunities for and Obstacles to Obtaining Evidence in France for Use in the United States*, 13 INT'L LAW. 35, 37 (1979).

[91] *Cf.* Murray & Stürner, *supra* note 16, at 293–297; Chase, *supra* note 83, at 4–5.

direct and cross examinations are extremely important.[92] This example illustrates the weakness of the variable and its definition.

The seventh variable, "Authenticity and weight of [documentary] evidence defined by law", is again a complicated one. First, one can wonder whether only a rule assigning "full probative value" to a document or also a presumption fulfills the variable. Even in cases of "full probative value" typically there are exceptions for fraud etc., and the term "presumption" is sometimes used interchangeably for both cases. Therefore, a uniform treatment seems to be appropriate. Is this the way the variable has been interpreted? We do not know.

Second, it is not fully clear whether the variable is meant to be limited to statutory provisions or also includes otherwise settled law or a uniform court practice. On the one hand, traditional statutory rules favoring documentary evidence have often been diminished remarkably by courts.[93] On the other hand, documents for which no statutory rules exist may still be treated as prima-facie-evidence, or the courts may use presumptions, what in practice may have the same consequences as a statutorily fixed probative value. Not to take into account these cases would overemphasize the law in the books and thereby necessarily create a bias against written systems.

Third, there are countries in which the probative value of certain, but not all documents is specified, often distinguishing as to the scope of what is to be seen as proven between private documents and documents emanating from a public authority or a notary.[94] Although there were times when the weight of virtually all evidence was fixed,[95] these systems have disappeared today. Therefore, it should be sufficient for an affirmative answer that just some documents have a probative value defined by law. But it is uncertain how the answering lawyers have treated these ambiguities and whether their interpretation was consistent. This once more throws a shadow on the reliability of the collected data.

---

[92] *Cf.* Murray, *supra* note 19, at 345–348; Lay, *supra* note 56, at 75 et seq.; for a good overview on the trial process, see Friedenthal et al., *supra* note 55, at 488 et seq. On Japan's reciprocal examination system, introduced in 1948, *see* Kojima, *supra* note 16, at 706–707.

[93] *Cf.* Stürner, *supra* note 20, at 239–240.

[94] *See, e.g.,* for Austria §§ 292 et seq. ZPO, for France Art. 1319 et seq. Code Civil, for Germany §§ 415 et seq. ZPO, for Switzerland Art. 9 Zivilgesetzbuch (ZGB). On documents certified by a civil law Latin Notary, see generally Pedro A. Malavet, *The Foreign Notarial Legal Services Monopoly: Why Should We Care?*, 31 J. MARSHALL L. REV. 945, 954–57 (1998).

[95] On the times when Europe as a whole (i.e., including England) was governed by the idea of a "filter of super-individual rationality", see Stürner, *supra* note 18, at 19; for Germany ("Beweisregeln"), see Murray and Stürner, *supra* note 16, at 26.

For the eighth variable, the questionnaire wants to know whether the recording of all evidence introduced at trial is mandatory. At first sight, this is a clear-cut question. But are we really surprised to find that in the majority of all the assessed countries, that is, in 83 of the 109 countries, there is such mandatory recording? Wouldn't it be more significant to ask how this recording looks like? It is here where we find the more characteristic and significant differences. There are countries where the record contains a literal transcript or another form of verbatim recording of the witness's statements.[96] In other countries, however, the record encloses only the judge's summary of what the witness said.[97] It is even conceivable that there be nothing more but the bare statement that the court heard a certain witness.[98] These remarkable differences, which appear to be more significant than the mere fact whether there is recording or not, are everything but unknown to civil procedure scholars.[99] Here again, it seems as if the question does not come to the really important point. This once more re-

---

[96] *Cf.* for the U.S. Rule 30 of the Federal Rules of Civil Procedure: "(b) … (2) The party taking the deposition shall state in the notice the method by which the testimony shall be recorded. Unless the court orders otherwise, it may be recorded by sound, sound-and-visual, or stenographic means, and the party taking the deposition shall bear the cost of the recording. Any party may arrange for a transcription to be made from the recording of a deposition taken by nonstenographic means. … (c) Examination and Cross-Examination; Record of Examination; Oath; Objections. … The officer before whom the deposition is to be taken shall put the witness on oath or affirmation and shall personally, or by someone acting under the officer's direction and in the officer's presence, record the testimony of the witness. The testimony shall be taken stenographically or recorded by any other method authorized by subdivision (b)(2) of this rule. … In lieu of participating in the oral examination, parties may serve written questions in a sealed envelope on the party taking the deposition and the party taking the deposition shall transmit them to the officer, who shall propound them to the witness and record the answers verbatim. …"

[97] This is the usual way of recording witness testimony in many civil law countries; for France cf. Art. 220, 221 NCPC and SERGE GUINCHARD & FRÉDÉRIQUE FERRAND, PROCÉDURE CIVILE 965-967, ¶¶ 1270–1272 (28th ed., 2006); for Germany cf. § 260(2), (3) no. 4 ZPO. For Switzerland (Zurich) see §§ 145, 146, 151, 152 ZPO and Franz Hasenböhler, *Beweisrecht, vorsorgliche Maßnahmen und Schutzschrift*, *in* DIE KÜNFTIGE SCHWEIZERISCHE ZIVILPROZESSORDNUNG 25, 30 (Thomas Sutter-Somm & Franz Hasenböhler, eds., 2003) (mentioning the variety of solutions in the different Cantons of Switzerland).

[98] This is the rule for criminal proceedings not before the lowest courts in Germany, *cf.* § 273(2) StPO. Note also that in France, under certain circumstances only the judgment contains the names and results of the witness's deposition, *see* Art. 219(2) NCPC and Guinchard & Ferrand, *supra* note 97, at 966, ¶ 1271.

[99] *See, e.g.*, Robert B. Acomb, Jr., *Foreign Depositions: The Problems, Pitfalls and Procedures*, 14 THE FORUM 440, 440–441 (1978/1979); Harry Leroy Jones, *International Judicial Assistance: Procedural Chaos and a Program for Reform*, 62 YALE L.J. 515, 531 (1953).

veals an unfortunate ignorance of comparative civil procedure on the part of the questions' drafters.

6. Control of Superior Review

Under this headline the questionnaire addresses some features of a possible review. Indeed, the importance and relative frequency of appeal in continental European proceedings and the finality of first instance decisions, subject to more sporadic appeals, in common law countries, are sometimes highlighted as characteristic features.[100] In reality, however, the differences are not that obvious, and they do not fully reflect the civil versus common law divide.[101] The Study's three variables have in common that they combine the question whether appeal is possible at all with specific questions about the suspension of enforcement, the scope of review, and a particular type of review, interlocutory appeals. The following discussion first addresses the variables' common aspect whether appeal is possible at all; then it focuses on the individual variables.

All variables about appeal take into consideration that appeals may be allowed or not. It is certainly true that in one and the same case, the answer can be either yes or no. Therefore, if applied to the two model cases, this approach seems reasonable. However, looking only on the two model cases considerably restricts the picture. In many if not most countries, there are provisions that a judgment may be appealed only if the appeal has been allowed by the trial court (*iudex a quo*) or the appellate court (*iudex ad quem*), or if the amount at stake exceeds a certain sum.[102] It is not clear if the first two variables (suspension of enforcement; scope of review) just investigate whether the decision in the respective model case can be appealed, or if they want to be understood in a broader sense, embracing all check collection or all eviction cases or even any cases.[103] In addition, it is

---

[100] *See, e.g.*, Damaška, *supra* note 14, at 30, 48–50, 58–61, 215; Goldstein, *supra* note 54, at 8 et seq.

[101] J.A. JOLOWICZ, ON CIVIL PROCEDURE 303–306 (2000) (noting that whereas in the U.S., it is the old common law writ of error that lies behind modern appeal, in most other common law countries appeal is based on the equity concept of a rehearing).

[102] *See only* J.A. Jolowicz, *Introduction*, *in* RECOURSE AGAINST JUDGMENTS IN THE EUROPEAN UNION 1, 5–8 (J.A. Jolowicz & C.H. van Rhee, eds., 1999) and the national reports in that volume.

[103] The Study itself implicitly acknowledges the necessity of departing from the mere application of the procedural rules on the model cases in the explanation of the variable on interlocutory appeals. Obviously the two model cases cannot address all possibilities of interlocutory appeals, even more if they only provide factual (as opposed to procedural) details. It follows that the question of whether interlocutory appeals are allowed necessarily cannot be answered other than in a general way, abstracting from the two

not clear whether the variables only concern so-called "ordinary" appeals or also cover appeals in cases where exceptional mistakes like violations of constitutional rights are alleged and which go to special courts like constitutional courts. Such distinction may be inexistent in many countries, especially in countries without specialized courts, but it is quite important in others. The Study completely ignores this feature. If follows from these observations that the question of whether the judgment can be appealed at all – a question common to the definitions of the first two variables of this sub-index – is problematic. Consequently, for this reason alone the significance of the results of both variables is doubtful.

Apart from these concerns, which are common to the variables about suspension of enforcement and scope of review, each of the three variables of this sub-index has its own difficulties. The first variable asks whether the enforcement of the judgment is automatically suspended until resolution of the appeal. If the judgment cannot be appealed at all, this is seen as corresponding to a case where no such automatic suspension exists. Not only could one wonder how "automatic" the automatic suspension has to be: Is it still an automatic suspension if we need a merely declaratory court order, leaving the judge with no discretion? And, more importantly, how should we deal with systems where there is no automatic suspension, but where special conditions must be met before enforcement is admissible? In Germany, for example, the general rule is that as long as an appeal is possible, judgments can only be enforced after the enforcing party has provided some form security. This security is designed to make sure that the appellant can recover from any damages suffered from a "premature" enforcement if the judgment is overruled on appeal.[104] However, there exist elaborated statutory provisions containing exceptions for claims that can be enforced without such security.[105] The judge determines the amount of the security, if any, in the original judgment. Still, this order can be modified on application of the appellant or the appellee, respectively, arguing that the case at issue involves special circumstances which necessitate a deviation from the statutory provision.[106] Is such a system close to an automatic stay, because without security the judgment cannot be enforced, or is it the opposite, because it lies in the power of the parties to meet the requirements necessary for starting (or avoiding) enforcement? In addition, we face the problem that the two hypothetical cases somewhat distort the picture. Taking once more Germany as an example, there is an express

model cases. Indeed, the definition determines that it be decisive whether such appeals are allowed or *always* prohibited.

[104] § 709 ZPO.

[105] § 708 ZPO.

[106] §§ 710, 712 ZPO.

exception from the requirement of posting security for eviction cases;[107] as to the check collection case, the answer depends on whether the claim has been adjudicated by the first instance court in the ordinary proceedings or in the special and accelerated proceedings for check collection.[108]

The second variable asks whether there is comprehensive review in appeal. Indeed, this is a meaningful feature which has long received much attention from comparative law scholars. It seems to be a worldwide phenomenon that wherever limitations on the scope of review exist, it is extremely difficult to draw the line between what can and what cannot be reviewed.[109] One tricky issue is the distinction between law and fact, another concerns limitations on pleading new facts on the appellate level, adding the intricate question of when facts are new. Moreover, we observe a tendency of appellate courts to expand their power of review, usually trying to hide that under abstract deductions that are more or less convincing.[110] Thus, it is difficult enough to correctly describe the scope of review for one and the same country. Even more difficult it is to compare the various national solutions. Although scholars tend to distinguish several types of review and have arranged the many countries into different groups, the delineations are not completely fixed. The Study differentiates between countries where "issues of both law and fact (evidence)" can be reviewed, and countries where "only new evidence or issues of law" can be reviewed. By using these words, the Study's definition seems to absorb all the difficulties in determining the borders between law and fact and the question of when evidence is new. How should this definition be applied then? Should we use the words in the way courts in the respective country use them, or should we develop independent categories?[111] One clear-cut solution would be to assign the same value to all systems with any limitation whatsoever on pleading "old" facts. However, it is doubtful whether

---

[107] § 708 no. 7 ZPO.

[108] § 708 no. 4 ZPO; on the non-mandatory special proceedings for check collection cases see supra sub III.A.3.

[109] *See generally* Peter E. Herzog & Delmar Karlen, *Attacks on Judicial Decisions*, *in* INTERNATIONAL ENCYCLOPEDIA OF COMPARATIVE LAW, VOL. XVI, CIVIL PROCEDURE, CH. 8, ¶¶ 8-94 through 8-100 (Mauro Cappelletti, chief ed., 1982); for France and Germany, see Stürner, *supra* note 85, at 335. *See also* ALI/UNIDROIT Principle 27.2 and 27.3 and Comments P-27A and P-27B.

[110] *See, e.g.*, MARTIN SHAPIRO, COURTS: A COMPARATIVE AND POLITICAL ANALYSIS 40 (1981) (calling the distinction between questions of law and facts in the U.S. "a notorious slippery one", mentioning the category of "mixed questions of fact and law" and talking of a worldwide "pull of appellate courts toward the facts").

[111] In principle, this question could be asked concerning any of the legal terms used in the definitions. Comparative law scholars have been familiar with this problem since a long time; *see only* KONRAD ZWEIGERT & HEIN KÖTZ, INTRODUCTION TO COMPARATIVE LAW 34–47 (Tony Weir, trans., 3rd ed., 1998).

this can lead to meaningful results, as the two historical extremes have disappeared.[112] At any rate, as neat as the definition may seem at first sight, its application is all but easy.

The third variable pertaining to superior review concerns interlocutory appeals. The questionnaire defines interlocutory appeals as "appeals against interlocutory or interim judicial decisions made during the course of a judicial proceeding in first instance and before the final ruling on the entire case."[113] The distinction is whether such appeals are always prohibited or not. It must be acknowledged that this simple criterion may be the only way to get a reliable set of answers. However, even if interlocutory appeals are not completely excluded in a civil procedure system, this does not say much about which role they actually play in practice. Particularly where only certain interlocutory or interim court decisions can be the object of an interlocutory appeal, it can well be that such appeals do not occur very frequently and therefore are not characteristic at all for a system.

7. Engagement Formalities

The questionnaire wants to determine here what steps are to be taken to engage court proceedings. The first variable addresses mandatory pre-trial conciliation or mediation. One could wonder whether a mandatory "settlement conference" before the court, which if unsuccessful is immediately followed by the trial stage of the proceedings,[114] satisfies this criterion. The definition only encompasses a conciliation or mediation before filing the lawsuit. Indeed, such in-court mediation, even if provided as a separate step of the proceedings, may look very different than any independent mediation or conciliation. "Settlement conferences" will often be combined with preliminary hearings. It therefore seems correct not to include them at all, be it in this or a separate variable. What is most problematic here, though, is that in some countries, there is mandatory pre-trial conciliation only for a certain set of cases.[115] With just two hypothetical cases, which

---

[112] *Cf.* ALI/UNIDROIT Principles Comment P-27B.

[113] Djankov et al., *supra* note 11, at 467.

[114] *See, e.g.,* Italy: Art. 320 Codice di Procedura Civile; Germany: §§ 278(2)–(5), 279(1) ZPO; Murray & Stürner, *supra* note 16, at 259–260; Stürner, *supra* note 85, at 333; *see also* § 54 Arbeitsgerichtsgesetz (ArbGG) for claims brought in the labor law courts (there, the trial usually cannot follow immediately because the lay judges, which need not participate in the court's conciliation attempt, are not instantly available).

[115] *See, e.g.,* Germany: § 15a EGZPO (deference to the German states to order mandatory conciliation proceedings for claims with a value up to 750 Euro and certain other claims) and the relevant state law provisions; for Switzerland cf. Art. 191–193 Vorentwurf (expert draft of June 2003) of the future Swiss Civil Procedure Code and Christoph Leuenberger, *Das ordentliche Verfahren*, *in* DIE KÜNFTIGE SCHWEIZERISCHE ZIVILPROZESSORDNUNG 51, 52–54 (Thomas Sutter-Somm & Franz Hasenböhler, eds., 2003).

due to their special settings may even involve considerable particularities,[116] the Study is far from covering a representative set of proceedings. Therefore the results collected under this variable should not be generalized.

The next two variables concern the questions of whether service of process and notification of judgment need to be done through the intervention of a judicial officer. Again, the definition has to be interpreted. What is meant by "intervention of a judicial officer"? In many countries, although the actual delivery of the respective documents can be done using the normal postal service, a judge or judicial officer is involved at an earlier stage. It cannot be expected that this question has been resolved by all the answering lawyers in the same sense.

8. Independent Procedural Actions

A last set of variables counts the number of "independent procedural actions" for the three stages of the proceedings: filing and service, trial and judgment, and enforcement. The idea behind this set of variables apparently is to find out how many steps are to be taken until the plaintiff gets what she wants. The questionnaire provides a relatively detailed description of what should be seen as an "independent procedural action".[117] Nevertheless, the considerable divergence in the numbers collected from the various countries[118] suggests that the application of this definition proves difficult.

Looking closer to the Study's definition of what constitutes an independent procedural action, this cannot surprise. On one hand, every step of the procedure demanding interaction between the parties or between the parties and the judge or court officer shall be deemed an independent procedural action. The next sentence explains that the authors "also" count as such action every judicial or administrative writ or resolution. The use of the word "also" seems to propose that the authors do not see such writ or resolution as a step demanding interaction. This, in turn, could mean that the authors have a rather narrow understanding of the term "interaction". Yet, interpreted that strictly, which procedural step at all really requires interaction, if this is not the case for a court writ or resolution which, of course, the parties must have received before it can take effect?

---

[116] *See, e.g.,* Germany: § 15a(2) no. 4 EGZPO prohibits states from ordering mandatory conciliation proceedings for check claims pursued in the special check proceedings.

[117] Djankov et al., *supra* note 11, at 469.

[118] For the check collection case, the numbers range from 2 to 20 (filing and service), 1 to 16 (trial and judgment), and 3 to 16 (enforcement); for the eviction case, the numbers range from 1 to 16 (filing and service), 1 to 17 (trial and judgment), and 2 to 12 (enforcement).

On the other hand, the questionnaire requires the answering attorneys to assume actions to be simultaneous if possible, so that procedural events which may be fulfilled in the same day and place be only counted as one action. The "same day and place" requirement and its illustration in the text (where the meeting of judge, claimant and defendant in which following a discussion the judge issues a decision is counted as one single action)[119] suggest that the pure fact of actions happening simultaneously in a merely temporal respect is not decisive. Rather, some form of communication between the actors seems to be required. Even with this clarification, though, the meaning of what are "simultaneous actions" remains somewhat unclear. In an optimal case, many different steps may be taken during one day and in one and the same place, i.e., the courthouse. However, it is possible that for practical reasons, this virtually never happens. Should, in such case, attention be paid to a merely theoretical possibility under the relevant rules? The definition seems to demand just that.

How difficult it is to apply the Study's definition becomes particularly obvious in the context of enforcement. The Study assumes without any further illustration that enforcement can happen in one single procedural action,[120] and consequently takes this as the ideal under the neighbor model. But how should we imagine enforcement in a single action? Even in a model, such immediate enforcement is hardly plausible, for when the defendant does not obey, but resists the judgment entered against her – what the claimant first has to find out –, the use of force or the involvement of the judge will be inevitable. And if the defendant does not resist, there is no need for enforcement and therefore no enforcement at all. Finally and most importantly, does it really make sense to use the absolute minimum of steps in an *optimal* case and not the much more realistic number in an *average* case? Or, on a higher level of abstraction, should we base our comparison on the law in the books or the law in action? We have alluded to this problem several times already. Comparative law scholars have since long argued that under normal circumstances, it is the law in action rather than the law in the book that matters.[121] The Study, however, here apparently decides the other way in that it counts the minimum numbers. Of course, this is not strange or even wrong per se. To the contrary, there can be a good reason for using the "law-in-the-books" approach. In our case, it could have been argued that minimum numbers are more significant for the purpose of comparing procedural formalism – although we

[119] Djankov et al., *supra* note 11, at 475–476.

[120] Djankov et al., *supra* note 11, at 476.

[121] *See only* RUDOLF B. SCHLESINGER, HANS W. BAADE, PETER E. HERZOG, COMPARATIVE LAW 987–998 (6th ed., 1998); Zweigert & Kötz, *supra* note 111, at 36–39.

cannot find support for this argument.[122] It is regrettable that the Study is not explicit on this point.

In sum, whether the numbers collected under the headline "independent procedural actions" are meaningful, is hard to assess without knowing what steps have been counted and why. It seems that many if not most decisions on what is to be counted as an "independent procedural action", are subjective evaluations rather than objective facts.

9. Conclusion

It goes without saying that any comparison of legal systems cannot be done without a more or less high degree of simplification. It is widely accepted that the comparative lawyer has to look to the law from a higher level of abstraction. However, such abstraction should not be done without a profound knowledge of potential "hot issues" in the various legal systems under examination. If she is taking too general an approach, the researcher risks overlooking the most striking and characteristic features of the different legal systems.

At first sight, the variables used in the questionnaire look promising. Most of them address issues which have long been discussed in comparative civil litigation. On closer scrutiny, though, serious doubts arise whether the questions are actually phrased in a way as to reveal the characteristic and distinctive features of the various legal systems. This is even more true taking into consideration that the two hypothetical cases seem to draw a somewhat distorted picture of the procedural reality. Moreover, and relatedly, many of the variables' definitions are unclear or ambiguous. Almost all of them leave considerable room for interpretation – be it by the answering lawyers or the Study's authors, who after a first coding and a second round of questions did the "fine-tuning".[123] Such interpretation

[122] Admittedly, the pure law in the books may give useful information about the model and the theoretical ideas the legislature or the court which decided the relevant precedent had in mind. In addition, there are areas of the law where the law in action and the law in the books are virtually identical. However, it seems that both is not the case for the number of "independent procedural actions": Actual court practice not only reflects the law, but is largely determined by the most various external factors. The actual number of procedural actions usually is by no means fix and predictable ex ante, but depends on individual circumstances like the judge's general workload and her preferred way of handling cases, the availability of the parties and their attorneys and diverse externalities. As a prominent example, in many countries the law permits that the judgment be rendered "sur le siège" immediately at the end of the trial hearing, but in reality this happens most rarely. What, then, is more significant in a comparison of various civil procedure systems – actual practice or a mere theoretical possibility? We believe that the arguments for the former solution prevail.

[123] *Cf.* Djankov et al., *supra* note 11, at 461.

necessarily involves subjective decisions.[124] The Study does not disclose whether it specified the definitions consistently across the countries, and if so, according to which criteria. Therefore, one may question whether these variables are suitable for the purpose of mapping the reality.

C. The Supplementary Questions

The Study not only wants "to explain theoretically and to measure empirically the determinants of procedural formalism", but also claims "to assess its consequences for the quality of dispute resolution in courts".[125] It therefore collects data for a whole bunch of other variables. Some of them stem from external sources. The authors group these data under the headlines "other judicial quality measures" and "other variables".[126] Data on incentives of the parties and on duration in practice, however, have also been collected from the participating law firms. I will therefore discuss the latter here, as this part is dedicated to the questionnaire, calling them the "supplementary questions".

1. Incentives of Parties

Among the incentives of parties – the term "parties" obviously is used by the Study in a broad sense, including the judge and the court – mandatory time limits unquestionably take a very important place. The questionnaire distinguishes between mandatory time limits for admission, to present evidence, to present defense, for judgment, and for notification of judgment. It goes without saying that mandatory time limits can be a very important incentive to act within a certain time, thereby preventing excessively long duration of proceedings. This is true not only for plaintiff and defendant, who are under threat of procedural disadvantages like preclusion with some piece of evidence or even a default judgment, but also for the judge, who may risk disciplinary measures, negative influences on his career in countries with career judges, or that after remand on appeal she must try the whole case *de novo*.[127] On closer scrutiny, one has to wonder what ex-

[124] *Cf.* Holger Spamann, *On the Insignificance and/or Endogeneity of La Porta et al.'s 'Anti-Director Rights Index' under Consistent Coding*, HLS John M. Olin Center for Law, Economics, and Business Discussion Paper No. 7, 3/2006, p. 8–11, *available at* <http://papers.ssrn.com/sol3/papers.cfm?abstract_id=894301> (last visited July 17, 2006).

[125] Djankov et al., *supra* note 11, at 455.

[126] These other sources will be discussed *infra* sub VI.

[127] *Cf., e.g., Coate v. Omholt*, 203 Mont. 488, 622 P.2d 591 (1983) and the other cases reported by Neil C. McCabe, *Four Faces of State Constitutional Separation of Powers:*

actly is meant with "mandatory": Is only a time limit that cannot be extended under any circumstances "mandatory", or is it sufficient that the time limit exist as a general rule, allowing for extensions for good cause? In order to catch the characteristics of a procedural system, the latter seems preferable. But the questionnaire's definition need not necessarily be understood in this sense. For Germany, for example, the answering attorneys found no mandatory "time limit for judgment" in check collection cases, although § 310(1) ZPO provides in its second sentence (without containing an exception for check collection), that the judgment shall be entered no longer than three weeks from the final hearing, unless special circumstances, like the scale or the difficulty of the case at issue, require a longer period of time.[128]

Another incentive the Study identifies is the admissibility of contingency fee agreements. The questionnaire wants to know whether these agreements are prohibited by law "in all cases" or not. This way of posing the question takes into account that such agreements may be admissible only in some cases and be prohibited in others. However, it does not clearly address conditional fee agreements and fee agreements which combine a fixed fee with a contingent fee. It therefore remains unclear from the questionnaire's definition how one should answer if in a country a pure quota litis agreement is prohibited, but a contingent component or a non-contingent, but conditional, bonus or uplift which adds to a fixed fee is allowed.[129]

The last incentive the Study investigates is the existence of a loser-pays rule. The variable flatly asks whether the loser is required to pay all the costs of the dispute. This question is unambiguous. However, two remarks

---

Challenges to Speedy Trial and Speedy Dispositoin Provisions, 62 TEMP. L. REV. 177 (1989); for Germany, see Dieter Leipold, *Prozeßförderungspflicht der Parteien und richterliche Verantwortung*, 93 ZZP 237–265 (1980); Bundesgerichtshof [BGH] 39 NEUE JURISTISCHE WOCHENSCHRIFT [NJW] 2958 (1986); 46 NJW 2603 (1993); for Russia, see Vladimir Yarkov, *Contemporary Problems of Russian Civil Procedure*, 10 ZZPINT 371, 379–380 (2005).

[128] *See also* § 315(2) and the decisions of the BGH, *supra* note 127.

[129] *See, e.g.,* for France: Loi no. 71-1130 Art. 10(3), as modified by Loi no. 71-647 Art. 72: "Toute fixation d'honoraires, qui ne le serait qu'en fonction du résultat judiciaire, est interdite. Est licite la convention qui, outre la rémunération des prestations effectuées, prévoit la fixation d'un honoraire complémentaire en fonction du résultat obtenu ou du service rendu." The answering French lawyers decided that this is no prohibition of quota litis "in all cases". On England's conditional fee agreements, which usually specify that the lawyer can receive a "success fee" exceeding his ordinary charge, see Andrews, *supra* note 53, at ¶¶ 35.02–35.64; *generally* MICHAEL BREYER, KOSTENORIENTIERTE STEUERUNG DES ZIVILPROZESSES 41–43 (2006). The Dataset's value for the United Kingdom is "zero", what means that quota litis agreements are not prohibited by law in all cases.

should be made. First, the range of possible cost-shifting rules is large. The American Rule, according to which each party bears its own costs,[130] and the loser-pays rule (also called the English Rule), pursuant to which the loser – be it the plaintiff or the defendant – bears his opponent's legal fees as well as his own,[131] only mark the most important cornerstones. In addition to these two rules, other forms of fee-shifting, like plaintiff-favoring fee-shifting,[132] defendant-favoring fee-shifting, or so called offer-of-settlement rules,[133] are possible. Taken literally, the variable distinguishes between the English Rule and all other types of rules.

Second, most countries do not follow one rule for all types of cases. Rather, we find exceptions and special provisions which typically incorporate policy decisions. It does not follow from the Study's definition whether the variable only asks who is required to pay the costs in the two model cases or whether it is to be understood as a general question. The first interpretation would once more raise the question of whether the two model cases can claim to be representative for a country's whole system; the second interpretation would either discern only "pure" loser-pays rule countries from all the other countries – countries which follow a "pure" American Rule and countries with a mixed system – or require an evaluation of which rule is predominant in and characteristic for a given country. Not only may it be difficult to determine which rule prevails, but such de-

---

[130] *See only Alyeska Pipeline Serv. Co. v. Wilderness Soc'y*, 421 U.S. 240, 247 (1975) (stating that "[i]n the United States, the prevailing litigant is ordinarily not entitled to collect a reasonable attorneys' fee from the loser."); John Leubsdorf, *Toward a History of the American Rule on Attorney Fee Recovery*, 47 LAW & CONTEMP. PROBS. 9 (1984).

[131] *Cf.* Peter Hurst, *Civil Procedure: Costs including conditional fees in England and Wales*, 10 ZZPINT 39, 40–42 (2006) (noting that since the introduction of the Civil Procedure Rules in 1998, this is no longer an all or nothing provision).

[132] *See, e.g.*, 15 U.S.C. § 15 (1982) (Clayton Act – Antitrust); 15 U.S.C. § 1640(a)(3) (1995) (Truth in Lending Act); *see also* 5 U.S.C. § 552a(g)(2)(B), (3)(B), (4)(B) (2004) (Privacy Act); 42 U.S.C. 1988(b) (2000) (Civil Rights Attorney's Fees Awards Act) and *Christiansburg Garment Co. v. Equal Employment Opportunity Commission*, 434 U.S. 412, 416 et seq. (1978).

[133] *See, e.g.*, Federal Rules of Civil Procedure Rule 68, which reads in part: "At any time more than 10 days before the trial begins, a party defending against a claim may serve upon the adverse party an offer to allow judgment to be taken against the defending party for the money or property or to the effect specified in the offer, with costs then accrued. If within 10 days after the service of the offer the adverse party serves written notice that the offer is accepted, either party may then file the offer and notice of acceptance together with proof of service thereof and thereupon the clerk shall enter judgment. An offer not accepted shall be deemed withdrawn and evidence thereof is not admissible except in a proceeding to determine costs. *If the judgment finally obtained by the offeree is not more favorable than the offer, the offeree must pay the costs incurred after the making of the offer. ...*" (emphasis added). *See also* Part 36 of the English Civil Procedure Rules, ALI/UNIDROIT Principle 24.3 and comment P-24B.

termination would also be doubtful because intermediate forms could be expressed numerically by using a number between zero and one. In the light of these several weak points, there is reason to question the usefulness of the so-defined variable.

2. Duration in Practice

It has constantly been pointed out by civil procedure scholars that duration is an important dimension of justice.[134] It follows that by taking duration as a determinant of judicial quality,[135] the Study is in good company. It collects data about the duration for three phases of the proceedings: duration until completion of service of process, duration of trial, and duration of enforcement.

As to the first phase, the duration from the moment of filing of the complaint until service of process, ambiguities can hardly arise. Also, it is interesting to define this phase separately, because apparently there are enormous differences.[136] The amplitude of these differences, in turn, involves differences in the exactitude of the data: The higher the numbers are, the less precise is the estimate.

Regarding the second phase, duration of trial, it should be mentioned that "trial" is not meant in a technical sense, but embraces the time between the moment of service of process and the moment the judgment is issued. This definition would include a pre-trial discovery. However, as already mentioned above, in none of the two model cases is it likely that an extensive pre-trial discovery takes place. Therefore, one characteristic aspect of the (Anglo-)American civil procedure which typically provokes extremely long duration of proceedings does not come into play in the collected data at all.

---

[134] *See, e.g.,* Jeremy Bentham's famous aphorism "Justice delayed is justice denied" (*cf.* Jeremy Bentham, *Principles of Judicial Procedure, with the outlines of a Procedure Code, in* THE WORKS OF JEREMY BENTHAM, Reprod. of the Bowring ed. of 1838–1843, vol. 2, at 17–18 (1962)); Adrian A.S. Zuckerman, *Justice in Crisis: Comparative Dimensions of Civil Procedure, in* CIVIL JUSTICE IN CRISIS 3, 6–7 (Adrian A.S. Zuckerman, ed., 1999) (arguing that justice has three dimensions: the dimension of truth in the sense of rectitude of the decision, the time dimension and the cost dimension); Konstantinos D. Kerameus, *Relevance and Computation of Time in Civil Procedure, in* FESTSCHRIFT FÜR FRANZ MATSCHER ZUM 65. GEBURTSTAG 241 (Oskar J. Ballon & Johann J. Hagen, eds., 1993); Thomas Sutter-Somm, *Schwerpunkte und Leitlinien des Vorentwurfs zur Schweizerischen Zivilprozessordnung, in* DIE KÜNFTIGE SCHWEIZERISCHE ZIVILPROZESSORDNUNG 11, 13 (Thomas Sutter-Somm & Franz Hasenböhler, eds., 2003); ALI/UNIDROIT Principle 7 and Comments P-7A, P-7B.

[135] Djankov et al., *supra* note 11, at 456.

[136] For the check collection case, duration ranges from 0 (Belgium) to 180 (Greece) days; for the eviction case, from 1 (Anguilla) to 160 (Gibraltar, Lebanon, Uganda) days.

The third phase, duration of enforcement, is defined as the duration between the moment of issuance of judgment and the moment the landlord repossesses the property (for the eviction case) or the creditor obtains payment (for the check collection case).[137] By focusing only on the result, that is, the fulfillment of the plaintiff's claim, without addressing the means by which this result is achieved, this definition seems to include the case that the defendant fulfills the judgment voluntarily. However, this interpretation somewhat conflicts with the notion of "enforcement" used to describe this phase. Enforcement excludes voluntary performance by the defendant. Whatever the correct interpretation, both possibilities are problematic: First, enforcement in the technical sense – enforcement assisted by state authority, be it through courts, bailiffs or marshals or any other state official – may only start after a separate application[138] and sometimes other actions[139] of the winning plaintiff.[140] Typically, the plaintiff will not immediately make such application, but wait for a certain period of time to give the defendant the possibility to fulfill the judgment. Should this period, the duration of which depends on the patience of the individual plaintiff, be counted? Second, it is worth mentioning that at least in the check collection case, there may be more than one way of enforcement. For example, the plaintiff-creditor could seize and foreclose on real estate or tangible property or seek an attachment-of-earnings order to get the money owed by the defendant. It seems that in most legal systems, it is in principle the winning plaintiff who decides what ought to be done.[141] Not only does this again bring about the necessity of a separate action by the plaintiff, but also the ultimate duration depends exclusively on the particularities of the case at issue, like the question of whether there are earnings that can be attached, or what type of property, if any, is available for seizure and how long it takes to foreclose – bank deposits or securities can be realized instantaneously whereas foreclosing on real estate, in particular if inhabited by others, may take a very long time. Even if we assume that all relevant details had been described in the model cases used in the ques-

---

[137] Djankov et al., *supra* note 11, at 471.

[138] *See, e.g.,* for England Andrews, *supra* note 53, at ¶¶ 39.20, 39.28, 39.46, 39.58 et seq.; for Germany §§ 753, 754 ZPO.

[139] An example is providing security to assure compensation of the other party in the case that the judgment be reversed on appeal; *see, e.g.,* for Italy Art. 478 (for the cases specified in Art. 35, 373 comma 1, 642 comma 2, 648 comma 2, 663 comma 3, 665 comma 2) Codice di Procedura Civile; for Germany §§ 709, 720a, 751(2) ZPO.

[140] *See also, e.g.,* Shapiro, *supra* note 110, at 13 (noting that courts typically do not monitor compliance and that they reintervene to exact compliance only at the request of one of the parties).

[141] *See only* for France Art. 22 Loi n°91-650 du 9 juillet 1991 portant réforme des procédures civiles d'exécution; for England Andrews, *supra* note 53, at ¶¶ 39.14, 39.15.

tionnaire, we here get into an area where significant comparisons are difficult to make. Third, if "enforcement" only encompasses cases where state officials have been involved to obtain fulfillment of the judgment, we should be aware that the number of these cases is much smaller than the number of all cases of the respective type brought into and decided by courts. Furthermore, these cases are special in that there is a defendant who even disrespects the court judgment, and this apparently for reasons other than her inability to fulfill (because the definition measures the duration *until repossession or payment*). Not only are these cases rare, but also they presumably involve extreme settings. Consequently, it is very doubtful whether any estimate of duration is possible, and whether such number can be seen as characteristic. If on the other hand "enforcement" includes cases in which the defendant fulfills the judgment voluntarily, the duration is not only a question of the relevant legal rules, but also and foremost a question of mentality. Needless to say that mentality – here: the willingness to obey a court decision – is different in different countries. Finally, a continuous and intense involvement of lawyers in the enforcement phase is not the rule but the exception, and it is even more doubtful that lawyers of the prestigious Lex Mundi member firms ever have to do with enforcement of such "small" cases as check collection and eviction. It is, then, questionable whether their answers on questions about the duration of enforcement are sufficiently reliable.

It follows that the duration variables by their numbers suggest a precision that is not realistic. All numbers are based on just two cases with their particularities, especially as to the phase of enforcement. It can hardly be expected that the answering lawyers ever followed a bigger number of cases similar to the model cases from the filing of the complaint until the end of the enforcement. Therefore, we must assume that the estimates are highly subjective. Using them for the purpose of comparing legal systems and drawing conclusions is daring. At least the Study should have contained an explicit caveat.

3. Conclusion

We have seen that likewise with respect to the supplementary questions, the definitions of the questionnaire are not as clear and unambiguous as they might appear to be at first sight. Consequently, the data collected under these questions is also not beyond all doubt.

Part IV

The Classification

In the foregoing third part of this book, we have discussed the questionnaire, focusing on the two model cases and the variables used to numerically analyze two model cases. In this part, we take a closer look at how the Study constructs the formalism index from the data collected through the questionnaire. Therefore, this part first revisits the understanding of formalism on which the Study is based. It then discusses the application of this concept: the Study's classification or "coding" of what is formalistic with regard to the individual variables.

A. The Neighbor Model

1. General Remarks

In order to determine whether a particular rule of an individual country's civil procedure is formalistic or more formalistic than another rule, one needs a point of reference. Two possible approaches are conceivable.

First, one can independently define which legal solution is formalistic for each specific aspect and step of the proceedings. Such an approach has the advantage that each rule could be examined individually, taking into consideration its context and the solutions which have been developed in the different legal systems of the world. This would probably best approximate the classic functional method in comparative law, which also is basic for comparative civil procedure.[142] But the described approach also has two major drawbacks. The one is that every single definition would contain an evaluation, would need to be justified or at least explained and therefore could be attacked as arbitrary, inconsistent, or biased. The other is that the absence of a general reference point raises the question whether any combination of the data collected under the several questions into a single general index is admissible.

[142] *Cf.* Stürner & Stadler, *supra* note 30, at 264–265, 290 (endorsing the functional approach for the field of comparative procedural law). But note that a comparison not of distinct legal institutions, but of the measure of a broad concept like "formalism" is somewhat at odds with the functional approach in comparative law.

Second, one can describe a general picture or concept and then decide whether a rule is formalistic or not with regard to the deviation of the rule from the general picture. To permit an easy application, such picture must be located at either end of the scale: formalistic or not formalistic. As formalism can take many different forms and is open-ended in the sense that in principle, the possibilities to add formalism to a system are endless, the only practicable location of such picture is at the zero, the non-formalistic, point. The use of such a general picture avoids the potential lack of consistency which inheres in the first approach. However, it may not furnish answers for all aspects, and in some cases may lead to results that are inadequate or at least counter-intuitive.

2. The Study's Approach: The Neighbor Model

The Study has chosen the second approach. It uses a general baseline, a concept which it calls the "neighbor model". The idea of this concept is relatively simple. Its basis is a hypothesis of how a dispute between two neighbors would be resolved in the absence of elaborated legal systems and courts. It is assumed that such disputes would be resolved by a third person on fairness grounds. This third person would not need to have special knowledge about the law; there would not be specialized lawyers, procedural requirements of written submissions or procedural constraints on the presentation of evidence, and no appeal.[143]

---

[143] Djankov et al., *supra* note 11, at 455, 457. When introducing its reader to the neighbor model, the Study references generally Martin Shapiro's important 1981 book COURTS: A COMPARATIVE AND POLITICAL ANALYSIS (*supra* note 110). Shapiro there proposes that courts derive their basic legitimacy from the social logic of the triad: They are part of a triadic structure of conflict resolution (p. 1, 36–37). When discussing the "mediating continuum", Shapiro speculates that "in tribal or village societies, [the go-between] may be any person, fortuitously present and not connected with either of the households ..." (p. 3). Maybe this or similar, relatively short descriptive speculations about archaic forms of dispute resolution (*see, e.g.*, p. 6) are the passages in which the Study's authors find support for their neighbor model. However, this picture is used to describe the *negotiator* (not the judge), and here as well as in the context of comparable sketches of archaic dispute resolution, Shapiro mentions the consensual character of these institutions, as opposed to today's courts. In addition, Shapiro immediately remarks that "a substantial portion of the total behavior of courts in all societies can be analyzed in terms of attempts to prevent the triad from breaking down into two against one" (p. 2). It seems that this "portion of behavior" is "procedural" behavior, the respect of certain procedural rules – and thus a deviation from a completely informal neighbor model. The connection between Shapiro and the neighbor model therefore seems to be rather loose. Nevertheless, is must be conceded that the Study is not the only text which cites Shapiro when referring to a neighbor model: *see, e.g.*, Owen M. Fiss, *Against Settlement*, 93 YALE L.J. 1073, 1075 (1984); Laura Margolis Warshawsky, *Objectivity and Accountability: Limits on Judicial Involvement in Settlement*, 1987 U. CHI. LEGAL F. 369, 370 (not

It follows that the Study uses a very simplistic and one-dimensional concept of formalism. Under the neighbor model, virtually any mandatory procedural rule or constraint can be seen as formalistic. It does not matter whether there is a good reason for the rule or not. In this respect, the Study's concept of formalism differs from the popular use of the term, where formalism usually has per se a negative connotation, suggesting that a restriction is not justified by the purpose, if any, it serves.

It may seem appealing to see in this "neighbor model" the predecessor of today's courts and to interpret the existence of lay as opposed to professional judges in certain areas as remnants of this type of proceedings. However, we do not have clear historical evidence of systems based on single laymen acting ad hoc and awarding judgments which are binding for the parties. Binding dispute resolution by a neutral third person presupposes the appearance of an authority.[144] It is a "mechanism [...] by which that authority is exercised."[145] When in early societies there was a single judge, this typically was the king, lord, or tribal leader. Laymen rather acted in a group, be it the folkmoot or a jury.[146] In both cases – single leader-judge or popular court – we have to suspect that these judges sought to resolve the disputes applying a body of traditional or customary rules and that certain procedural constraints were quite important, even more so if religiously motivated. As far as the jury is concerned, at least for the past two and a half centuries this institution has been accompanied by extremely formalistic and complicated rules, in particular in the field of evidence,[147] which account for many of today's differences between civil jus-

---

referencing Shapiro, *supra*, but excerpts of the same text *in* THE STRUCTURE OF PROCEDURE 284, 285 (Robert M. Cover & Owen M. Fiss, eds., 1979)).

[144] *See, e.g.*, SERGE GUINCHARD ET AL., DROIT PROCESSUEL 36, ¶ 15 (3rd ed., 2005). But note that it has been suggested that in imperial China, village elders and others imposing their mediation services on conflicting parties and employing preexisting written or customary rules were more lay judges than mediators because of the threat of severe social and economic sanctions (Shapiro, *supra* note 110, at 187, 192).

[145] James et al., *supra* note 57, at § 6.2, 362.

[146] *See, e.g.*, Shapiro, *supra* note 110, at 56 et seq.

[147] Langbein, *supra* note 54, at 1170 et seq. (inferring from the small importance of "unwritten evidence" in Geoffrey Gilbert's Treatise of 1726/1754 and Dudley Ryder's Notebooks of 1754–1756 that today's law on evidence is more recent than John H. Wigmore had proposed. But note that these sources' descriptions of "written evidence" and the "solemnities of an oath" sound also highly formalistic. In addition, judges at the time apparently could "reject a proffered verdict, probe its basis, argue with the jury, give further instruction, and require redeliberation." *Id.*, at 1190–1193, referencing John H. Langbein, *The Criminal Trial before the Lawyers*, 45 U. CHI. L. REV. 263, 291 (1978) and concluding that "[t]he impression that one derives from studying Ryder's civil practice is that the judge routinely dominated jury verdicts." This much more important role

tice in the U.S. and more or less the rest of the world.[148] Moreover, the jury is not alone in the courtroom – it is the fact finder, but the responsibility for the proceedings and the legal instructions of the jurors lies with the judge.[149] This separation of functions otherwise assumed by a single judge or uniform panel of judges does not appear to be a simple, informal setting. To say, as the Study does, that "neighborly dispute resolution by juries [comes] closer to Shapiro's ideal"[150] is therefore quite doubtful a statement, at least if "Shapiro's ideal" is associated with minimal formalism. In sum, the historical evidence we have seems to suggest that binding dispute resolution typically was all but an informal event of minor importance. In addition, even if the neighbor model were the ancestor of today's courts, the neighbor model would be as far away from most countries' contemporaneous civil procedure as, say, the Aurignacien homo sapiens from one of the 980 today's inhabitants of this place in France. Even if a completely informal "neighbor justice" ever existed, since then both Common Law and Civil Law traditions experienced an important period of time when the activity of courts was much more influenced by formalistic procedural rules than it is today: the separation of procedural law and substantive law is a relatively recent development. Both the Roman *legis actiones* and the English writs were first and foremost procedural tools, each good for one specific type of conflict;[151] both the Roman praetor and the English com-

---

of the judge as opposed to the laymen jury is obviously no informal neighborly dispute resolution.).

[148] *See supra* note 54 and accompanying text.

[149] *See generally* Damaška, *supra* note 14, at 25 (noting that a system based on "temporary officials" is typically associated with the development of a "cast of professionals" who "assist the 'inexperienced' decision maker, supply him with information, and maintain tenuous continuity within the apparatus of authority. Specialization [...] can be found in their midst. In short, a symbiotic relationship thus develops between a cast of nonauthoritative professionals and the amateurs in positions of power."); Carrington, *supra* note 56, at 44 (noting that "[g]roup lay decisionmaking necessitates professional leadership in the conduct of proceedings; the role of that officer is an unavoidable issue.").

[150] Djankov et al., *supra* note 11, at 459.

[151] On the English forms of actions, *see, e.g.*, FREDERICK POLLOCK & FREDERIC WILLIAM MAITLAND, 2 THE HISTORY OF ENGLISH LAW 562 (2nd ed., 1968) (observing that "[t]o-day we can say much of actions in general and we can say little of any procedure that is peculiar to actions of particular kinds. On the other hand, in the middle ages one could say next to nothing about actions in general, while one could discourse at great length about the mode in which an action of this or that sort was to be pursued and defended."); Shapiro, *supra* note 110, at 93–94 (noting that the writs were basically procedural in character, and that it was a system of law that was essentially a series of special procedures); on Roman law, *see, e.g.*, MAX KASER & KARL HACKL, DAS RÖMISCHE ZIVILPROZESSRECHT 23–148, in particular 34 et seq., 70, 75 (2nd ed., 1996); FRITZ SCHULZ, CLASSICAL ROMAN LAW 28–58 (1951); Shapiro, *supra* note 110, at 127. *See*

mon law and equity courts required the parties to respect relatively strict formal rules.[152] The English and the continental European procedure of the Middle Ages both were much more formalistic than procedures today. There is no straight line from informal neighborly dispute resolution to our civil procedure systems.

In any event, today's world is obviously very different from "intensely interdependent agricultural communities" in which "active neighborhood investigators" could perform their role.[153] It is hardly arguable that all other things being equal, we could even consider going "back to the roots" in the field of civil procedure. It follows that the neighbor model is, as the Study itself says, a theoretical model, and a very theoretical one at that. All this raises the question of whether using as a baseline the neighbor model is a wise approach.

The purely theoretical nature of the neighbor model has another implication. Whenever in a particular situation it is not obvious which solution is formalistic and which is not, there is no real-world system to have resort to for an answer. Rather, for such questions, one needs to make additional theoretical assumptions in order to complete the neighbor model, a model one pretends to just apply. In other words, the neighbor model used by the Study is the sum of what follows from the Study's own classifications. This, in turn, somewhat devalues its ability to provide a general picture. We will see this in the following, when we discuss the classifications for the variables of the questionnaire.

---

also Fritz Pringsheim, *The Inner Relationship between English and Roman Law*, 5 CAMBRIDGE L.J. 347, 358–359 (1935) (describing the striking analogy between classical Roman and traditional English procedure).

[152] On England, *see, e.g.,* Pollock & Maitland, *supra* note 151, at 558 et seq. (noting that "in the middle of the twelfth century the old, oral and traditional formalism is in part supplanted and in part reinforced by a new, written and authoritative formalism, for the like of which we shall look in vain elsewhere, unless we go back to a remote stage of Roman history. Our *legis actiones* give way to a formulary system." [Emphasis in original]); Shapiro, *supra* note 110, at 95 (arguing that in the sixteenth and seventeenth centuries equity developed its own highly artificial, complex, and rigid rules and practices which could be mastered only by specialists at equity pleading) and 101 (pointing out the bizarre complexity of common law and equity proceedings in the eighteenth century). *See also* Paul D. Carrington, *Teaching Civil Procedure: A Retrospective View*, 49 J. LEGAL EDUC. 311, 317 (1999) ("...common law pleading was a task for which common sense was useless."). On the *legis actiones*, see Kaser/Hackl, *supra* note 151, at 34, 75 et seq.

[153] *Cf.* Langbein, *supra* note 54, at 1170.

B. The Application of the Neighbor Model to the Questions Which Are the Basis for the Formalism Index

1. General Remarks

A numerical "formalism index" can only be constructed from the individual answers if a numerical value is attributed to each and any answer. This in turn presupposes that the answers be classified as to the degree of procedural formalism of a country's civil procedure in the particular context. The formalism index and its sub-indices are only correct if the classifications of the answers to the individual questions are correct. We will therefore now turn our attention to the way the Study classifies the individual answers on a "formalism scale". In doing so, let us ignore for the purpose of this subsection the problematic aspects of some of the questions as such, discussed in part III, and focus exclusively on the Study's classifications.

The basic method for the classification is that a particular variable equals "zero" for a country if the answer to the respective question describes a situation which corresponds best to the hypothetical solution under the neighbor model. In all other cases, the variable equals "one". Thus, the Study employs a very simple binary approach.

Yet the Study's classification of what is formalistic and what is not, as well as its binary approach, are not unproblematic.

2. Professionals versus Laymen

The coding of the first variable perfectly illustrates how problematic it can be to apply the neighbor model to a particular variable. Arguing that the resolution of disputes in specialized as opposed to general jurisdiction courts "generally entails procedural simplification aimed at 'mass production'", the Study assigns the value "zero" to this variable if the respective model case is tried before a court of limited jurisdiction, and "one" for a court of general jurisdiction. Not only is this classification counter-intuitive, it also is or at least comes close to a *petitio principii*.

First, if we want to take the neighbor model seriously, it is hard to integrate in this model something like a specialized court. Of course, we could imagine that there be neighbors specialized in the resolution of certain types of disputes. However, this qualification clearly departs from the idea of a most simple, unregulated dispute resolution by any neutral third person. It not only supplements the neighbor model in the context of a variable for which an application of the model could not have been derived easily from its initial description. Rather, it modifies the model by taking the opposite solution of what one would have expected. Therefore, the coding of this variable is not consistent with the Study's claim of the neighbor model as single, straightforward baseline for classification.

Second, it is most probably true that specialized courts generally act under procedural rules particularly adapted to their limited jurisdiction. However, this does not necessarily mean that these rules are less formalistic than the rules governing the procedure of general jurisdiction courts. The rules of a housing court, for example, may be much more complicated than the rules of a general jurisdiction court due to procedural safeguards to ensure the protection of the tenant. And any specialization presupposes rules determining which court is competent to try a particular case. Not only does this add to procedural complexity, but these rules as such might also be formalistic. Yet above all, whether the rules applied by the relevant court are formalistic or not is just to be proven.[154]

Turning now to the second variable, it cannot surprise that the Study classifies professional judges as more formalistic than nonprofessional judges – this follows from the name even of the neighbor model. One could wonder, though, whether this is consistent with the classification regarding the previous variable: There, specialized courts were seen as less formalistic than general jurisdiction courts. As courts consist primarily of one or several judges, this could be read in the sense that specialized judges are less formalistic than generalist judges. Judges, in turn, are specialists in conflict resolution by binding decisions, whereas neighbors, merchants and other "private" persons asked to resolve a dispute are not. This seems to suggest that for the two variables the coding should go in the same direction. Admittedly, as nonprofessional judges usually do not have general jurisdiction, this would bring about diametrically opposed results for the two variables in countries with laymen judges only for specified sets of cases ("zero" for limited jurisdiction, "one" for laymen). Surprisingly enough, however, the Dataset shows that this need not be so.[155]

The coding of the third variable, which results in saying that the absence of mandatory legal representation is closer to the neighbor model, is indeed evident.[156] It may also be true that in the absence of legal represen-

---

[154] The only way to escape from the reproach of circular argumentation is to point out that the Study wants to prove formalism not in comparison to other courts within the same country, but in comparison to the competent courts in other countries. However, in view of the fact that the index combines the data from two cases and considering the uniform standard of the neighbor model, this argument would not be fully convincing.

[155] For check collection cases, in 1 (Indonesia) of the 12 countries with nonprofessional judges a general jurisdiction court is competent; for eviction cases, this is true for 2 (Indonesia, Malawi) of the 8 countries with nonprofessional judges.

[156] But note that mandatory representation can also be justified by the intent to avoid unmeritorious claims and to promote smooth proceedings; *see, e.g.*, LEO ROSENBERG, LEHRBUCH DES DEUTSCHEN ZIVILPROZESSRECHTS 72 (2nd ed., 1929).

tation, the judge is more likely to act as a mediator and guide the parties to an agreement. This statement, however, is outside the scope of the Study, for its two model cases both do not address a resolution of the dispute other than by judgment.

3. Written versus Oral

From the basis of the neighbor model, it seems to be compelling to argue that any mandatory use of written form is formalistic. Notwithstanding this general idea, one point where that can be questioned is the fourth variable, which deals with evidence, in particular documentary evidence. The definition states that the variable equals "zero" if most of the evidence, including documentary evidence, is presented at oral hearings before the judge.[157] But it could perfectly be seen as *less* formalistic if the judge is allowed to read documentary evidence herself and *more* formalistic to require that any documentary evidence, for example lengthy excerpts of commercial correspondence or tables of accountants, be presented orally by the party or its attorney reading them to the judge.

4. Legal Justification

The coding for the variables under the headline "legal justification" is based on the assumption that "the neighbor model presumably does not call for such legal justifications".[158] This certainly is a possible interpretation of the neighbor model and may be somewhat corroborated by the experiences with the American jury system, insofar as traditionally it is the judge who tells the fact finder in her instructions what the law is[159] and that the jury does not write a justification. However, it is telling that the Study's authors use the word "presumably": The neighbor model in itself gives no definite answer on this question. In particular, one would assume that even in a very informal setting, a party would try to justify her claim or defense, and a third person would try to justify her decision by referencing rules or customs – at least orally.[160] This illustrates once more that the neighbor model sometimes needs to be supplemented by a best-guess assumption, what involves a subjective moment.

---

[157] Djankov et al., *supra* note 11, at 464.

[158] *Id.*, at 473.

[159] *See, e.g.,* Friedenthal et al., *supra* note 55, at 495–497, 515; James et al., *supra* note 57, at 451 et seq.; *see also* the illustration and critical remarks of STEPHEN J. ADLER, THE JURY 226 et seq. (1995) and Lay, *supra* note 56, at 135–136.

[160] Note that the judge's instructions to the jury somehow fulfill the function of providing a justification – what is illustrated by the fact that they can give rise to a new trial or an appeal (*see, e.g.,* Friedenthal et al., *supra* note 55, at 593, 639). It seems that a legal system in which courts would not provide any justification could not survive.

5. Statutory Regulation of Evidence

The coding of the variables on evidence rests on the idea that any statutory limitation or constraint on who can introduce evidence, what can be introduced, how this has to occur and how the evidence is to be weighted is formalistic.[161] If one endorses such a most extreme interpretation of the Study's one-dimensional concept of formalism, this appears to be correct.[162] Moreover, there is good reason to believe that some of the restrictions in this field are formalistic also in the sense that the purpose they want to serve does not justify them. This can be said of rules preventing the judge from rejecting the collection or admission of irrelevant evidence; of the hearsay rule, at least in cases which are not tried before a jury; of limitations on who is allowed to interrogate witnesses; and of rules admitting only original documents and certified copies as documentary evidence.[163] As to rules prohibiting the judge from freely introducing evidence that had not been requested, offered or introduced by the parties, a more nuanced position seems to be appropriate. By focusing only on the formal aspects of these rules, the Study can avoid taking any position on their necessity.

The classification of the variable on documentary evidence shows how extreme the Study interprets its own concept of formalism here. Rules on the authenticity and probative value of documentary evidence certainly are a restriction. Yet if covering only a small number of documents which actually can claim to be authentic or having a true content, such rules may avoid inefficient disputes and thereby simplify the proceedings.[164] It is doubtful whether the classification of this variable and the variable on general or limited jurisdiction of courts are consistent.

---

[161] *See* Djankov et al., *supra* note 11, at 474 (using the somewhat pathetic expression "judicial freedom in the neighbor model").

[162] Note, however, that the Study's classification of the variables on the judge's role in the taking of evidence may be difficult to reconcile with the neighbor model if neighborly dispute resolution is understood as a stage in the development towards more formalistic proceedings. Distinguished scholars believe that the role of the judge initially was completely passive and that the court was "a non-violent substitute for the duelling ground" (Jolowicz, *supra* note 83, at 281–282). This would suggest that restrictions on the powers of the judge to take evidence are closer to the neighbor model.

[163] *See also* Murray & Sheldon, *supra* note 54, at 30 et seq. (proposing that "[j]ustice can be done by judges here, just as it is in Europe, without complex rules regulating the admissibility of proof.").

[164] *See also* Stürner, *supra* note 18, at 21 (suggesting that the increased use and value of electronic documentation may influence the law of evidence at the expense of personal means of evidence). On the impact of computer technology on civil procedure, in particular evidence, see also Paul D. Carrington, *Virtual Civil Litigation: A Visit to John Bunyan's Celestial City*, 98 COLUM. L. REV. 1516, 1533–1534 (1998).

6. Control of Superior Review

The variables on appeal proceedings are the most striking example for a procedural aspect on which it is difficult to apply the neighbor model. For it cannot be deduced from the neighbor model as such whether this model includes superior review, and if yes, how superior review in a world of neighborly dispute resolution would look like. The coding of the first two variables – automatic suspension of enforcement upon request for appeal and scope of the review – demonstrates this difficulty: On one hand, the variables equal "zero" if the judgment cannot be appealed at all. On the other hand, under certain circumstances these variables equal "zero" even if there is an appeal.

That the absence of superior review is classified as non-formalistic is anything but self-evident. First, from a pure formal point of view, the lack of rules providing for an appeal can also be understood as a complete prohibition of appeal. Under the Study's concept of formalism, in particular as applied to the variables on evidence, restrictions of any type are considered as formalistic. Intuitively, one would rather qualify the prohibition and not the possibility of an appeal as procedural "intervention". Second, the general phenomenon of at least one appeal to a higher instance, excepting only cases of minor importance, seems to be shared today throughout most legal cultures of larger societies.[165] Particular weight has usually been given to the availability of superior review where the first instance court consists of nonprofessional judges. It is certainly true that appellate review is a form of control over the trial court proceedings which might be used by the sovereign to sustain its power. However, this is only one aspect, and an aspect which has been emphasized only lately, for the most part by scholars in the field of political science. Another aspect, which has since hundreds of years dominated literary discussion, is the benefit for the parties and the society as a whole of such superior control.[166] Against this background, it

[165] *See* Kojima, *supra* note 52, at 581; Shapiro, *supra* note 110, at 37–56 (suggesting, *inter alia*, that one of the functions of a right of appeal may be to provide a psychological outlet and a social cover for the loser at trial) and 194 et seq. (describing the courts of Islam and the problem of appeal); Herzog & Karlen, *supra* note 109, at 8-14 through 8-17; CHARLES PLATTO (ED.), CIVIL APPEAL PROCEDURES WORLDWIDE (1992).

[166] *See generally* Herzog & Karlen, *supra* note 109, at ¶ 8-7; James et al., *supra* note 57, at 740 et seq.; Guinchard & Ferrand, *supra* note 97, at 1143, ¶ 1582; ADOLF WACH, VORTRÄGE ÜBER DIE REICHS-CIVILPROCESSORDNUNG 243 (2nd ed., 1896); Rosenberg, *supra* note 156, at 440. Even Shapiro, who discusses appeal with the intent to show that "it yields great advantages to the regime in terms of increased legitimacy and hierarchical control", describes this aspect only "in addition to [the significance of appeal] to contributing to the stability of the triadic structure (Shapiro, *supra* note 110, at 194) and, as a theoretical explanation, suggests that one of the functions of a right of appeal may be to provide a psychological outlet and a social cover for the loser at trial (*id.*, at 49). Surpris-

would seem a bit naïve to believe that without a sovereign whishing to expand its control appeal would not exist.

Even where there is an appeal, the variable concerning the enforcement of the judgment equals "zero" if the suspension of the enforcement is not automatic. This as well is not obvious under the neighbor model. Of course, an "automatic" suspension in a certain sense contains a restriction on a completely free proceeding. But it first and foremost expresses that the legal system values the protection of the loser from premature enforcement higher than the interest of the winner in assuring fulfillment of her claim as soon as possible. And in a simple procedural setting, wouldn't it be less complicated to stay any enforcement for the short period until a judgment is final than to make such stay dependent on a second, separate motion of the appellant to this effect?

With regard to the coding of the variable on the scope of review, we encounter the same uncertainty. Here again, the neighbor model gives no clear hint. By determining that the absence of appeal would be the ideal under the neighbor model, the Study has maneuvered itself in an awkward situation: In order to be consistent with this standpoint, the authors apparently felt bound to see any limitation on the superior review as closer to the neighbor model. This, however, is clearly in contradiction with the one-dimensional concept of formalism employed elsewhere, pursuant to which any restriction and limitation is considered as formalistic. The Study decides to accept this inconsistency and determines that it is "more compatibl[e]" (sic!) with the neighbor model if only new evidence or issues of law can be reviewed on appeal.[167]

In addition to this lack of consistency, the coding itself raises doubts. As has been mentioned in the preceding part,[168] there is panoply of national solutions on both the level whether and when appeals are possible and whether and when there is suspension of the enforcement. The solutions mostly are quite close to each other, but differ in details. This suggests a coding which, as difficult as this might be, reflects to a certain degree the many nuances that can be found. Yet the variable only offers "one" or "zero". No matter how an individual country is classified, it is inevitable that such a black or white solution overstates some differences and understates others, thereby potentially separating countries which from

---

ingly enough, while the Study (maybe mistakenly, *see supra* note 143) references this work when introducing the neighbor model, it makes no reference to it when determining that the control of judges by a superior court is inconsistent with the neighbor model. Instead, it references the work of Damaška, *supra* note 14, which in this regard is built on Shapiro's ideas.

[167] Djankov et al., *supra* note 11, at 474.

[168] *Supra* sub III.B.6.

a neutral and informed observer's point of view could be grouped together. This problem is exacerbated by the unclear delineations of the decisive terms used in the definition – "issues of law", "issues of fact", "new evidence".

Finally, it is just the difficulty of determining which issues can be reviewed by appellate courts which has rendered this area of procedural law extremely difficult and has in many countries led to the formation of a smaller group of lawyers specialized in appeals proceedings. It is therefore hardly convincing to classify such limitations as less "formalistic" (in the sense this word is used by the Study) than a general and blunt admission of appeals based on all issues of law and facts – what, as mentioned above, doesn't seem to exist in reality in a pure form.[169]

The third variable, which concerns interlocutory appeals, is inflicted with similar problems: Again, the prohibition of such appeals is seen as the solution which is closer to the neighbor model, and the allowance for such appeals is classified as formalistic. Intuitively, interlocutory appeals indeed would not to fit into the image of informal dispute resolution by a neighbor. Once more, however, the classification of a restriction as non-formalistic seems inconsistent with the way formalism is interpreted elsewhere. Moreover, the definition – here the definition of what is an interlocutory appeal – again is far from being clear. And again, we find a black and white solution, so that the variable cannot take into account that a country may allow interlocutory appeals only in certain circumstances.

7. Engagement Formalities

These days, regulations providing for pretrial conciliation are often acclaimed by the legislature as an important improvement, introducing modern and efficient mediative forms of dispute resolution into civil procedural law, which was traditionally focused on litigation.[170] Therefore, one

---

[169] *See supra* text accompanying note 102.

[170] On the introduction of mandatory pre-trial conciliation in Germany, *see, e.g.*, the explanatory statement of the federal government, BT-Drucks. 14/4722, p. 59, 62. *But see* the negative comment of the Bundesrat (Federal Council), BT-Drucks. 14/4722, p. 147–148, and the critical remarks of legal scholars, *e.g.* Joachim Münch, *Die "neue" ZPO: bedeutende Änderungen im zivilgerichtlichen Verfahrensrecht (Teil I)*, 40 DEUTSCHES STEUERRECHT 85, 91 (2002) (noting that in Germany, mandatory conciliation had been introduced in 1924 for local courts, but had been abolished in 1950 because of a lack of success and significance, to be reintroduced with hoopla in 2002). According to recent data, the results of pre-trial conciliation in Germany are modest, *see* Reinhard Greger, *Die ZPO-Reform – 1000 Tage danach*, 59 JURISTENZEITUNG (JZ) 805, 806–807 (2004); KLAUS F. RÖHL & MATTHIAS WEIß, DIE OBLIGATORISCHE STREITSCHLICHTUNG IN DER PRAXIS (2005); CHRISTOPH HOMMERICH, HANNS PRÜTTING, THOMAS EBERS, SONJA LANG & LUDGER TRAUT, RECHTSTATSÄCHLICHE UNTERSUCHUNG ZU DEN AUSWIRKUN-

might think that mandatory pretrial conciliation is closer to the neighbor model. However, under the one-dimensional concept of the Study, a requirement to attempt a pretrial conciliation or mediation before filing the lawsuit must be seen as formalistic, even if this in some cases avoids that the parties proceed to the other much more formalistic steps of litigation in courts. Also, under the Study's concept, mandatory intervention of a judicial officer in the service of the complaint and the notification of judgment must be regarded as formalistic – between neighbors, there would probably be no need to formally serve a complaint, and the neighbor would pronounce the decision orally.

8. Independent Procedural Actions

The last three variables of the formalism index are special in several ways. At a first glance, what happens under these variables is not "coding" but "counting". The possible values are not limited to "zero" and "one"; the single variables as such give pure numerical sums and do not contain any information as to whether a country is formalistic or not. This information emerges only with the sub-index on independent procedural actions, which is basically construed as the ratio of a country's number of independent procedural actions to the maximum number of independent procedural actions. This implies that the more independent procedural actions a country shows, the more formalistic it is.

Indirectly, however, there is a classification or aggregation issue also on the level of the three variables: Any "independent procedural action" at the three different stages of the proceedings – filing and service, trial and judgment, and enforcement – is assigned the same weight.

Differently to what one might believe when first reading it, the Study does not use the neighbor model here. To the contrary, it suddenly accepts a concept whose general application it has, by electing for the neighbor model, rejected at the outset: the comparison not with a theoretical, idealistic picture – the very neighbor model – but with the real world.[171] For it calculates the sub-index on independent procedural actions not on the basis of numbers derived from a comparison with the neighbor model, but using the real numbers collected by means of the questionnaire. As comprehensible and sensible this may be, it is worth mentioning that instead of making this methodological switch clear, the Study purports to stick with the neighbor model.[172]

GEN DER REFORM DES ZIVILPROZESSRECHTS AUF DIE GERICHTLICHE PRAXIS – EVALUATION ZPO-REFORM 58–82 (Bundesministerium der Justiz, ed., 2006).

[171] *Cf. supra* sub IV.A.1.

[172] The Study declares that in the neighbor model, there would only be three procedural actions: (1) the claimant's request of judicial intervention, (2) a meeting of judge,

9. Conclusion

Except for the variable "Independent procedural actions", the Study classifies the possible outcomes of the different questions by assigning them either the value "zero" or "one". Equals "zero" the solution that is closest to the neighbor model, a model in which a neighbor resolves a dispute between two parties in a most informal way. It follows from this model that the Study employs a one-dimensional concept of formalism. This concept basically takes any constraint and any mandatory rule as formalistic without regard to a possible justification of such a restriction.

For many variables, the application of the neighbor model poses no difficulty. However, as to important sets of questions, the model shows weaknesses. Sometimes, the model provides no clear indication on how a variable should be classified; sometimes, contradictory classifications can be derived from the model. In such cases, it was left to the authors to determine how to classify a variable.

Another drawback of the Study's approach is that variables can only be "zero" or "one" even in cases where such black and white solutions seem inappropriate if one were taking into account the smooth transitions from one country's procedural law to another's. It follows that a good number of the Study's classifications are problematic and, due to necessarily subjective interpretations of the incomplete neighbor model, can by no means claim complete objectivity.[173]

---

claimant and defendant, where after a discussion the judge issues the decision, and (3) the enforcement (Djankov et al., *supra* note 11, at 475–476). It is clear that these numbers do not give any maximum that could be used to normalize the various results to fall between "zero" and "one". But in addition, as follows not from the text but from the definition of the variables in Table I (*id.*, at 469), the Study does not take the "one" from its description of the situation under the neighbor model as the minimum number. Instead, it takes the minimum number of independent procedural actions among the countries in the sample. Thus, the formula used to determine the sub-index on independent procedural actions has no connection to the numbers derived from the neighbor model.

[173] It seems obvious that even without these problems on the level of classification, this Study as well as any other empirical study cannot claim to be completely objective. Note, however, that the Study claims just such objectivity, although in a subtle way; *see* Djankov et al., *supra* note 11, at 456–457 (Relating the general statement that "[f]inding *objective measures* [emphasis added] of institutional structure is sometimes more useful than just focusing on survey assessments of quality..." to the Study, which "takes the measurement of institutions in a new direction: the study of courts.").

C. The Classification Regarding the Supplementary Questions on Incentives

1. Duration in Practice

As to the supplementary questions on duration, no classification issues are involved: The Study simply counts the estimated calendar days from filing of the complaint to completion of enforcement.

2. Incentives of Parties

Unlike with duration, classification plays a certain role with regard to the incentives of the parties. As we will see shortly, classification here may involve a theoretical problem.

It cannot be seriously contested that mandatory time limits create incentives for the parties or the judge to fulfill or complete the required action by a specified date. As already mentioned, the parties are under the threat of procedural disadvantages, ranging up to a default judgment; the judge may fear disciplinary measures, negative influences on his career and, last but not least, that he will have to start the proceeding from the very beginning after remand from the appellate court. The Study assigns to all mandatory time limits the value "one". This implies that "one" is the value expressing the existence of an incentive.

It is just this classification which causes a theoretical problem for the two other variables on incentives, namely quota litis and loser-pays rules. The Study determines that the quota-litis-variable equals one if quota litis or contingent fee agreements are prohibited by law in all cases and that the loser-pays-variable equals one if the loser is required to pay all the costs of the dispute.[174] From this and the time-limit-variables, one would derive that the Study's authors take the absence of quota litis and the presence of the loser-pays rule as incentives, thereby denying that the presence of quota litis and the absence of the loser-pays rule are incentives. However, in a later discussion, the Study explains that "prohibitions of contingency fees may dis-incentivize lawyers and thus delay proceedings".[175] It appears that either with regard to this statement or in the coding of the quota litis variable a lapse occurred.

Regardless of the somewhat confusing coding, the whole approach is more than doubtful. Concerning the time-limit variables, it is clear that the incentive has just one immediate consequence, that is, the performance of the specified act within the specified time. However, unlike for time limits,

---

[174] Djankov et al., *supra* note 11, at 470.
[175] *Id.*, at 509.

neither do quota litis and the loser-pays rule have one single and clearly defined, immediate consequence which could serve as reference, nor does their influence on the parties' behavior go only in one direction, in the sense that only their absence or presence, respectively, has an effect. Consequently, these two variables cannot be classified in a scheme of "incentive" and "no incentive". The following discussion will illustrate this point.

For a long time, scholars have discussed the consequences of different forms of lawyer compensation on parties' behavior. Contingency fee agreements are only one salient form of compensating lawyers for their work. Other forms of compensation are conditional fees, hourly fees, flat fees and fees fixed by statute based on various factors, like the amount in controversy and the stage of a litigated case.[176] Each and any of these forms of compensation influences the attorney's and her party's behavior in different ways. Under an hourly fee agreement, lawyers will have incentives to accept cases regardless of the outcome and to go to trial instead of settling the case at an early stage if this involves more work. Under contingency fees, lawyers will only take a promising case and often press for early settlements to avoid spending a lot for litigating the case.[177] Flat fees as well as statutory fixed fees depending on the stage of litigation tend to limit lawyers' effort to an amount of activity which can be reasonably compensated by the flat or statutory fee.[178] The positive effect of such a compensation rule on duration can be even greater than that of a contingent

[176] On Germany, where lawyers' compensation has traditionally been determined by a comprehensive statute prescribing fixed fees, see Murray & Stürner, *supra* note 16, at 112–115 and 346–349 (discussing the former Federal Attorneys Fee Law [Bundesrechtsanwaltsgebührenordnung, BRAGO], which has been replaced by the Attorney Compensation Law [Rechtsanwaltsvergütungsgesetz, RVG] in 2004. The RVG leaves more room for agreements; the basic structure, however, is the same as under the BRAGO). For a comparison of the traditional prohibition of quota litis agreements in Germany with the development in England and the U.S., see Alexander Bruns, *Das Verbot der quota litis und die erfolgshonorierte Prozeßfinanzierung*, 55 JZ 232, 233–240 (2000).

[177] For an economic analysis, see Shavell, *supra* note 9, at 435–436 (summarizing that "relative to the benchmark of maximizing the expected gain minus legal costs, the incentive to take cases under the hourly fee is excessive, and the incentive to take cases under the contingency, outcome-based arrangement is inadequate", that "relative to the benchmark of maximizing the expected gain minus legal costs, the incentive to go to trial under the hourly fee is excessive, and the incentive to go to trial under the contingency fee contract is too low", and finally, that "under the hourly fee arrangement, the lawyer will want to work more than may be worthwhile... [while] under the contingency fee arrangement, ... the lawyer will tend to work less than would be worthwhile ..."). In practice, things are much more complicated, as there are not only "pure" contingency fee agreements, but also statutory limitations or "sliding scales", *see, e.g.;* Bruns, *supra* note 176, at 234–236.

[178] Murray & Stürner, *supra* note 16, at 115.

fee agreement,[179] under which the lawyer who has invested a lot in a case may have an incentive to do whatever is possible in order not to loose the whole investment, what in turn can cause delays. It follows that all these different forms of compensation create various different incentives, which can be of crucial importance on aspects like duration[180] and even be correlated with procedural formalism.[181] Thus it would be an error to say that only one of these forms of lawyer compensation creates an incentive, and to regard the other forms as incentive-neutral. Regrettably, the Study furnishes no explanation for why it just picked out the contingency fee and why it takes the absence (or presence?) of a contingency fee arrangement as creating an incentive. The classification is even more surprising because the Study, when introducing the "'incentive' theory", presents contingency fees as a factor improving court performance.[182]

The situation is similar for the loser-pays rule. Apart from the fact that, as mentioned above, there exist more forms of fee shifting than just the loser-pays rule and that many countries have special rules for certain circumstances, here again none of the rules is incentive-neutral. What incentives a particular rule creates usually depends on the individual constellation. Among the factors to be taken into account are the minimum award, the probability of victory, the amount of the plaintiff's and the defendant's litigation costs and their relation to each other.[183] A risk-neutral plaintiff who believes that she would win is more likely to bring suit under the loser-pays rule than under the American Rule, for due to fee-shifting she expects the defendant to pay her legal expenses. Conversely, a plaintiff who has doubts on whether she would win has stronger incentives to sue under the American Rule because she then does not need to fear that she would have to bear the opponent's expenses. Once suit has been brought,

---

[179] Apparently, the Study assumes that only contingency fees create incentives to avoid delays (Djankov et al., *supra* note 11, at 509). This is incorrect.

[180] For example, lawyers who are paid by the hour may have an incentive to increase the duration of the trial by making unnecessary motions.

[181] For example, in a flat fee system an additional fee for a motion to leave automatic suspension of the enforcement in case of an appeal may be enough an incentive to make such a motion to protect the plaintiff, whereas in a contingency fee system it may make sense not to have automatic suspension of enforcement if the enforcement stage of the proceeding is not part of the contingency fee agreement, so that the lawyer would have no incentive to make a motion for a permission of enforcement.

[182] Djankov et al., *supra* note 11, at 455; *see also supra* text accompanying note 175. "Court performance" obviously is used by the Study in a broad sense, encompassing the whole proceedings.

[183] For an interesting figure comparing the incentives on the plaintiff's decision to file, see Edward A. Snyder & James W. Hughes, *The English Rule for Allocating Costs: Evidence Confronts Theory*, 6 JOURNAL OF LAW, ECONOMICS & ORGANIZATION 345, 352 (1990).

the loser-pays rule creates incentives for risk-neutral parties to go to trial and makes a settlement less likely because an optimistic party will not only expect to win but also to escape legal fees.[184] With regard to duration, it may well be that a defendant who is at fault is discouraged from delaying the proceedings if she has to expect bearing the cost.[185] Yet the opposite could also be true: The defendant has an incentive to invest more in her defense as long as there is a slight hope of winning the case. This in turn can cause enormous delays. Generally spoken, each rule brings about various incentives, and the incentives of two different rules typically diverge. As with the compensation rules and contrary to the time limits, there exists no solution that was free of incentives. Thus, here again, it would be incorrect to conclude that only one or the other rule creates incentives. The Study's classification, though, implies exactly this, namely that only the loser-pays rule creates incentives. Absent any explanation, one may be tempted to believe that the Study just took the American Rule – which from an international perspective is exceptional –[186] as a baseline and overlooked that this rule also generates incentives.

In addition, different forms of lawyer compensation and cost allocation/fee shifting rules should not be regarded independently of one another, and the same is true for the incentives they may create. Rather, these features of a country's civil procedure should be analyzed comprehensively, and such analysis must also include the availability and efficiency of legal aid and legal expenses insurance.[187] By isolating these aspects and treating

---

[184] For an overview on economic analysis, see Shavell, *supra* note 9, at 428–432; for more details, see Ronald Braeutigam, Bruce Owen & John Panzar, *An Economic Analysis of Alternative Fee Shifting Systems*, 47 LAW AND CONTEMPORARY PROBLEMS 173 (1984) (concluding that under the assumptions made by the authors, it is unclear whether the English model discourages meritless litigation); Snyder & Hughes, *supra* note 183, at 353–355 (discussing plaintiffs' decisions whether to continue with their claims or to drop them at an early stage); James W. Hughes & Edward A. Snyder, *Litigation and Settlement under the English and American Rules: Theory and Evidence*, 38 JOURNAL OF LAW AND ECONOMICS 225, 227–234 (1995) (suggesting, *inter alia*, that under the English Rule, courts will be biased in favor of plaintiffs to avoid making them liable for legal costs, and will award more small judgments; and that under the English Rule parties tend to spend more, what may counteract this rule's incentive in favor of numerous small, meritorious claims).

[185] This is the assumption of the Study, *see* Djankov et al., *supra* note 11, at 509.

[186] *See, e.g.*, Hughes & Snyder, *supra* note 184, at 225.

[187] For an excellent comprehensive analysis, see Breyer, *supra* note 129, at 2 et seq. (distinguishing *Finanzierungslast* [the burden of financing the proceedings in advance], *Investitionsrisiko* [the risk that the investment in the proceedings may prove futile because the party finally looses] and *Haftungsrisiko* [the risk that the party may be obliged to compensate the opponent, in particular if she finally looses]). Obviously, the incentives created in a particular case by the various possible legal regimes for lawyer com-

two of them separately while completely omitting the other two and the relationship between all four elements, the Study seems to go too far in its desire to reduce complex systems to simple binary numbers.

Probably, the reason for the Study's confusion is that it fails to be fully precise on the kind of incentives it attributes to the different forms of lawyer compensation and cost allocation. In its short presentation of the "incentives theory", the Study mentions delays created by careless judges, lawyers who prolong the proceedings and defendants who seek to avoid judgment.[188] This suggests that only incentives to speed up proceedings would matter.[189] However, we have seen that rules on lawyer compensation and cost allocation also have an impact on the number and type of cases that are filed at all, and on who can afford to file them. The number and type of cases and plaintiffs, in turn, affect duration: Whether a judge deals with cases expeditiously depends last not least on the caseload and the difficulty of the cases and the characters of the plaintiff and the defendant. For all these reasons, the Study's classification of when the variables on lawyer compensation and cost allocation show the presence or absence of incentives is very problematic.

3. Conclusion

In our review of the Study's classification regarding the supplementary questions, we observed at the outset that classification plays no role regarding the variables on duration. However, classification is an issue for the variables on incentives.

Among them, the coding of the variables on mandatory time limits is self-explaining. The coding of the quota litis variable and the loser-pays variable, however, would have deserved an explanation. In particular, it is unclear why just and only the absence (or presence?) of outcome-related lawyer compensation and the presence of the loser-pays rule shall be seen as creating incentives. Even with a clarification, though, it seems implausible that the theoretical problem of incentives and counter-incentives could have been resolved without defining the direction of those incentives

---

pensation and cost allocation depend on how the parties evaluate the respective risks and estimate the prospective costs.

It can only be mentioned here that lawyers compensation, fee allocation, legal aid and legal expenses insurance are part of an even bigger picture, in which a country's preference for public or private law enforcement plays an important role.

[188] Djankov et al., *supra* note 11, at 455.

[189] But note that later in the Study, the variables on incentives are also linked to the "subjective measures of the quality of the legal system" (Djankov et al., *supra* note 11, at 509). It is unclear, though, what kind of relationship there could be apart from satisfaction or dissatisfaction with duration.

that should matter. As has been pointed out, other forms of lawyer compensation and cost allocation also influence the parties' behavior; the only difference lies in the different and typically divergent effects. Whether the respective incentives are positive or negative for "court performance", cannot be determined abstractly and in isolation, but depends on the case, the parties and the legal environment at issue.

Part V

The Aggregation of the Data

A. The Study's Approach

Obviously, a study about procedural formalism cannot simply collect comparative data on various questions and present these data without any further processing. Rather, an important part of its value lies in the aggregation of the individual answers into comprehensive figures which permit more general statements. It follows that the way of aggregating the data is crucial for the Study's conclusions.

1. The Formalism Index

Among the many different possibilities, the Lex Mundi Study has chosen the following approach: The variables do not enter directly the formalism index. They all belong to one of several sub-indices of variables. These sub-indices each concern a discrete feature of civil procedure. The values from the individual variables belonging to one and the same sub-index are added up. For all but one sub-index, this sum is divided by the number of variables. The one sub-index, where the procedure is different, concerns the variables on independent procedural actions. There, the sum is normalized to fall between zero and one whereby the index is zero for the minimum number among the countries in the sample and one for the maximum number.

The result of the relevant operation constitutes the sub-index for the respective procedural feature. The formalism index for each country is just the sum of these sub-indices. It therefore ranges from zero to seven, with seven indicating the highest level of formalism.

This approach has some remarkable consequences. Within one and the same sub-index of variables, every individual variable is given the same weight.[190] However, as has become apparent from the foregoing parts, not all sub-indices contain the same number of variables. This means that

[190] Where all variables of a sub-index can be either "zero" or "one", they exert an equal impact on this sub-index. For the sub-index "independent procedural actions", however, this would only hold if each of the three variables were assigned a weight equal to the inverse of its standard deviation.

within the ultimate formalism index, not all variables have the same weight. Conversely, the sub-indices are all weighted equally[191] for the computation of the formalism index.

Another aspect which becomes relevant on the level of the aggregation, concerns all that is *not* covered by the variables. Any missing procedural feature that would have deserved attention in a comparison under the aspect of formalism distorts the ultimate results – not only directly in the sense that its answers would have had an effect on the result, but also indirectly by its absence, which unduly increases the relative weight of the actual variables.

2. The Supplementary Questions

It is obvious that the total duration is the sum of the duration of the different steps of the proceedings. With regard to the incentives, the Study distinguishes between time limits, quota litis and loser-pays rule. For the latter two, there is no aggregation at all. For the time limits, the Study employs the same method as for the formalism variables: the sub-index "mandatory time limits" is the average of the variables concerning the diverse time limits.

B. The Aggregation of the Data for the Formalism Index

1. General Remarks

As a matter of principle, nothing can be said against a judgmental weighting of various variables collected in a survey. To the contrary, it would be rather exceptional if in the evaluation of data concerning complex sociological phenomena like court proceedings, all variables could be given the same weight. The way the collected data is weighted is clearly of extreme importance. One would therefore expect a study to be explicit on this point.

Unfortunately, this is not the case for the Lex Mundi Study. Neither is there any explanation for the weighting of the variables within the formalism index, nor for the lack of weighting of the variables within the sub-indices. All we know is that the authors of the Study used the section on French civil procedure in the Kluwer International Encyclopaedia of Laws

---

[191] However, as the sub-indices are not binary, this does not mean that the sub-indices exert an equal impact on the index.

– Civil Procedure[192] as a guide in their choice of the areas investigated.[193] But as the Study did not just copy the headlines from the Encyclopaedia, this does not really help us. After all, we can only speculate whether the weighting done by the Study is on purpose or merely the consequence of the calculation method it applies.

Without any doubt, any weighting typically involves subjective judgments. Where in the following it is proposed to assign weights different from those in the Study to variables or sub-indices, these proposals cannot and do not claim to be objective, better or more correct. But they reflect legitimate deliberations upon the difficult question how to evaluate the significance of the diverse variables.

2. *Professionals versus Laymen*

According to the Study's definition, this sub-index measures the degree of participation by professionals. It seems arguable to integrate the first variable, which asks whether a court of general or limited jurisdiction would hear the case, in this group. A better headline would maybe just have been: "General characteristics of the court system and roles of the participants". Under so broad a headline would fit another salient feature for which the Study understandably provides no variable: the question of the *roles* of laymen in the court, or, in other words, the question of the jury. Admittedly and as mentioned above, in both model cases there would most likely not be a jury trial in any jurisdiction. However, as also mentioned above, it is widely accepted among scholars that the mere possibility of juries in civil matters massively affects the whole procedural law of the country at issue, even in cases which are not tried before a jury.[194] In a jury trial, the role of the neutral third (the "neighbor") is shared by two institutions: the jury as the fact finder and the judge as a watchdog over what is presented to the fact finder. It is obvious that such an allocation of the third's tasks is only possible where there is a relatively strict framework determining the respective competencies in sufficient detail. It is doubtful whether a study measuring procedural formalism without taking into account this important procedural feature can claim that its results may be generalized.

---

[192] Raymond J. Martin & Jacques M. Martin, *France*, *in* INTERNATIONAL ENCYCLOPAEDIA OF LAWS – CIVIL PROCEDURE (Roger Blanpain, gen. ed., Piet Taelman, ed., looseleaf; the Study used the 1994 version).

[193] Djankov et al., *supra* note 11, at 461.

[194] *See supra* note 54 and accompanying text.

3. Written versus Oral

Of this sub-index's variables, the variables "Judgment" and "Notification of judgment" seem most problematic. They concern steps of the proceedings that are so closely related to each other that the "judgment" aspect de facto has double weight. Of course it cannot be said that this is clearly excessive. But the Study furnishes no justification for why just this aspect receives more importance than the aspects covered by the other variables.

Bundling all the variables concerning written form in one sub-index and assigning this sub-index the same weight as the foregoing index about the participants of the proceedings seems to be defensible. The same is true for the fact that the single variables, eight in number, for this reason only have a rather small weight in the ultimate formalism index. Mark, however, that the sub-index covers various steps of proceedings. We will see that this can have implications for the other variables.

4. Legal Justification

The sub-index "Legal justification" contains only three variables. They therefore have a considerable weight in the formalism index. For example, the question of whether the complaint must be legally justified is given more than twice the weight of the question of whether the judge can introduce evidence. As mentioned above, the Study furnishes no explanation for this. In substance, it seems doubtful whether the aspects in this sub-index really deserve so much attention. This holds particularly for the problematic variable "Judgment must be on law (not on equity)". Not only is the meaning of this variable very unclear (what becomes the more problematic, the higher its weight), but also the variable, regardless of its precise meaning, is only very loosely connected to the question of formalism, because it rather concerns the substance of the judgment and not its form.[195] In our opinion, the Study would have done better to omit this variable, of course without increasing the already high weight of the remaining two variables in this sub-index

5. Statutory Regulation of Evidence

The sub-index on evidence perfectly illustrates how problematic the aggregation of the collected data can be: We find a variable for which it is doubtful whether it really fits into to this sub-index. We find a variable that is part of another sub-index, but could also have found its place here. We do not find variables which could perfectly be used to measure formalism in the context of taking evidence. And we have reason to discuss the lack

---

[195] *See supra* sub III.B.4 (text accompanying note 77).

of weighting within the sub-index and the weighting within the ultimate formalism index.

Let us start with the final variable under the headline "Statutory regulation of evidence". This variable asks whether there is mandatory recording of evidence. It goes without saying that under the Study's concept of formalism, a rule requiring that the taking of evidence be recorded must be seen as formalistic. Why this variable deserves a remark, is that it does not completely fit together with the other variables this sub-index contains. As opposed to them, this variable does not pertain to the procedural rules regulating the admissibility of and dealing with the evidence itself, but only concerns the recording. Recording is merely a by-product of this phase of the proceedings. It may add to the duration of this phase, but has no material influence on the way the court proceeds. Its real significance, as the Study correctly remarks,[196] lies in the availability of an official recording for potential appeal proceedings. Thus, this variable could perfectly have been included in the sub-index "Control of superior review", even more as the variables on review do not address the availability and use of a trial court recording. Of course, if one believes that recording of evidence is a characteristic feature, it is better that the variable be part of the sub-index on evidence than that it be omitted. However, to which sub-index a variable is assigned makes a difference. It influences the result of the relevant sub-index directly, by its "zero" or "one" value, and indirectly, because it reduces the weight of the other variables within this index and within the ultimate formalism index. A flawed location of a variable therefore potentially distorts the results. Including the recording of evidence in the sub-index on evidence and not the sub-index on superior review is at least questionable.

The opposite case, a variable which we find elsewhere, but which would perfectly fit in this sub-index, is the variable "Evidence" in the sub-index "Written versus oral". Recall that this variable asks whether "evidence is mostly submitted to the court in written form, in the form of attachments, affidavits, or otherwise" or whether "most form of evidence, including documentary evidence, is presented at oral hearings before the judge".[197] It shall not be questioned that this is one aspect of "written versus oral". Also, this variable does not concern the questions of admissibility of evidence or of who can introduce it, and in the way it is defined is not limited to statutory regulations, but looks at the actual court practice. Nevertheless, it is obvious that the variable belongs to the salient procedural characteristics with regard to evidence. To decide which of the two sub-indices has a better right to host the variable is not just difficult, but seems impos-

---

[196] Djankov et al., *supra* note 11, at 474.

[197] *Id.*, at 464.

sible, for the two sub-indices use different levels of abstraction. The question of whether steps of the proceedings require written form or can be accomplished orally can be asked throughout the whole proceedings. Conversely, the sub-index "statutory regulation of evidence" concerns the treatment – especially the introduction, admissibility and weight – of evidence, questions which mainly concern one separate element or phase of the proceedings, i.e. the presentation of evidence. It is consequently anything but surprising that the two sub-indices overlap. In the case at issue, the overlap means that if the Study had chosen to integrate this variable differently, both sub-indices and – as a consequence of the change in the weight of the individual variables – the formalism index would look slightly different.[198]

The Study ignores two other procedural aspects which could perfectly figure among the variables on formalism with regard to evidence. First, the Study could have asked whether the procedural law requires that witnesses swear an oath in all cases. In some countries, the oath is seen as a substantial formality.[199] In other countries it is not mandatory and rare in practice.[200] Needless to say that if an oath is mandatory, this would be qualified as formalistic under the Study's approach. This does not necessarily mean that it could also be seen as formalistic in the sense that it is a rule creating an unjustified and superfluous burden, because depending on the importance and force of the oath in the respective country's culture and society, it may be a valuable institution to find the truth. Perhaps the Study did not address this issue in order to avoid variables with a high cultural sensitivity.

Second, neither the variables on statutory regulation of evidence nor any other variable cover the important field of evidentiary privileges.[201] Tech-

---

[198] As an example, all other things equal, relocating the "evidence" variable from the sub-index "Written versus oral" to the sub-index "Statutory regulation of evidence" would change the results for France in the check collection case in the following sense: The value of the sub-index "Written versus oral" would increase from 0.75 to 0.857, the value of the sub-index "Statutory regulation of evidence" would decrease from 0.125 to 0.111; the formalism index would increase from 3.234 to 3.328.

[199] For the U.S., see Rule 603 Federal Rules of Evidence; for France, see Guinchard & Ferrand, *supra* note 97, at 965 n. 2, ¶ 1270 ("formalité substantielle") and Art. 211(1) NCPC (Persons heard as witnesses must take an oath to tell the truth).

[200] Austria: §§ 336(2), 337(2) ZPO and WALTER H. RECHBERGER & DAPHNE-ARIANE SIMOTTA, ZIVILPROZESSRECHT. ERKENNTNISVERFAHREN 362–363, ¶ 631 (6th ed., 2003); Germany: § 393 ZPO (Oath after the testimony only if court deems it necessary with regard to the importance of what the witness said or to ensure truthful testimony, and if the parties do not renounce on an oath). For Switzerland (Basel) see ADRIAN STAEHELIN & THOMAS SUTTER, ZIVILPROZESSRECHT 163, § 14 ¶ 38 (1992).

[201] *See only* Kerameus, *supra* note 14, at 499–501 (describing the rules governing the admissibility of evidence as a "striking feature of common law rules of evidence").

nically, privileges belong to the category of regulations about what evidence is admissible. With regard to the evidence in question they reach even further than the hearsay rule or a rule prohibiting other than original documents and certified copies: They not only prevent the judge or jury from using a certain means of evidence, but they exclude that the information, no matter in which form it could be introduced in the proceedings, can be used at all. With the variable about regulation of the weight of certain types of evidence, they have in common that they imply a particular definition of the weight of evidence, in that they prescribe a weight of zero for any evidence concerning the privileged information. It follows that the natural place for privileges would have been under the sub-index on statutory regulation of evidence. The importance of evidentiary privilege rules is illustrated, for instance, by the battle about the inclusion of such rules in the U.S. Federal Rules of Evidence[202] and by Principle 18 of the ALI/ UNIDROIT Principles.[203] Therefore, the reader would have expected to find this feature addressed by a study which claims to make general statements, even more as there are not only similarities, but also important differences – mostly as to the range and the technical and conceptual bases of privileges – between the Anglo-American and the continental European solutions.[204] An explanation for the Study's omitting these variables might be that in check collection or in eviction cases, witness testimony and even more privileges usually play no role, and in particular might not have played a role in the two hypothetical cases.[205] Nevertheless, this should not

[202] *See, e.g.*, Kenneth S. Broun, *Giving Codification a Second Chance – Testimonial Privileges and the Federal Rules of Evidence*, 53 HASTINGS L.J. 769, 772–779 (2002) (tracing the legislative history which led to evidence rules that include no codification of privileges).

[203] On the background of ALI/UNIDROIT Principle 18, *see* Rolf Stürner, *Discorvery and Sanctions Against Non-Compliance*, VI UNIF. L. REV. NS 871, 878–880, 885 (2001-4).

[204] *Cf., e.g.*, MIRJAN R. DAMAŠKA, EVIDENCE LAW ADRIFT 12–13 (1997) and Richard D. Friedman, *Anchors and Flotsam: Is Evidence Law "Adrift"?*, 107 Yale L.J. 1921, 1925 & n. 23 (1998) (book review); Damaška, *supra* note 14, at 211 and n. 64; Murray & Sheldon, *supra* note 54, at 31; Rolf Stürner, *U.S.-amerikanisches und europäisches Verfahrensverständnis*, *in* FESTSCHRIFT FÜR ERNST C. STIEFEL ZUM 80. GEBURTSTAG 763, 773–774, 780–781 (Marcus Lutter, ed., 1987); Stürner, *supra* note 20, at 241–243; Stürner, *supra* note 54, at 1081; DAGMAR COESTER-WALTJEN, INTERNATIONALES BEWEISRECHT 388–406 (1983); ALI/UNIDROIT Principles Comments P-18A, P-18B. On Japan, cf. Kojima, *supra* note 16, at 702. According to the Study's approach, a variable about privileges would be coded the higher the more privileges are accorded to parties and witnesses by a country's civil procedure. Presumably this would have led to higher values for the civil law countries than for the common law countries.

[205] A more trivial explanation is that this topic escaped the attention of the Study's authors because the International Encyclopaedia's section on France (*supra* note 192) fails to mention the oath and evidentiary privileges.

have prevented the Study to at least mention this point, as it covers other questions which also are not necessarily related to the two hypothetical cases.

Finally, the Study's weighting of the variables on evidence deserves some attention. As for the single variables, they are all assigned the same weight for this sub-index. An alternative approach could have taken into account that rules on the judge's power to introduce or reject evidence have a broader scope, for they apply to any (or at least more than one) type of evidence, whereas rules on the admissibility (original documents), the procedure (prequalification of questions, interrogation only by the judge) and the probative value of documentary evidence only pertain to one type of evidence.[206] Admittedly, it would have been difficult if not arbitrary to decide in which way some of the variables should have been given more weight than others. Therefore, valuing all variables equally may indeed be the most feasible solution. Yet the reader of the Study should be conscious of these alternatives.

Whether the Study's implicit weighting of the evidence variables is correct is more doubtful on the level of the formalism index. In their aggregated form, i.e. as expressed in the sub-index "Statutory regulation of evidence", the eight variables on evidence together have the same importance as the combined variables of all other sub-indices, for example the three variables of the sub-index "Legal justification". Together with the eight variables of the sub-index "Written versus oral", the eight variables on evidence have the smallest individual weight per variable within the formalism index. At first-instance trials, though, the determination of the facts is typically one, if not the most, important task of the court. It takes most of the time and effort of the parties and the judge. Facts, in turn, are determined by proving them with relevant evidence. Moreover, comparative law scholars agree that probably the most significant difference between systems of civil justice concerns the process of fact-finding.[207] Therefore, it seems inevitable to conclude that the Study assigns far too low a weight to the sub-index on evidence, no matter how difficult it would have been to determine the correct relation of the sub-indices. At any rate, this again is an example that the asserted objectivity of the Study is subject to many qualifications.

---

[206] The hearsay rule would have deserved a weight somewhere in between, as it concerns any introduction (be it oral or in writing) of an out-of-court statement which is hearsay.

[207] *See, e.g.*, Langbein, *supra* note 54, at 1168 (noting that "[t]he great chasm that separates the modern Continental legal systems from the Anglo-American systems is largely about the conduct of fact-finding.").

6. Control of Superior Review

Under the aspect of aggregation of the data, the variables on superior review are problematic as well.[208] First, both the variable on suspension of enforcement and the variable on the scope of review are to equal "zero" if the judgment cannot be appealed at all; the same is true for the third variable if interlocutory appeals are always prohibited. This means that the prohibition of appeals has a very high weight. For a country which does not allow any appeal, all three variables and consequently the sub-index are "zero". One might say that indeed any appeal is formalistic per se. But should such a prohibition really account for one seventh of the formalism index? This seems unbalanced and would mean that different interpretations, which cannot be excluded because of the variables' somewhat unhandy descriptions, have an immense effect.

Moreover, as has been mentioned, there is no variable which covers in a general manner restrictions to the right of appeal. The information gathered from the attorneys seems to concern only situations of superior review in the two model cases. Yet what is correct for the two model cases need not be characteristic for the entire civil procedural law in a country. Rather, it is doubtful whether the answers for the two model cases with their particularities reflect the general existence and the character of restrictions to the right of appeal. Thus there is reason to argue that the Study should have contained a variable covering generally any restriction on the right to appeal.[209]

7. Engagement Formalities

Two points must be made here about the sub-index "Engagement formalities" and its variables. First, two variables cover aspects so close to those covered by other variables that the weight of the respective phase of civil procedure seems excessive. Second, and related, it is questionable whether the whole sub-index should be given so important a weight.

The sub-index "Written versus oral" contains the variable "Service of process". This variable wants to detect whether the defendant's first notice of the complaint is most likely received in writing. On the other hand, the second variable of the sub-index "Engagement formalities" asks whether

---

[208] Remember that according to this paper's methodology, we ignore for the purposes of this part, concerned exclusively with data aggregation, the deficiencies of the definitions and classifications as to the "Superior review" sub-index.

[209] The coding of such a variable is not obvious, for the neighbor model does not provide an unequivocal answer: One would have to wonder, for example, whether it is more formalistic if a judge has to decide on the admissibility of an appeal or if there is a clear rule allowing appeals as soon as a certain amount is at stake.

the complaint has to be served through the intervention of a judicial officer. Not only do both variables concern two aspects of one and the same phase in the proceedings, that is, service of process. They are also interdependent in the sense that it is hardly imaginable to find service of the complaint through a judicial officer without a written complaint. Indeed, all countries with service of process by a judicial officer also have a written complaint.[210] Moreover, it should be mentioned that receiving the first official notice of the complaint in writing is most likely in nearly all countries.[211] Therefore, the Study could have renounced on this variable without missing a characteristic point, but instead could have avoided an excessive emphasis on the service of process-phase of the proceedings.

The situation is similar for the variables "Notification of judgment" in the "Written versus oral" sub-index and "Notification of judgment by judicial officer required" in the "Engagement formalities" sub-index. Not surprisingly, we find virtually no country where there is notification by an officer without written form of the judgment. Although there is no uniformity as to the "written form" variable, so that it cannot be claimed that this variable was superfluous, it remains true that both variables concern aspects of one and the same phase of the proceedings – the notification of the judgment. Again it is very doubtful whether this increased weight is justified as compared to other phases of the proceedings.

With two variables concerning service of process and notification of the judgment, these two phases clearly have a higher weight than, for example, the question of whether legal representation is mandatory. This does not seem to be very convincing. In addition, as a more fundamental question, it can be asked whether the three variables the Study identifies as "Engagement activities" really deserve their own sub-index. Does it make sense to combine mandatory pretrial conciliation with the requirement of a judicial officer's intervention in the service of process and the notification of the judgment? And does the question of whether there is involvement of a judicial official in these two phases of the proceedings merit to account for two thirds of a sub-index?

---

[210] But note that according to the Dataset, in Greece in the eviction case and in Italy, Monaco and Tunisia in the check collection case there is service of process by a judicial officer but no answer for the form of the complaint.

[211] For no country, the value of the "Written versus oral" variable is "zero". In addition to the countries mentioned in the previous footnote, there is no answer on the form of the complaint for Greece in the check collection case (but also no service by judicial officer).

8. Independent Procedural Actions

We have already seen that the variables in this particular sub-index are determined by adding the number of procedural actions in each of the three phases of the proceedings. Therefore, they can, in principle, take the value "one" or any higher natural number. In this sense they are different from the other variables with their two alternatives, "zero" or "one". The sub-index on independent procedural actions, in turn, is not just the average of these numbers, but requires are more complex calculation: The sum of the variables is normalized to fall between zero and one using the minimum and maximum numbers from the countries in the sample. Hence, the sub-index on independent procedural actions, although combining only three variables, can take various different values between zero and one – and not just the four possibilities which exist for other sub-indices with three binary variables.

Nonetheless, for the calculation of the formalism index, the Study adds the value of this sub-index to the values of the other sub-indices without qualms. If adding up sub-indices with different numbers of variables is seen as methodologically questionable unless the differences in weight are justified or at least explained, this problem is exacerbated here: Each variable can also be understood as a sub-index of its own. This means that the sub-index on independent procedural actions is itself a combination of sub-indices, and a problematic one at that.[212]

---

[212] The number of independent procedural actions for the respective step of the proceedings – filing and service, trial and judgment, enforcement – could also be expressed as a fraction of the difference of the maximum and the minimum of actions for all steps of the proceedings from the countries of the sample. In turn, one would have to determine the sub-index on independent procedural actions as the sum of these fractions less a certain fraction to adjust the result to the "elevated" zero level. In other words, let *max* be the maximum number of independent actions and *min* be the minimum number of independent actions, and let *a* be the number of independent actions for the filing and service step, *b* the number of independent actions for the trial and judgment step, and *c* the number of independent actions for the enforcement step of a particular country. Then the sub-index on independent procedural actions equals $1/(max - min) \times (a + b + c - min)$. This is the same as $a/(max - min) + b/(max - min) + c/(max - min) - min/(max - min)$.

However, even if we ignore the adjustment for the "elevated" zero level, two inconsistencies with the methodology used for the other sub-indices remain. To illustrate, imagine for a moment the maximum of actions as a catalogue containing a description of all independent procedural actions, where for each country the answer can be "yes" or "no", or "one" and "zero", and ignore the fact that the country with the maximum number does not necessarily combine all the independent actions of the other countries. In this simplified picture, each variable could be interpreted as combining (as sub-variables) the described independent procedural actions for the respective step of the proceedings, each sub-variable having a value of either "zero" or "one". This looks identical to the methodology employed elsewhere. But even this picture cannot be upheld: First, only some of

9. Mandatory Time Limits Missing

The Study *does* collect data about mandatory time limits. However, it uses this data only in the context of incentives and not as a sub-index of the formalism index. Under the generalizing approach of the Study, there is no reason why this important characteristic should not be significant for measuring formalism.[213] Moreover, it seems to be easy to apply the neighbor model, as mandatory time limits would certainly not exist in a simple triadic structure resolving disputes among neighbors.[214]

10. The Formalism Index

It has already been mentioned at various occasions that adding up sub-indices, which contain different numbers of variables, attributes different weights to the variables within the formalism index, and that the Study furnishes no explanation for these differences. What has not been discussed so far is the method of constructing the formalism index by a simple summation of the sub-indices. From a pure mathematical standpoint, the problem of different weights of the variables could be resolved by multiplying each sub-index with an appropriate factor.[215] However, we have

---

the variables could be checked for each of the three different steps of the proceedings, although the others would remain relevant to constitute the denominator (and the adjustment fraction). Consider that $a \geq 1$, $b \geq 1$, $c \geq 1$ and $a + b + c \geq min$ and $a + b + c \leq max$. Second, the idea of the catalogue does not fit with the calculation of the Study, because the Study takes the minimum and – in particular – maximum number to normalize the sum to fall between zero and one. Therefore, the variables for the different steps cannot be seen as fractions of the maximum, but as fractions of the difference of maximum and minimum minus the adjustment number. This and the above-mentioned fact that the country with the maximum number does not necessarily combine all the independent action of the other countries shows that our catalogue cannot contain fix descriptions, what is different from the approach used for the other formalism variables.

Nevertheless, the three variables of the sub-index on independent procedural actions are in a certain sense a complex combination of various simple "yes" and "no" questions and therefore special sub-indices themselves rather than "yes" and "no" variables.

[213] *Cf. only* MAX VOLLKOMMER, FORMENSTRENGE UND PROZESSUALE BILLIGKEIT 1–2 (1973) (noting that formal requirements in the field of procedural law are closely connected to the procedural time schedule).

[214] Obviously, if one intends to create an outcome where formalism is bad, this would mean that such time limits were seen as negative – what would go against conventional wisdom according to which mandatory time limits are an efficient means to avoid excessive duration. It is, of course, pure speculation to suggest that just for this reason the authors of the Study did not use time limits as a formalism variable. Nevertheless, this data being available, one may be surprised not to find even a short explanation.

[215] This factor could bet the least common denominator divided by the number of variables.

seen that assigning the same weight to all variables is no convincing solution either.

The idea of multiplying each sub-index with a factor is interesting, though. First, one could wonder whether it is possible to determine factors which would assign the "correct" weight to each individual variable. This, however, seems to be doubtful, because still all variables of one and the same sub-index would have the same weight. Second, one can consider an alternative, top down approach, according to which in a first step, the weight of the different sub-indices is determined, and in a second step, the individual variables are assigned an appropriate weight balancing any inconsistencies within the sub-index. For example, on the top level one would hardly have assigned the same value to the sub-index "Engagement formalities" and the sub-index "Written versus oral" or "Statutory regulation of evidence". We do not want to propose that this alternative method necessarily would have been preferable. But under such an approach, it would have been inevitable to more carefully consider and disclose the consequences of the chosen method of aggregating the data.

11. Conclusion

The Study does not explicitly assign weights to the variables or the sub-indices. To the contrary, the Study avoids the question of how significant each of the variables and sub-indices really is. Nevertheless, neither each variable nor each sub-index exerts an equal impact on the formalism index.[216] To the contrary, the variables are attached different weights merely as a consequence of the aggregation method. It seems impossible to discern in this approach a clear concept. The Study itself does not provide any overt explanation for the described differences in the weights. Not surprisingly, the results of this aggregation method are questionable in many respects.

In addition, the Study completely ignores some procedural features which appear to be significant in comparing formalism on the basis of the Study's approach. Other procedural features gain increased, and presumably excessive, impact, because they are covered by more than one variable and therefore tend to influence the formalism index twice in the same direction. Finally, the Study's allocation of variables to sub-indices is not fully convincing and definitely not the only possible approach.

---

[216] *Cf.* JAMES D. GWARTNEY, ROBERT LAWSON & WALTER BLOCK, ECONOMIC FREEDOM OF THE WORLD 1975–1995 37–38 (1996) (proposing that "[t]he simplest alternative would be to take the position that since we do not know the weight that should be attached to the various components, each should exert an equal impact on the index" and noting that "[o]nly one adjustment is required to achieve this objective – each variable must be assigned a weight equal to the inverse of its standard deviation".).

In sum, our review of the Study's aggregation of the data for the formalism index adds to the doubts on whether the Study can provide reliable results that are adequate to be generalized.

C. The Aggregation of the Data for the Supplementary Questions on Time Limits

As mentioned above, among the data collected from the supplementary questions, only the variables on mandatory time limits are aggregated. With the variables taking the value of either "zero" or "one" and the sub-index being calculated as the average of the variables, each of the variables is implicitly assigned the same weight. This seems to be justified, as the concept of time limits is very clear and narrow and the only difference between the variables is in the step of the proceedings and the respective period.

Part VI

The "Other Judicial Quality Measures" and the "Other Variables"

The Study does not only collect and aggregate data on procedural formalism, incentives and duration in the two model cases. It also combines these data with data from other empirical studies and data sources. Most of the data from the external sources concern "other judicial quality measures". The remaining "other variables" cover various topics like the gross national product, the average years of schooling and ethnic fractionalization. The selection of these other, "external" sources is motivated by the aim of proving or refuting the "three broad theories" which according to the Study offer an explanation for differences in courts' performance – the "development" theory, the "incentive" theory, and the "formalism" theory.[217]

Several significant differences between the Lex Mundi Study's formalism index and these other studies and sources can be pointed out upfront. First, the other studies do not cover the same countries, but typically only a fraction of the countries examined by the Lex Mundi Study.

Second, they are not based on data provided by the same attorneys, by law firms or even lawyers generally, but mostly rely on the answers of businessmen or the findings of researchers of the respective institution or organization providing the data.

Third, these other studies are obviously not based on the Lex Mundi Study's two model cases. To the contrary, they contain very general and broad statements about the situation in the various countries.

Fourth, some of the other sources are "perception indices", that is, indices not based on data about the actual situation in a country, but based on the subjective perceptions of a more or less clearly defined group of individuals, like industry leaders, in that country. This concerns in particular the broad and not very specific questions about the attributes of a country's legal system – fairness, impartiality, honesty and corruption, affordability, consistency, confidence, and law and order. Such "trust scores" vary substantially among cultures[218] and groups of people dependent on their pro-

---

[217] Djankov et al., *supra* note 11, at 454–455.

[218] *See only* EUROPEAN COMMISSION FOR THE EFFICIENCY OF JUSTICE, EUROPEAN JUDICIAL SYSTEMS 2002 12 (2005), *available at* <http://www.coe.int/t/e/legal_affairs/le

fessional background.[219] In addition, externalities like coverage by the local news media and a culture of investigative journalism might play a decisive role.[220] On the other hand, the formalism index and other studies are focused on relatively specific and precise questions and seek to rely on facts rather than mere perceptions.

Finally, the other sources' data are not in all cases based on the years 1999 and 2000, the years for which the authors of the Lex Mundi Study collected their data, but partly are older or younger.

It seems worth mentioning these differences because the Study – despite, for the formalism index, limiting itself to data concerning the two hypothetical cases – fully and uncritically relies on these other, general sources for its conclusions. This is the more important as it is just these other sources which provide the material for evaluating the legal systems of the various countries.

The present section discusses these external sources and how the Study uses their data. Before going into detail, one general caveat cannot be repeated often enough: Measuring judicial quality in an objective way is extremely difficult, if not impossible. Leaving behind the field of factual observations, as for example data on duration or cost, only subjective estimates remain, which are prone to be influenced by a strong "home bias" – the preference of what one is familiar with.[221] Therefore, whoever uses such estimates as input for an own study should not claim objectivity for that study's results.

A. The "Other Judicial Quality Measures" and their Sources

1. Measuring Judicial Quality

Legal scholars and policymakers have since long discussed what determines the quality of adjudication. Diverse standards have been proposed, ranging from the enforcement of individual rights or the substantive law over convenient – including cheap and fast – dispute resolution or litigant satisfaction, to social cohesion or the controlled exercise of state power,

---

gal_co%2Doperation/operation_of_justice/efficiency_of_justice/systeme%20judiciaire %20A.pdf> (last visited July 17, 2006).

[219] *See, e.g.*, Vollkommer, *supra* note 213, at 5–11. *Cf. also* Gilles, *supra* note 30, sub II.3.b.

[220] Davis, *supra* note 23, at 150.

[221] Detlev Vagts, *Comparative Company Law – The New Wave*, *in* FESTSCHRIFT FÜR JEAN NICOLAS DRUEY 595, 602 (Rainer J. Schweizer, Herbert Burkert & Urs Grasser, eds., 2002).

encompassing combinations of these factors.[222] The Study seems to ignore this discussion and to choose its "judicial quality measures" rather eclectically according to the availability of data from other sources. It so happens that this is mostly "litigant satisfaction" data.

Of course, one must not expect a statistical study to enter deeply into the discussion about when a particular form of procedure is "good". And the factors chosen by the Study are clearly meaningful. However, it is once more obvious that the Study's selection cannot claim objectivity.

2. Business Environmental Risk Intelligence (Enforceability of Contracts)

In order to measure the enforceability of contracts, the Study employs a scale from zero to ten and uses data collected by "experts" on behalf of Business Environmental Risk Intelligence S.A. (BERI). Unfortunately the source of the data is not fully specified: Neither do we know the year nor the precise index. BERI measures the enforceability of contracts for the Operation Risk Index (ORI), which covers 53 countries from 1980 to 2003. The ORI scale ranges from zero to four.[223] However, contract enforceability is also relevant for BERI's Financial Ethics Index (FEI).[224] Although results might not differ significantly, a full indication of the source and the method of transformation, if any, of its ratings to the Study's scale from zero to ten would have increased the Study's trustworthiness.

Moreover, one could wonder why the Study uses data on the enforceability of contracts from BERI and not from the World Business Environment Survey, on which it relies for many other "external" variables. That survey contains a variable on the enforceability of decisions. It is true that the BERI data concentrates on contracts, and our two hypothetical cases

---

[222] *See only* John Leubsdorf, *The Myth of Civil Procedure Reform*, *in* CIVIL JUSTICE IN CRISIS 53, 54–56 (Adrian A.S. Zuckerman, ed., 1999), with references to RONALD M. DWORKIN, A MATTER OF PRINCIPLE 72–103 (1985); Cynthia R. Farina, *Conceiving Due Process*, 3 YALE J.L. & FEMINISM 189 (1991); Jerry L. Mashaw, *Administrative Due Process: The Quest for a Dignitary Theory*, 61 B.U. L. REV. 885 (1981); Robert S. Summers, *Evaluating and Improving Legal Processes: A Plea for "Process Values"*, 60 CORNELL L. REV. 1 (1974). *See also* Zuckerman, *supra* note 134, at 48–49 (proposing a reappraisal of the balance between the factors truth, time, and cost); Jolowicz, *supra* note 101, at ix–x (urging that "we should give more attention to the purposes [civil litigation] serves, and should serve, in society" and criticizing that "it must not be assumed, as it so often seems to be, that the whole panoply of (civil) courts, judges and lawyers amounts to no more than one of a number of institutions whose business is simply to settle those disputes which fail to settle themselves, and that the only question is how courts and judges can deal with the cases that reach them as quickly and as economically as possible.").

[223] BERI S.A., *Historical Ratings Research Package User Guide* p. 1–2.

[224] BERI Marketing Team, E-Mail of January 2, 2006 (on file with the author).

concern contractual settings. Therefore, one plausible reason could be that these data are more closely related to the two hypothetical cases. Nevertheless, the very general approach of the Study, in particular regarding the "other judicial quality measures", would not have excluded resorting to the more general data of this other survey. It would certainly be exaggerated to ask for a detailed explanation of the selection of all "external" sources of empirical data. However, in the present case, where similar data is available form a source widely used for other variables, it can be argued that an explanation would have been desirable.

The Study uses the data about the enforceability of contracts – and the same is obviously true for all other data under the headline "Other judicial quality measures" – to determine the judicial quality of the respective country's court system, and links the result with the formalism index. That formalism has something to do with enforceability, seems plausible, even more because the variables of the formalism index encompass the enforcement stage of the proceedings. Nevertheless, it should be kept in mind that procedural formalism is only one aspect which might influence the ability and willingness of the parties to enforce a contract, and a less important one at that.

3. World Business Environment Survey (Legal System Is Fair and Impartial, Honest and Uncorrupt; Affordable; Consistent; Confidence in Legal System)

According to the Study, the data for five of the variables on judicial quality stems from the World Bank's World Business Environment Survey (WBES).[225] The Study's references include two such surveys, one of 2000 and another of 2002. As to the 2000 survey, the relevant data is readily available.[226] The WBES 2000 is based on data collected from firm managers and owners in 80 countries.[227] In addition to the WBES 2000, however, the Study apparently also uses data from a 2002 survey.[228] We could not identify such a survey. Yet the data for the WBES 2000 are in part derived from the 1999 Business Environment and Enterprise Performance Survey (BEEPS), a survey jointly owned by the European Bank for Reconstruction

---

[225] It can only be mentioned here that instead of using a variable on impartiality, the Study could also have used a variable of judicial independence – a field where much research is being done; *see only* World Bank, *Judicial Independence: What It Is, How It Can Be Measured, Why It Occurs*, <http://www1.worldbank.org/publicsector/legal/judicialindependence.htm> (last visited November 27, 2006), and the references therein.

[226] *See* World Bank, World Business Environment Survey (WBES) 2000 Webtool Interactive, <http://info.worldbank.org/governance/wbes/> (last visited July 17, 2006).

[227] *Id.*

[228] Djankov et al., *supra* note 11, at 471.

and Development and the World Bank. The BEEPS collects data from managers and owners of firms in Eastern European countries, countries of the former Soviet Union and Turkey.[229] As there is also a 2002 BEEPS (the so called BEEPS II),[230] we suppose that the Study used the data from this survey.

Assuming that the data are based on these two surveys, two qualifications must be made. First, the Study classifies the countries on a scale from one to six. The surveys do not use a scale. Rather, they give the percentage of people who, for a relevant question, associate one of the following descriptions with their country's court system: "Never", "Seldom", "Sometimes", "Frequently", "Usually", "Always". In addition, the BEEPS also allows to show the "Don't Knows".[231] On the basis of these data, it is not completely clear how the Study came to the results that are shown in its Dataset.[232] Second, both the WBES and the BEEPS ask owners and managers of firms about their estimation of the legal system concerning "business disputes".[233] The two hypothetical cases, however, can hardly be seen as typical business disputes. To the contrary, it seems unlikely that such cases came into the mind of the owners or managers when asked about their evaluation of the legal system in resolving business disputes. Of course, if the aspects of formalism in the two model cases are seen as representative for the whole civil procedure in a country, any combination

---

[229] World Bank, The BEEPS Interactive Dataset, <http://info.worldbank.org/governance/beeps/> (last visited July 17, 2006).

[230] World Bank, The BEEPS II Interactive Dataset: Enterprise Survey in Transition, <http://info.worldbank.org/governance/beeps2002/> (last visited July 17, 2006).

[231] *Cf.* the various questionnaires: World Business Environment Survey, "Measuring Conditions for Business Operation and Growth", Private Enterprise Questionnaire, p. 5, *available at* <http://www.ifc.org/ifcext/economics.nsf/AttachmentsByTitle/IC-WBESCoreQuestionnaire/$FILE/wbescore1.pdf>, and World Business Environment Survey Screener Questionnaire, p. 12, *available at* <http://www.worldbank.org/wbi/governance/pdf/beeps_questions.pdf> (BEEPS) and Business Environment and Enterprise Performance Survey Screener Questionnaire, p. 14, *available at* <http://info.worldbank.org/governance/beeps2002/beeps2_questions.pdf> (BEEPS II) (last visited July 17, 2006).

[232] One would expect that values from 1 to 6 were attributed to each of the possible answers from "never" to "always", and that the value on the scale for a given country equaled the sum of the values multiplied with the respective percentage. Also, one would suppose that for countries which were included in both surveys the average of the results was used. However, the results of spot tests on the basis of the data from the surveys and calculated accordingly do not exactly match the Study's numbers. E.g., the Dataset exhibits for "law and order" in Argentina 2.13. Calculating on the base of the WBES data as proposed, we find 2.1% x 6 ("always") + 9.3% x 5 ("mostly") + 10.3% x 4 ("frequently") + 34% x 3 ("sometimes") + 20.6% x 2 ("seldom") + 23.7% x 1 ("never") = 2.672.

[233] *See* the questionnaires, *supra* note 231.

with surveys covering other types of cases is possible and not problematic. However, we have seen that this assumption can be questioned for good reasons. From this point of view, the fact that WBES and BEEPS are limited to business disputes suggests that the link between the Study's formalism index and the data from these surveys might be rather loose.

4. Transparency International (Corruption)

The Study claims to use the "composite index for the year 2000" prepared by Transparency International (TI).[234] Surprisingly, though, it seems that the data in the Dataset cannot be attributed to any of the indices published by TI.[235] The description of the index, "a composite index for the year 2000 that draws on fourteen data sources from seven institutions", and the seven institutions listed[236] match with the TI Corruption Perceptions Index 2001 (2001 CPI).[237] Also, the 2001 CPI uses a scale from zero to ten, with ten being the score for an uncorrupt country. However, the scores assigned to the various countries in the Study's Dataset differ extremely from the results of the 2001 CPI. For this reason, it is hard to imagine that the authors of the Study had actually used the 2001 CPI data.[238] Even more, the fact that the discrepancies are so important suggests that this cannot simply be the result of a different method of aggregating the results from the various sources, but rather that the Study used another source with quite different results.[239]

---

[234] Djankov et al., *supra* note 11, at 472.

[235] Regrettably, the Study omits any mention of the TI index in the references, while it lists some – not all – of the other sources of "external" data.

[236] Djankov et al., *supra* note 11, at 472.

[237] *See generally* Transparency International, Corruption Perceptions Index 2001, <http://www.transparency.org/policy_and_research/surveys_indices/cpi/2001#source> and Annual Report 2001, p. 13, <http://www.transparency.org/content/download/2282/14290/file/TI%20Annual%20Report%202001.pdf>; for the sources, see JOHANN GRAF LAMBSDORFF, FRAMEWORK DOCUMENT. BACKGROUND PAPER TO THE 2001 CORRUPTION PERCEPTIONS INDEX 3, 10–11 (2001), <http://www.transparency.org/content/download/1936/11436/file/methodology.pdf> (last visited July 17, 2006).

[238] *Cf.* the following examples (for each country, the first number is the 2001 CPI score, the second stems from the Dataset, rounded to one decimal place): Chile 7.5/5.3; China 3.5/6.5; Costa Rica 4.5/8.3; Czech Republic 3.9/7.2; Ecuador 2.3/5.2; France 6.7/9.0; Greece 4.2/7.3; Malawi 3.2/6.3; Malaysia 5.0/7.4; Poland 4.1/7.4; South Africa 4.8/8.9.

For some countries, the Dataset contains no data, although there is a CPI score. This is the case, e.g., for Croatia, Estonia, Latvia, Lithuania, and Slovenia.

[239] With regard to some sources, the 2001 CPI "combines assessments from the past three years to reduce abrupt variations in scoring" (Graf Lambsdorff, *supra* note 237, at 3). It seems possible that the Study did not follow this approach, but used exclusively

Note also that corruption is already included in the variable "Legal system is honest or uncorrupt", which is based on the WBES, and that data from the WBES is one of the indices used by TI to construct its composite index. The Study gives no information, let alone explanation, concerning the increased weight of corruption, the use of different sources and the inclusion of the one source in the composite index of the other.

5. PRS Group International Country Risk Guide (Law and Order)

Since 1980, PRS Group has been publishing the International Country Risk Guide (ICRG), which rates financial, political and economic risk for 140 countries.[240] The Study defines the variable "law and order" as measuring the "integrity of the legal system in 2000" and draws on the data in the "law and order" component of the Political Risk Points table,[241] but modifies them from a scale ranging from zero to six to a ten-point scale.[242] Here again, we are missing a precise description of exactly which data has been used; moreover, it seems that not all the data in the Study's Dataset can be explained with the data from the source.[243] In addition, it is noteworthy

---

data for the year 2000. However, even if this were the case, some discrepancies would remain; moreover, we see no reason for departing from TI's sound approach.

[240] PRS Group, International Country Risk Guide, <http://www.prsgroup.com/icrg/icrg.html> (last visited July 17, 2006).

[241] Table 3B. This table lists the points for twelve political risk components (A–L); the law and order component is component I. The components on which the political risk rating is based are weighted; the maximum points are either 4, 6 or 12 (the minimum number of points is zero). The maximum points of the law and order component are 6. The law and order component is the sum of the sub-component "law" (assessing the strength and impartiality of the legal system) and the sub-component "order" (assessing popular observance of the law). Each of them comprises zero to three points. *See* PRS Group, About ICRG, <http://www.icrgonline.com/page.aspx?page=icrgmethods> (last visited July 17, 2006).

[242] Djankov et al., *supra* note 11, at 472. The Study seems to use a linear modification, multiplying the data from the ICRG by 10/6.

[243] First, the ICRG contains data for each month of the year 2000. Without being explicit about that (the Study only mentions very generally "various issues"), the Study apparently only looks at the last month(s) of the year 2000 and ignores earlier changes: for Bangladesh, the ICRG value from February through December 2000 is 2, what if multiplied by 10/6 equals the Dataset's 3.33; however, Bangladesh shows an ICRG value of 3 for January 2000; *see also* China (ICRG: October through December 4; Dataset: 6.67; ICRG January through September: 5); Colombia (ICRG March through December: 1; Dataset: 1.67; ICRG January and February: 2), Germany (ICRG September through December: 5; Dataset: 8.33; ICRG January through August: 6), Hungary (ICRG March through December: 4; Dataset: 6.67; ICRG January and February: 6), Japan (ICRG February through December: 5; Dataset: 8.33; January: 6), Malta (ICRG July through December: 5; Dataset: 8.33; ICRG January through June: 6), Philippines (ICRG October through December: 2; Dataset: 3.33; ICRG January through April: 4, May through Sep-

that the "law and order" variable of the ICRG contains once more an assessment of the impartiality of the legal system,[244] a feature to which the Study dedicates an own variable based on WBES data. Finally, the criticism on this variable expressed by Professor Vagts, colorfully illustrated with the example that "[a] cosmopolitan lawyer would surely prefer to litigate a complex corporation case before the Tribunal Commercial de la Seine than before a randomly chosen jury and elected judge in rural Mississippi"[245] holds as well in the context of the Lex Mundi Study.

6. Conclusion

It is no question that the sources which the Study uses in order to combine the formalism index with "other judicial quality measures" must, in principle, be seen as reliable – although one might have doubts as to the signifi-

---

tember: 3), Turkey (ICRG February through December: 4; Dataset 6.67; ICRG January: 3), and Zimbabwe (ICRG April through December: 2; Dataset: 3.33; ICRG January through March: 4).

Second, there is no explanation for the values for the Dominican Republic (ICRG: 4; Dataset: 5, but 4 multiplied by 10/6 is 6.67), Lithuania (ICRG: 4; Dataset: 8.33, but 4 multiplied by 10/6 is 6.67), and Vietnam (ICRG: 5, but no value in the Dataset). Having compared with ICRG data from PRS Group's online data as of February 21, 2006, <http://www.countrydata.com/>, it cannot be excluded that the data available at the time of the Study was different.

Note also that the Study's reference to another "source" is puzzling. The Study defines the variable "Integrity of the legal system in 2000 [...] based on the Political Risk Component 1 (Law and Order) from the PRS Group's International Country Risk Guide", but then gives as a source "GWARTNEY, LAWSON, AND BLOCK", ECONOMIC FREEDOM OF THE WORLD, and indicates as year for this reference 2001 (Djankov et al., *supra* note 11, at 472) as well as – in the references – 1975–1995 (*id.*, at 516). Obviously, giving Gwartney et al. as source contradicts the definition of the variable (according to which the variable is based on the PRS Group's ICRG), unless the reference is interpreted as a source for the modification to a ten-point scale. However, this reference is not very helpful: The Fraser Institute has published annual reports with the title "Freedom of the World" for (among others) the years 2000 and 2001; yet its authors are either James Gwartney, Robert Lawson and Dexter Samida (annual report 2000) or James Gwartney, Robert Lawson, Walter Park and Charles Skipton (annual report 2001). The authors of ECONOMIC FREEDOM OF THE WORLD 1975–1995 (1996), in turn, are indeed James Gwartney, Robert Lawson and Walter Block. In this latter work, Chapter 1 on the "Construction of the Economic Freedom Index" explains three alternative methods to derive the ratings from the underlying data (Gwartney, Lawson & Block, at 15–16; *see* also the explanations of ratings in Appendix II, *id.*, at 243–308). However, the Economic Freedom Index does not use the ICRG component "law and order". Therefore, the reference does not make clear what kind of modification has been used. We assume that the Study multiplied the ICRG values with 10/6 (*see supra* note 242). But we do not see why such a simple linear modification deserves a reference at all.

[244] *See* PRS Group, *supra* note 240.

[245] Vagts, *supra* note 221, at 602.

cance of these studies' results. Regrettably, however, to the reader who is interested in comparing the Dataset with the data in these external sources, the Study does not provide a sufficient amount of information. The reader is left alone with ambiguous and imprecise references and dissatisfying explanations of how exactly the data from the external sources have been modified for the Study. The doubt and frustration this might create could easily have been avoided.

B. The "Other Variables" and their Sources

1. World Development Indicators/CIA World Factbook (Log of GNP per capita)

In order to determine a potential relationship between procedural formalism and economic development, the Study uses a variable "log of GNP per capita". It is defined as the "logarithm of GNP per capita in 1999, Atlas method, expressed in current US dollars."[246] The data for this variable stem mostly from the World Bank's World Development Indicators 2001 (WDI 2001) and, where no WDI data was available, from the CIA World Factbook.

Indeed, the hard copy of the WDI 2001 contains measures of the gross national income per capita in 1999 in current US dollars, calculated using the World Bank Atlas method.[247] It is also true that 1999 income data are not available for some of the countries in the Study's sample, and that such data are available for the indicated years either in other WDI statistics or in the CIA World Factbook, which only provides GDP per capita (purchasing power parity).[248] The Study does not mention the CIA World Factbook in the references and does not specify the Factbook's year in the text. The interested reader therefore has to derive from the qualifications in the variable's definition[249] that the Study uses the CIA World Factbook 2000.[250] Although the variable is abbreviated "log" and the definition only speaks

[246] Djankov et al., *supra* note 11, at 473.

[247] World Bank, World Development Indicators 2001, 12–14 and 32 (2001). Apparently, the Study uses the terms "gross national income" and "gross national product" interchangeably, what is common.

[248] Note that although 1999 data for Kuwait and Bahrain is available on WDI online, these data were not included in the hard copy of the WDI 2001 (*see id.*, at 13 and 32).

[249] 1997 data for the Cayman Islands, Gibraltar and the Turks and Caicos Islands; 1998 data for Anguilla and the Netherlands Antilles; 1999 data for Monaco and the British Virgin Islands.

[250] CIA, CIA World Factbook 2000, *available at* <https://www.cia.gov/cia/download2000.html> (last visited July 17, 2006, formerly *available at* <http://odci.gov/cia/download.html>).

of "logarithm", the Study does not use the logarithm with the base 10, as one could have assumed, but the natural logarithm – the logarithm with the base *e* – which is oftentimes denoted *ln*.[251] It seems that it would have been helpful if the Study had been more precise.

2. La Porta et al. [1999] (Legal Origin)

The Study classifies the countries into five groups of legal origin: English, French, Socialist, German, and Scandinavian. In support of this classification, it refers to La Porta et al. [1999].[252] While being presented as if it were a survey based on more or less objective data, this is not a source like most of the other external sources; for it is not a survey but a paper. The Study's description of this variable, borrowed from La Porta et al. [1999], says that it "[i]dentifies the legal origin of the company law or commercial code of each country (English, French, Socialist, German, Scandinavian)".[253] He who expected to find in the 1999 La Porta article an explanation for why the authors believe that this or that country was assigned to this or that legal origin, would be disappointed. The cited article uses the same classification, but refers to other sources: "La Porta et al., 1998, extended using 'Foreign Laws: Current Sources of Basic Legislation in Jurisdictions of the World', and CIA World Factbook 1996".[254] It is only in this other La Porta article of 1998, that we find the source of the Study's classification of countries according to legal origins: a brief summary of the various concepts of legal families in comparative private law and the authors' decision for one of these concepts.[255]

---

[251] The authors have turned to this abbreviation in a more recent study: Djankov et al., *The Law and Economics of Self-Dealing*, NBER Working Paper 11883 (2005), 44 et seq. ("Residual Ln (Firms-to-Population)"; "Ln GDP/POP" et cet.), <http://papers.nber.org/papers/w11883.pdf> (last visited July 17, 2006). However, most computer programming languages use *log* to denote the natural logarithm.

[252] Rafael La Porta, Florencio Lopez-de-Silanes, Andrei Shleifer & Robert Vishny, *The Quality of Government*, 15 J. OF LAW, ECONOMICS AND ORGANIZATION 222–279 (1999).

[253] Djankov et al., *supra* note 11, at 473.

[254] La Porta et al., *supra* note 252, at 238.

[255] Rafael La Porta, Florencio Lopez-de-Silanes, Andrei Shleifer & Robert Vishny, *Law and Finance*, 106 JOURNAL OF POLITICAL ECONOMY 1113, 1117 et seq. (1998), first published as NBER Working Paper No. 5661 (1996), p. 8 et seq., <http://papers.nber.org/papers/w5661.pdf> (last visited July 17, 2006). This article can also be found in the references of our Study. All the more, it could have been cited directly. Note that this article only classifies 49 countries at the exclusion of socialist or transition economies (*id.*, at 1117).

In this article, the authors state that their classification relies on Thomas H. Reynolds & Arturo A. Flores, Foreign Law: Current Sources of Codes and Basic Legislation in Jurisdictions of the World (1989) without explaining their choice. Actually, determining

First of all, it should be mentioned that in the last years, distinguished comparative law scholars seem to have agreed on a declining importance of the traditional distinction of legal families. For this reason, the fact that the quantitative studies of the "new comparative economics" link their results with the traditional distinction of legal families has recently been described as a "revival of 'legal families' [... that] may surprise modern comparative lawyers."[256] This exclamation seems a bit strong, considering that these studies are interested in "legal origins" rather than "legal families". Nevertheless, this observation indicates a gap between these studies and modern comparative law.

Second, note that the first La Porta article [La Porta et al., 1999] resorts to legal origins in the context of a "strategy for evaluating political theories" of institutions,[257] the second [La Porta et al., 1998] focuses on the protection of corporate shareholders and creditors.[258] Thus, the purpose of these articles is obviously very different from the purpose of the Lex Mundi Study. Also, the 1998 article – which provides the basis for the classification – concentrates on commercial law, while the Lex Mundi Study is about civil procedure. This does not necessarily mean that the Study cannot adopt these articles' classification of legal origins – provided that they were correct for the purposes of these studies, what is quite doubtful.[259] However, it advises a careful scrutiny as to whether their classification also fits for the Study's purpose.

It is a commonplace among comparative law scholars that different areas of the law of a country do not automatically have one and the same legal origin.[260] No thoughtful comparatist, interested in the legal origin of a *particular* area of the law, would simply conclude from one area of the law to another or indiscriminately use a general classification, but would always reassure herself by investigating into the legal history and character-

---

the legal origin of legal institutions and specific areas of law is all but easy. For an excellent overview on the difficulties in determining legal origins, see Kohler, *supra* note 14, at 9–12.

[256] Mathias M. Siems, *Legal Origins – Reconciling Law & Finance and Comparative Law*, Heinrich-Heine-University Düsseldorf Center for Business and Corporate Law Research Center Paper Series no. 0023 (01/2006), p. 4, *available at* <http://papers.ssrn.com/sol3/papers.cfm?abstract_id=879720> (last visited July 17, 2006).

[257] La Porta et al., *supra* note 252, at 231.

[258] La Porta et al., *supra* note 255, at 1113.

[259] *Cf.* Siems, *supra* note 256, at 8 et seq. (noting that "one cannot escape the conclusion that the law and finance categorization of legal families which aims to cover most countries of the world, is to a large extent just arbitrary." *Id.*, at 14).

[260] *See, e.g.,* Kojima, *supra* note 52, at 575 (raising the point "[t]o what extent a categorizing by legal families in the context of civil procedure should be different from one developed mainly in the area of private, substantive law"); *see generally* Zweigert & Kötz, *supra* note 111, at 66.

istics of the area of law at issue. This suggests that a study which focuses on civil procedural law should not blindly adopt existing general classifications, but should verify whether these qualifications also – and still – hold for the field of civil procedure.[261] Put differently, the correct determination of the legal origin depends on the level of comparison: A distinct legal institution, like a certain form of third-party proceedings or rules for documentary evidence, may have another legal origin than the field of the law, taken as a whole, to which this institution is seen to belong.[262] For what matters on the level of the field of the law is the basic structures and characteristics of this field of the law. That single legal institutions have another origin, is no longer decisive on this level. On an even higher level of abstraction, a country as a whole may be attributed to a legal family even if the legal origin of some fields of the law is another one.[263] Speaking of legal origins in a study on civil procedural law suggests that the relevant level of comparison is that of the field of procedural law. To be sure, this does not exclude to go to a higher or lower level of abstraction. However, as a matter of transparency, this ought to be made clear.

And indeed there is some reason to wonder whether the Study's distinction of legal origins is as unambiguous as it seems to be. Although one might have doubts as to whether in the field of civil procedural law, legal families have lately been losing importance, as this has been claimed for

---

[261] *See, e.g.,* the discussion on the 1995 World Conference on Procedural Law: Kojima, *supra* note 52, at 597–598, 601–607; Harald Koch, *Neuordnung der Rechtsfamilien im Prozeßrecht. Die Lehre von den Rechtskreisen (Rechtsfamilien) und das deutsche Zivilprozessrecht – Legal families in procedural law revisited –, in* TRANSNATIONALES PROZESSRECHT – TRANSNATIONAL ASPECTS OF PROCEDURAL LAW, GERMAN REPORTS FOR THE WORLD CONFERENCE ON PROCEDURAL LAW IN TAORMINA, SICILY, 1995, 119, 138–139 (Peter Gilles, ed., 1996) (noting that "[t]raditional classifications of legal families do not reflect the changing orientation of legal systems in countries and regions with new political orders and/or societies."). *See also* Stürner & Stadler, *supra* note 30, at 291 (emphasizing that "civil procedural law is a small and independent area of law which allows not only micro-comparison but even a consideration of the litigation as a whole.").

[262] For example, the French rules on the verification of documentary evidence are said to be inspired by the German Code; *see* Guinchard & Ferrand, *supra* note 97, at 918, ¶ 1176, although German procedural law as a whole has borrowed a lot from French procedural law (*see, e.g.,* Rosenberg, *supra* note 156, at 10–11).

[263] Traditionally, scholarly work on the methodology of comparative law distinguishes between "macro-comparison", whose objects are legal systems as a whole, and "micro-comparison", which deals with clearly defined problems and their solution in a country's legal and sociological environment. *See, e.g.,* Zweigert & Kötz, *supra* note 111, at 4–5; MAX RHEINSTEIN, EINFÜHRUNG IN DIE RECHTSVERGLEICHUNG 31–36 (Reimer von Borries, ed., 2nd ed., 1987); for an overview on macro- and micro-comparison in the field of civil procedural law, see Gottwald, *supra* note 30, at 235–241.

comparative (private) law in general,[264] many distinguished scholars think that in civil procedure the distinction between common law and civil law has to some extent blurred over the last decades.[265] One reason is that while in England, the jury not only has disappeared, but also its shadows no longer dominate the structure of civil procedure under the new Civil Procedure Rules, the jury still plays a very important role in the U.S.,[266] although this role might be more a conceptual than an actual one.[267] In many respects, U.S. civil procedure today is regarded as unique among the common law countries.[268] It has even been suggested that the differences between English and U.S. civil procedure nowadays are greater than the differences between English and continental European, i.e., civil law, civil procedure.[269]

A careful scrutiny of whether classifications from other fields of the law or other levels of comparison also hold for a country's civil procedure is particularly important if the comparison embraces "socialist countries". For the purpose of a survey on the quality of government based on political theories of institutions, it may, as a general matter, be true that "socialist

---

[264] *See supra* note 256 and accompanying text.

[265] *See, e.g.*, Kojima, *supra* note 16, at 720, 721; Kojima, *supra* note 52, at 603; Gottwald, *supra* note 83, at 717–718.

[266] *See only* Jolowicz, *supra* note 222, at 30 (noting that "in the United States jury trial still *presents itself* as the normal mode of trial in civil cases." [Emphasis added]).

[267] *See, e.g.,* Marc Galanter, *The Vanishing Trial: An Examination of Trials and Related Matters in* Federal *and State Courts*, 1 J. EMPIRICAL LEGAL STUD. 459 (2004); Justice Nathan L. Hecht, *The Vanishing Civil Jury Trial: Trends in Texas Courts an and Uncertain Future*, 47 S. TEX. L. REV. 163 (2005).

[268] *See, e.g.,* Stephen Goldstein, *Contrasting Views of Adjudication: An Israeli-American Comparison, in* GEDÄCHTNISSCHRIFT FÜR PETER ARENS 169, 182 (Dieter Leipold, Wolfgang Lüke & Shozaburo Yoshino, eds., 1993) (concluding that there is an "essential difference between the United States and Israel as to their expectations of the judicial process."). According to him, "it is characteristic of American scholarship in this field to look at the 'Anglo-American' or 'common-law' traditions from a very American perspective, thus ignoring some basic differences between England and the United States in terms of adjudication in general and civil procedure in particular." Goldstein, *supra* note 54, at 5; OSCAR G. CHASE, LAW, CULTURE AND RITUAL 47–71 (2005) (describing in chapter 4 "American 'Exceptionalism' in Civil Litigation").

[269] *See, e.g.*, Stürner, *supra* note 54, at 1076 (observing that the difference in structure between modern German procedure and the new English procedure is but relative; that the differences between English and German procedure on the one side and the "Romanic" systems on the other are greater in many respects; and that differences between U.S. civil procedure and the rest of the world are even much stronger). *See also* Stürner, *supra* note 18, at 9–10, 28–30. Note that this is an exception from the general observation that today's U.S. law seems to have "greater affinities with the continental European tradition than with the English common law." Cally Jordan, *The Conundrum of Corporate Governance*, 30 BROOK. J. INT'L L. 983, 1005 et seq. (2005).

law is a clear manifestation of the State's intent to create institutions to maintain its power and extract resources, without much regard for protecting the economic interest or the liberties of the population" and that "[t]he goal of socialist law is to keep the Communist Party in power, not to protect property or freedom."[270] However, as early as in the 1960s, it has been observed that not all legal institutions are affected to the same degree by socialist ideas. One of the areas, which were said not to be completely "system-conditioned", just is procedural law.[271] No doubt socialist civil procedure pursued other, "collectivist" goals besides dispute resolution and vindication of individual rights. Nevertheless, as far as fundamental and technical structures – the most important determinants of formalism – are concerned, it appears that in a number of socialist countries, the former style has to some extent been preserved during that period.[272] For this reason alone, one could wonder whether it makes sense to speak of a socialist legal origin when comparing formalism in the field of procedural law.

---

[270] La Porta et al., *supra* note 252, at 231.

[271] Dietrich A. Loeber, *Rechtsvergleichung zwischen Ländern mit verschiedener Wirtschaftsordnung*, 26 RABELSZ 201, 228 (1961); KONRAD ZWEIGERT & HEIN KÖTZ, INTRODUCTION TO COMPARATIVE LAW 38 (Tony Weir, trans., 2nd ed., 1992). *See also* Damaška, *supra* note 14, at 6–8 (emphasizing the strong similarities between socialist and conventional Continental systems and concluding that "most questions relevant to the study of procedural diversity lie beyond the opposition of capitalism, socialism and similar vague socioeconomic concepts [...]") and 201–204. *But see* Mauro Cappelletti & Bryant G. Garth, *Introduction – Policies, Trends and Ideas in Civil Procedure, in* INTERNATIONAL ENCYCLOPEDIA OF COMPARATIVE LAW, VOL. XVI, CIVIL PROCEDURE, CH. 1, ¶¶ I-10 through I-17 (Mauro Cappelletti, chief ed., 1987) (mentioning important particularities of socialist civil procedure like powers of the state attorney or the court to commence a proceeding without request of a party, and their affirmative duty to seek out counterclaims; however, these differences mostly have no important effect on the aspects of procedural formalism examined by the Study); Petr Chemlíček, *Einführung in das Tschechische Zivilprozessrecht*, 7 ZZPINT 429, 430–431 (2002) (describing the the influence of the socialist ideology on Czech civil procedure after World War II).

[272] For Eastern Europe, see generally János Németh, *Das deutsche Zivilprozeßrecht und seine Ausstrahlung auf die Rechtsordnungen der osteuropäischen Länder, in* DAS DEUTSCHE ZIVILPROZESSRECHT UND SEINE AUSSTRAHLUNG AUF ANDERE RECHTSORDNUNGEN 254–281 (Walther J. Habscheid, ed., 1991); for Poland Mieczysław Sawczuk, *Das deutsche und das polnische Zivilprozeßrecht in der Zeit von der ersten polnischen ZPO bis zur Gegenwart, in* DAS DEUTSCHE ZIVILPROZESSRECHT UND SEINE AUSSTRAHLUNG AUF ANDERE RECHTSORDNUNGEN 282–292 (Walther J. Habscheid, ed., 1991); for Hungary Miklós Kengyel, *Veränderungen des Inhalts der Dispositions- und Verhandlungsmaxime im ungarischen Zivilprozeßrecht*, 2 ZZPINT 273, 282–283 (1997); Miklós Kengyel, *Die Entstehungsgeschichte der fünfzigjährigen ungarischen Zivilprozessordnung, in* 1 FESTSCHRIFT FÜR KOSTAS E. BEYS ZUM 70. GEBURTSTAG 705, 706, 713–716 (Hideo Nakamura, Hans W. Fasching, Hans Friedhelm Gaul & Apostolos Georgiades, eds., 2003).

With regard to the Study's group of countries with "Scandinavian legal origin", some qualifications seem to be appropriate as well. It may be true that in the area of commercial law and maybe also with regard to institutions, there are considerable and characteristic similarities among the Scandinavian countries. However, despite textual differences, German and Austrian procedural concepts have played an important role in Scandinavian civil procedure.[273] By no means do we want to deny Scandinavian civil procedure its genuine character. One should be aware, though, that the links between civil procedure in countries of what the Study calls "Scandinavian legal origin" and countries of other legal origins can be very close – and might even be closer than between countries which, according to the Study, have one and the same legal origin.

These and other[274] examples illustrate that adopting, in a study on civil procedure, an existing general classification or a classification from studies

---

[273] *Generally* Rolf Stürner, *Gegenstand und Formen der Rezeption im neueren Prozeßrecht*, *in* LAW IN EAST AND WEST 287, 290–291 (Institute of Comparative Law, Waseda University, ed., 1988) and the articles of Per Olof Ekeløf (Sweden), Eva Smith (Denmark), Stefán Már Stefánsson (Iceland), Hans M. Michelsen (Norway), and Gustaf Möller (Finland) *in* DAS DEUTSCHE ZIVILPROZESSRECHT UND SEINE AUSSTRAHLUNG AUF ANDERE RECHTSORDNUNGEN 214–253 (Walther J. Habscheid, ed., 1991); for Sweden, see also Kohler, *supra* note 14, at 190 et seq., 536–550; for Finland Sakari Laukkanen, *Die Entwicklung des finnischen Zivilprozeßrechts und die Veränderung der Rolle des Richters*, 2 ZZPINT 227, 228, 231, 234–238, 244 (1997).

[274] It may be correct with regard to civil and commercial law to classify *Greece* as a country of French legal origin; yet with regard to civil procedural law, there have always been closer ties to German law, going back to the times of Georg Ludwig von Maurer. *See. e.g.,* Nikolaos K. Klamaris, *Das griechische Gesetzbuch über das Civil-Verfahren (1834) und die griechische Gerichts- und Notariatsordnung (1834)*, *in* GERICHTS- UND NOTARIATSORDNUNG UND GESETZBUCH ÜBER DAS CIVIL-VERFAHREN 1834, reprint of the original edition IX, X et seq. (2001); Rolf Stürner, *Das deutsche Zivilprozeßrecht und seine Ausstrahlung auf andere Rechtsordnungen – von Deutschland aus gesehen, in* DAS DEUTSCHE ZIVILPROZESSRECHT UND SEINE AUSSTRAHLUNG AUF ANDERE RECHTSORDNUNGEN 3, 27 (Walther J. Habscheid, ed., 1991); Kostas E. Beys, *Die Ausstrahlung des deutschen zivilprozessualen Denkens auf das griechische Recht der Privatrechtsstreitigkeiten, in* DAS DEUTSCHE ZIVILPROZESSRECHT UND SEINE AUSSTRAHLUNG AUF ANDERE RECHTSORDNUNGEN 300–328 (Walther J. Habscheid, ed., 1991). On Georg Ludwig von Maurer, see KARL DICKOPF, GEORG LUDWIG VON MAURER 1790–1872 – EINE BIOGRAPHIE (1960); Karl Dickkopf, *Friedrich Thiersch und Georg Ludwig von Maurer – Zwei Konzeptionen zum Neubau eines griechischen Staates in den Jahren 1833/1834*, 56 ZEITSCHRIFT FÜR BAYERISCHE LANDESGESCHICHTE (ZBLG) 165–174 (1993). For commonalities between Greek civil procedural law and German and Austrian civil procedural law, see, e.g., A. Rammos, *Der Gang des Erkenntnisverfahrens nach dem Entwurf der neuen griechischen ZPO*, 78 ZZP 241–264 (1965).

Another country for which the grouping is not obvious is *Japan*: Without any doubt, the basic structure and many legal institutions of Japanese civil procedure clearly have German origins, and ties between Japanese and German scholars have always been very

which pursue other purposes and focus on other areas of the law does not seem advisable.

Another problem of relying on earlier studies concerns the temporal dimension. First, it must be emphasized that, unlike the static approach of the Study may suggest, continuing influence of one legal origin over other legal systems is rather the exception than the rule.[275] Second, the Lex Mundi Study is based on a questionnaire and other data which mostly date from 1999 or 2000. The classification of the countries, however, uses concepts which, although not much older by years, have basically been developed before the fall of the Berlin Wall and the transition of many formerly socialist states to the "Western" model of capitalism and democracy.[276] This adds to the general question about the significance of socialism for procedural law. By the turn of the century, many of the former socialist states had in most areas of the law begun to eliminate concepts inspired by socialist ideas.[277] Quite often they returned to the basic legal structures of

---

strong. Nevertheless, one should be aware that over the last half century, other and particularly U.S. concepts and ideas have gained importance. *See, e.g.,* Kojima, *supra* note 16, at 694–695, 718–720; Hideo Nakamura, *Der Einfluss des amerikanischen Rechts auf den japanischen Zivilprozess und seine Begrenzung, in* 2 FESTSCHRIFT FÜR KOSTAS E. BEYS ZUM 70. GEBURTSTAG 1105, 1109–1119 (Hideo Nakamura, Hans W. Fasching, Hans Friedhelm Gaul & Apostolos Georgiades, eds., 2003). Whether procedural features measured by the Study are a consequence of German legal origin, of Common Law legal origin or of autochthonous developments in Japan is not always easy to decide, especially with regard to a variable like duration.

It should also be noted that regarding the structure of the proceedings, *Spain* (as well as the Código Procesal Civil Modelo para Iberoamérica of 1994) has turned from the traditional French model with its judicial instruction during a sequence of hearings to the modern German and English model with a "main hearing"; *see, e.g.,* Stürner, *supra* note 18, at 14, 17–18 (suggesting that the advance of this model "may be to a remarkable degree the result of a surmounting of traditional barriers of legal culture and of more pragmatic considerations of a worldwide procedural civilization which has developed independently from national preconditions.").

[275] Stürner, *supra* note 274, at 6.

[276] Note that after a brief summary of different approaches in comparative law, the 1998 La Porta article (which provides the basis for the classification of the countries in the 1999 article and the Study) refers to the 1989 loose-leaf edition of Thomas H. Reynolds & Arturo A. Flores, Foreign Law: Current sources of Codes and Basic Legislation in Jurisdictions of the World (*see* La Porta et al., *supra* note 255, at 1119). In 1989, the year of the fall of the Berlin Wall, identifying countries with socialist legal origin might still have made sense (subject to the qualifications made above). However, in the light of the developments in these countries in the 1990s, it cannot be assumed that the same was true 10 years later. *See also* Kojima, *supra* note 52, at 601 (noting on the 1995 World Conference on Procedural Law that "the status of the socialist legal family is highly uncertain.").

[277] For Poland, cf. Janusz Jankowski, *Die wesentlichen Grundsätze des Zivilverfahrens nach 40 Jahren der Geltung der polnischen Zivilprozessordnung*, 10 ZZPINT 227,

their pre-socialist law; in the meantime, they had started to catch up with developments that had taken place in their Western partners.[278] In addition, then prospective new member states of the European Union were in the process of adopting the "acquis communautaire", which – although to a limited degree – has direct and indirect influence on these countries' procedural law.[279] Sticking to the traditional classification with a "socialist legal origin" therefore seems doubtful; at least it would have required further justification. That this critique has its merits is confirmed by a more recent study of the same authors.[280] That study no longer uses a "socialist legal origin" in its classification of legal origins.[281] To the contrary, all former socialist countries have been integrated in one of the other legal origins, namely either the French[282] or the German[283] legal origin.[284]

230–232, 235–236, 240–241 (2005); for Hungary Miklós Kengyel, *Die Zukunft des ungarischen Zivilprozeßrechts nach der Zivilverfahrens-Novelle 1999*, 5 ZZPINT 361, 364 et seq. (2000); for Lithuania Valentinas Mikelénas, *Reform of Civil Procedural Law in the Republic Lithuanina during 1990–1996*, 2 ZZPINT 249 (1997).

[278] *See generally* Stürner, *supra* note 18, at 12; for Russia Dmitry Y. Maleshin, *Some Cultural Characteristics of the New Russian Code of Civil Procedure of 2002*, 10 ZZPINT 385 (2005); Yarkov, *supra* note 127; on the reformed civil procedure in the Czech Republic *see* Chemlíček, *supra* note 271, at 431 et seq.; on Lithuania Vyautas Nekrošius, *Grundlagen der neuen litauischen ZPO (das Erkenntnisverfahren)*, 7 ZZPINT 409 (2002).

[279] *Cf.* on the impact of Europan law on civil procedure in the member states Kazimierz Lubiński, *Eigenheiten der Prozeßrechtsvergleichung*, *in* TRANS-NATIONAL ASPECTS OF PROCEDURAL LAW 1093,1117–1118, 1131 (Int'l Ass'n of Procedural Law, ed., 1998); Kojima, *supra* note 52, at 601; Haimo Schack, *Wechselwirkungen zwischen europäischem und nationalem Zivilprozessrecht*, 107 ZZP 279–300 (1994); Herbert Roth, *Grundfreiheiten des EG-Vertrages und nationales Zivilprozeßrecht*, *in* RECHT UND RECHTSWISSENSCHAFT 351, 353 et seq. (Peter-Christian Müller-Graff & Herbert Roth, eds., 2000); Ulrich Ehricke, *Art. 12 I (ex 6 I) EG-Vertrag und das nationale Zivilprozessrecht – Bilanz und Perspektiven*, 19 PRAXIS DES INTERNATIONALEN PRIVAT- UND VERFAHRENSRECHTS [IPRAX] 311–323 (1999) with further references in note 1; Harald Koch, *Konvergenz der Rechte im Europäischen Zivilprozeß*, *in* 1 FESTSCHRIFT FÜR KOSTAS E. BEYS ZUM 70. GEBURTSTAG 733, 744 et seq. (Hideo Nakamura, Hans W. Fasching, Hans Friedhelm Gaul & Apostolos Georgiades, eds., 2003); Stürner, *supra* note 13, at 835–837.

[280] Djankov et al., *supra* note 251.

[281] Note that this study still mentions previous works, which used a classification "socialist legal origin" (*id.*, at 5), and gives no explanation or source for its "new" classification. Note also that this study deals with an issue of corporate law. According to what has been explained above (text accompanying notes 257–263), this does not necessarily mean that the same classification would hold for civil procedure. Nevertheless, it is noteworthy that the same authors have now abandoned the "socialist legal origin" classification. We think that they should already have given up this approach for the purposes of the Lex Mundi Study.

[282] Kazakhstan, Lithuania, Romania, Russia, Ukraine.

Obviously, errors in the classification of countries could have considerable effects for the overall results of the Study – even more, if one had to reallocate the 16 countries of the group "socialist legal origin" or the five countries of the group "Scandinavian legal origin".[285] We do not want to go so far as to say that some of the Study's classifications are clearly wrong. However, we want to alert the reader that these classifications are by no means absolute. This is another important observation which can be put forward against the Study's claim of objectivity.

3. CIA Factbook (Latitude)

The data for the variable "latitude", which the Study uses as a control for its other results,[286] stem from the "CIA Factbook"[287]. The variable is defined as measuring the location of the country's capital north or south of the equator, but data are modified to values between zero and one.

Indeed, the values we can find in the Dataset are calculated by multiplying the CIA World Factbook's "geographic coordinates" for each country with a factor of 1/90.[288] However, the Study's reference to the country's capital is not correct, for the Factbook data do not point to the capital, but purport to find the "approximate geographic center".[289]

---

[283] Bulgaria, China, Croatia, Czech Republic, Hungary, Latvia, Poland.

[284] Note that this new study does not cover Estonia, Georgia, Slovenia, and Vietnam, which were classified as countries with socialist legal origin in the Lex Mundi Study, but that it includes the Slovak Republic, clearly a (part of a) country with a socialist past, in the countries with German legal origin.

[285] For an interesting illustration (concerning other such "numerical comparative law" studies), see Siems, *supra* note 256, at 19–23.

[286] *See* Djankov et al., *supra* note 11, at 491, 501.

[287] *Id.*, at 473. We assume that the Study refers to the CIA *World* Factbook. Here again, the Study does not furnish the year of the Factbook; however, this is not so important in the present context as the data – latitude – should for most countries always be the same.

[288] In a few cases, there are minor differences. This is true, e.g., for the Czech Republic: On the basis of the Factbook the value should be 0.549; however, the Dataset displays 0.556.

[289] The CIA World Factbook defines the "geographic coordinates" as follows: "This entry includes rounded latitude and longitude figures for the purpose of finding the approximate geographic center of an entity and is based on the *Gazetteer of Conventional Names*, Third Edition, August 1988, US Board on Geographic Names and on other sources." *See* CIA World Factbook 2000 sub "Notes and Definitions". In some cases, this leads to striking differences: For Australia, e.g., the Factbook's geographic coordinates indicate a latitude of 27°S, whereas the latitude of Australia's capital Canberra is approximately 35°S.

The idea behind this variable apparently draws on the observation frequently put forward, according to which there is a correlation between latitude and wealth. Presumably, the Study's authors included this variable to verify what they call the "'development' theory", according to which courts and other institutions work better in richer countries with more educated populations.[290] The Study finds that "[l]atitude is generally unimportant".[291] Therefore, we do not really know what kind of conclusions the authors would have drawn from it, had it shown significant results.

4. Human Development Report (Average Years of Schooling)

Likewise for the purpose of verifying the "'development' theory", the Study measures the level of education of a country using data for 1992 from the United Nations Development Programme (UNDP) Human Development Report 1994.[292] Among the various variables in this Report which pertain to education, the Study has chosen the "average years of schooling".[293] The Study correctly states that for the average years of schooling, the last available data are from 1992. However, it fails to disclose the reason for that, which seems us to be important for evaluating the accuracy of any results based on this variable: After the 1994 Report, the indicator "mean years of schooling" has been replaced by combined school enrolment ratios because of serious concerns about the reliability of the data.[294]

The Study defines "average years of schooling" in the same way as the HD Report defines "mean years of schooling", i.e. the average number of

---

[290] Djankov et al., *supra* note 11, at 454.

[291] *Id.*, at 506.

[292] United Nations Development Programme (UNDP) Human Development Report 1994, New Dimensions of Human Security (1994), English version only without dataset *available at* <http://hdr.undp.org/reports/global/1994/en/>. The French and Spanish versions are fully *available at* <http://hdr.undp.org/reports/global/1994/fr/hdr_fr_1994.pdf> and <http://hdr.undp.org/reports/global/1994/sp/hdr_sp_1994.pdf> (last visited July 17, 2006). Hereinafter, "HD Report".

[293] UNDP, *supra* note 292, at 141–143 (pages refer to French version), Table 1. Other variables concerning education are adult literacy rate and educational attainment.

[294] Selim Jahan, *Measuring Human Development: Evolution of the Human Development Index*, Confidential Draft, 7, 15, <http://www.undp.org.in/hdrc/APRI/Event/Colombo/resources/bgppr/Measuring%20HD-Evolution%20of%20HDI%20.pdf> (last visited July 17, 2006) (noting that "the mean years of schooling were constructed in a fuzzy way and some of the data do not reflect reality" and that "[t]herefore, in 1995, it was replaced by combined gross enrolment at primary, secondary and tertiary level" [at 7] and adding that "there was serious methodological and data problems with mean years of schooling" [at 15]). Note that this paper is posted on the web as a "Background Paper" by the UNDP Human Development Resource Center (HDRC), *see* <http://www.undp.org.in/hdrc/APRI/Event/Colombo/resources/bgppr.htm> (last visited July 17, 2006).

years of schooling received per adult aged 25 or over.[295] Therefore, one would expect that the numbers for the variable "average years of schooling" in the Study's Dataset are identical with the numbers in the HD Report's indicator "mean years of schooling". However, this is not the case. To the contrary, not only do the numbers diverge significantly,[296] but also the Dataset omits countries for which there is data in the HD Report[297] and gives different numbers for countries with the same numbers in the HD Report.[298] There may be an explanation for this, but we cannot find one in the Study. It seems that the Study's Dataset does not rest on the HD Report.

5. Alesina et al. [2003] (Ethnic Fractionalization)

In their NBER Working Paper, Alesina and his co-authors claim to provide new measures of ethnic, linguistic and religious fractionalization, which are "more comprehensive than those previously used in the economics literature."[299] The Lex Mundi Study adopts the data from the "ethnic" column of the table in Appendix 1 of Alesina et al.'s paper.[300] This variable combines racial and linguistic characteristics and is based on multiple sources of data, mostly of the early to mid-1990s.[301]

A problem of the approach of Alesina et al. is that their study counts ethnic groups regardless of their actual distinctiveness in society.[302] A comparison of different ways to measure ethnic diversity in Africa shows that depending on the approach, there can be important divergences.[303] It

---

[295] Djankov et al., *supra* note 11, at 473 and UNDP, *supra* note 292, at 231 (French version).

[296] *Cf., e.g.*, Australia (HD Report: 12.0/Dataset: 9.977143), Austria (HD Report: 11.4/Dataset: 5.848571).

[297] E.g., Bangladesh, Barbados, Belize, Botswana, Estonia, and Georgia.

[298] For Germany and Switzerland, the HD Report shows 11.6, while the Dataset shows 8.238571 for Germany and 7.924286 for Switzerland.

[299] Alberto Alesina, Arnaud Devleeschauwer, William Easterly, Sergio Kurlat & Romain Wacziarg, *Fractionalization*, NBER Working Paper 9411 p. ii (2002), <http://www.nber.org/papers/w9411.pdf> (last visited July 17, 2006). Note that the correct date of the NBER Working Paper is 2002, but an amended version of the paper has since been published in 8 JOURNAL OF ECONOMIC GROWTH 155–194 (2003).

[300] *Id.*, at 27–32 = 8 Journal of Economic Growth, at 184–189.

[301] *Id.*, at 6–7 = 8 Journal of Economic Growth, at 159–160.

[302] *Cf.* Daniel M. Posner, *Measuring Ethnic Fractionalization in Africa*, 48 AMERICAN JOURNAL OF POLITICAL SCIENCE 849, 853 (2004). *But see* Alberto Alesina & Eliana La Ferrara, *Ethnic Diversity and Ethnic Performance*, 43 JOURNAL OF ECONOMIC LITERATURE 762, 793 (2005), first published as NBER Working Paper 10313, 27 (2004), <http://www.nber.org/papers/w10313.pdf> (last visited July 17, 2006) (criticizing in turn Posner's classification based on "politically relevant ethnic groups.").

[303] Posner, *supra* note 302, at 856 et seq.

follows that, as with nearly all statistics, using these data does not provide unshakable results.

6. Conclusion

What has been said before with regard to the "other judicial quality measures" also holds for some of the external sources on which the "other variables" draw: imprecise references and partly unexplained modification of data. One could have expected a more thorough presentation.

In addition, adopting from an older publication, which discussed a different field of law and pursued a different purpose, the determination of the legal origin of the countries in the sample is questionable. The fact that the Study does not address this issue at all raises the concern that its authors might not have been aware of basic questions with which every comparatist is familiar. Given the legal origins' fundamental importance for the results of the Study, the identification of which country belongs to which legal origin would definitely have deserved more attention.

Part VII

The Use of the Data and the Study's Interpretation

Having extensively reviewed the "input" to the Study in parts III to VI, this part addresses how the Study uses the collected data and, in particular, how it interprets the respective results. For the purposes of this part, we mostly assume that the data, on which the Study's calculations and their interpretation are based, are correct. This will allow us to focus on how the Study uses the data and how it interprets the results.

In a first step, the discussion is limited to the data concerning the formalism index. In a second step, it embraces the combination of the formalism index with the variables on duration, the "other judicial quality measures" and the "other variables". This distinction corresponds with the Study's parts IV, entitled "Formalism and its Determinants", and V, entitled "Determinants of the Quality of Courts". The third section of this part provides some comments on the Study's conclusion.

A. The Formalism Index and the Sub-Indices

1. The Study's Findings

In a large table (Table II, with Table I containing the definitions of the variables) the Study presents its data on procedural formalism for the eviction and the check collection case (Table IIa[304] and IIb,[305] respectively). The table does not list the results for all the individual variables,[306] but only the seven sub-indices (professionals versus laymen, written versus oral, legal justification, statutory regulation of evidence, control of superior review, engagement formalities, and independent procedural actions) and the formalism index for each country, with the countries being classified by legal origin.

In addition, the table contains several forms of combination of the data. First, it shows the means for each sub-index and the formalism index for the countries with the same legal origin, as well as the mean for all coun-

[304] Djankov et al., *supra* note 11, at 478–483 (reprinted *infra* Appendix 2).
[305] *Id.*, at 474–489 (reprinted *infra* Appendix 3).
[306] These results are available in the Dataset, *see supra* note 11.

tries, rounded to two decimal places. Second, the test of means in the end of the table compares the significance of the differences in these means. The Study finds that "for both check collection and eviction, common law countries have least formalized, and French civil law countries most formalized, dispute resolution, with other legal origins in the middle."[307]

The next table (Table III)[308] finds consistency of these results across the sub-indices and the two cases, with a remarkable exception for the sub-indices on evidence and superior review, which show no correlation with the others.

Finally, in a Table IV,[309] the Study includes the variable "[natural] logarithm of GNP per capita". It observes that "richer countries exhibit lower levels of procedural formalism than poorer ones" and sees the results of the other tables confirmed, as dispute resolution in French and socialist civil law countries – and to a lesser degree in German and Scandinavian civil law countries as well – shows a higher level of formalism also holding per capita income constant.[310]

2. *The Study's Interpretation*

The Study's basic interpretation of the results of these tests and calculations is that procedural formalism is directly linked to what the authors of the Study believe is a country's legal origin. In the relevant part IV of the Study, dedicated to "Formalism *and its Determinants*" (emphasis added), the Study communicates this to the reader in a quite interesting way.

The first paragraph of part IV, which refers to Table II, completely omits any discussion of whether the Study's classification of legal origins finds support in the data. To the contrary, it takes the classification as given and jumps immediately to a ranking of procedural formalism across the different legal origins. Having found that for both check collection and eviction,[311] French and socialist civil law countries regulate most heavily, German and Scandinavian somewhat less and common law countries are the clear "winner", it refers to the "thrust of the comparative law literature" with which these findings "are broadly consistent".[312]

In the second paragraph of part IV, addressing the results of Table III, the Study is more cautious. Although it finds "a clear picture of consis-

---

[307] Djankov et al., *supra* note 11, at 477.

[308] *Id.*, at 490 (reprinted *infra* Appendix 4).

[309] *Id.*, at 492–493 (reprinted *infra* Appendix 5).

[310] *Id.*, at 491.

[311] Note that in this paragraph, the Study does not speak of "*the* check collection *case*" and "*the* eviction *case*", but only generally of "check collection" and "eviction" and in particular of "dispute resolution", what obviously embraces any type of case.

[312] Djankov et al., *supra* note 11, at 477.

tency"[313] and strong positive correlations, it has to acknowledge that "[i]n contrast to the general pattern, the evidence and superior review subindexes are uncorrelated with the others."[314] The conclusion does not make any reference to the legal origin, but simply states that "[f]or most aspects of formalism, however, it appears that some countries regulate dispute resolution more heavily than others."[315]

It is not before the end of the third paragraph, dedicated to Table IV, that the reader finally finds the basic interpretation of the data regarding the classification of the countries. The beginning of this paragraph follows the pattern of the first paragraph, in that it compares the results for the different legal origins. The paragraph ends by stating that "nearly half of the residual variation in formalism (holding per capita income constant) is explained by the legal tradition."[316] It continues by mentioning that "[t]hese results are robust to inclusion of other controls such as latitude, average years of schooling, and ethno-linguistic and religious fractionalization."[317] The table does not exhibit the results for these other controls. Moreover, the attentive reader is surprised to read something about *religious* and *linguistic* fractionalization. Recall that the relevant variable is described as *ethnic* fractionalization; that the source of this variable, Alesina et al., splits its fractionalization data into the categories "Ethnic", "Language" and "Religion"; and that the data in the Dataset is a one-to-one adoption of the "Ethnic" data from Alesina et al.[318]

Part IV concludes with a two-sentence paragraph able to wipe away any doubts. In a first enthusiastic exclamation, the results are called a "striking support of the comparative law hypothesis that there are systematic differences in legal procedure across legal families."[319] Whether one can speak of a "striking support" depends of course on several factors: one has to agree that the Study got the identification of legal families right, that the two model cases are sufficiently representative for a country's legal sys-

---

[313] *Id.*, at 477.

[314] *Id.*, at 491.

[315] *Id.* Note that in this paragraph, the Study speaks first of the "two cases", but later of the "two types of cases" or generally of "check collection and eviction".

[316] *Id.*

[317] *Id.* Note that this paragraph speaks of "eviction" and "check collection" (not "*the* eviction *case*" or "*the* check collection *case*") only in the second sentence, but later only uses the general term "dispute resolution".

[318] In addition, somewhat hidden in a footnote we find what seems to be an important qualification in the eyes of the Study's authors: that the percentage of a country's population that is Catholic is a statistically significant determinant of formalism. The footnote states, without any numerical support, that "this variable becomes insignificant in a horse race with legal origin, which remains important." *Id.*, at 491 note 7.

[319] *Id.*, at 491.

tem, and that the results are sufficiently significant. Note that this sentence only speaks of "systematic differences in legal procedure". Therefore, it is possible to agree even if, with regard to procedural formalism, one does not believe that all of the variables as such make sense and that the classification and aggregation is fully correct. However, this is different for the second sentence. Here, the Study jumps to formalism and simply states that "civil law countries have more formal dispute resolution than do common law countries."[320] We do not want to say that this statement is clearly wrong. Yet one should not oversee that the Study's support for this statement is not necessarily as "striking" as its authors pretend, given the doubts and deficiencies we have discussed in the previous parts.

3. Additional Observations

Some other points deserve further comment. First, while the Study cares a lot about the correlations between the sub-indices,[321] it seems not to pay attention to correlations among the variables within one and the same sub-index. The Study does not apply the same statistical methods, which it uses to justify the combination of the formalism index from the sub-indices and the identification of legal families, on the combination of the sub-indices from the variables and the identification of which variable belongs to which sub-index. One reason for this could be that the variables of the questionnaire are "binary" or too basic. Even so, the different treatment is noteworthy.

Second, it should be pointed out that when comparing the different legal origins, the Study always uses the mean, not the median – maybe because the mean is needed for the tests of means, which are exhibited in the end of the tables. Admittedly, for the formalism index and its sub-indices the problem of outliers is not so acute: First, the results always remain within the range of the index,[322] and second, due to the fact that most questions are "binary" and some questions clearly head in one direction,[323] the actual range for differences is even smaller. Nevertheless, there are countries

---

[320] *Id.*

[321] *Id.*, at 477, 491.

[322] The range of the formalism index (from zero to seven) and for the sub-indices (from zero to one) does not offer too much room for a differentiation. Of course, one might argue that steps could be infinitesimally small. As a practical matter, however, this is not the case here due to the "binary" questions.

[323] One of the most striking examples for this is the variable "filing": according to the Dataset, in most countries, the complaint is normally submitted in written form (exceptions: Taiwan, Thailand and Turks and Caicos for the check collection case and Taiwan for the eviction case).

which show extreme results. Excluding them from the sample would have at least a quantitative impact on the comparison.

Third, it is not really remarkable that across the two model cases, the same sub-indices and the formalism index are moderately or even strongly correlated with each other. Typically civil procedure does not look to the substance of the case at issue.[324] Moreover, it was the intention of the Study to choose model cases which are not tried in special proceedings.[325] Therefore, one can draw only limited support for the Study's general approach from these strong positive correlations.

Fourth, it is very remarkable that the "evidence" and "superior review" sub-indices are uncorrelated with the other sub-indices. The reader may recall that we had expressed serious doubt with regard to the Study's approach to superior review and suggested that the sub-index on evidence be assigned a higher weight. It is of course impossible to predict how different definitions and classifications of the variables on superior review would have influenced the results. However, it appears to be clear that assigning a higher weight to the variables on evidence, as has been suggested here, could have completely changed the ranking of the countries on the formalism scale and, thus, the overall results of the Study. Presumably, the correlations between the formalism index, legal origins and the "judicial quality measures" would have been less strong and would maybe even have disappeared completely. This would have had a huge impact on possible interpretations of the researchers' findings.

Fifth, even if one can conclude from these tests that "nearly half of the residual variation in formalism [...] is explained by the legal tradition"[326], the actual accuracy of this statement presupposes that the theoretical model as such is correct. Given the many questions concerning the formalism index as well as the classification of legal origins, some reservation as to whether this statement reflects reality must be retained.

---

[324] *See only* the statement of Pollock & Maitland, quoted *supra* note 151. But remember that this may be different if there are procedural safeguards for a certain type of cases like, e.g., eviction cases (*cf. generally* James et al., *supra* note 57, at 2). Nevertheless, the consequences of such protective rules most probably do not affect all sub-indices, but particularly the sub-indices "independent procedural actions" and the variables on duration.

[325] The Study may not have fully succeeded, but again, presumably only some sub-indices would be influenced.

[326] Djankov et al., *supra* note 11, at 491.

B. Formalism and the Quality of Courts

1. The Study's Findings

The Study starts the section on the "determinants of the quality of courts" with a table on duration (Table V).[327] Again, the countries are classified by legal origin; the table shows the means for each legal origin and is followed by a test of means. Providing both the average and the median for the two cases, the Study deplores the "extraordinary length of time it takes [...] to pursue either claim in court". It goes on by illustrating the "tremendous variation in the estimated duration", mentions that countries of German legal origin are "comparatively more efficient at check collection than at eviction", but concludes in a brief sentence that "the bottom line of table V is the higher expected duration in civil law countries".[328]

Tables VI[329] and VII[330] exhibit ordinary least square regressions and instrumental variables regressions, respectively. The variables are the potential determinants of judicial quality – "Log GNP per capita", the formalism index, ethnic fractionalization, the average years of schooling, and latitude – on the one hand (independent variables), and judicial quality measures – "Log of duration", enforceability of contracts, "legal system is fair and impartial", "legal system is honest or uncorrupt", "legal system is affordable", "legal system is consistent", "confidence in legal system", corruption, and "law and order" – on the other hand (dependent variables). The Study finds no significant impact of the level of per capita income, ethnic fractionalization, the average years of schooling and latitude on expected duration, but observes that "expected duration is highly correlated with procedural formalism".[331] The effect of the average years of schooling on the "judicial quality determinants" is negative and in part statistically significant.[332] Latitude is found as generally unimportant[333]. Although insignificant, the Study expressly mentions that ethnic fractionalization "exerts

[327] *Id.*, at 494–500 (reprinted *infra* Appendix 6).

[328] *Id.*, at 501.

[329] *Id.*, at 502–503 (reprinted *infra* Appendix 7).

[330] *Id.*, at 504–505 (reprinted *infra* Appendix 8).

[331] *Id.*, at 501.

[332] In the words of the Study, its "measure of human capital, the average years of schooling, often enters with the 'wrong' (negative) sign and is statistically significant" (Djankov et al., *supra* note 11, at 506). This can be read as if the results were either "often" or always statistically significant. Only the first interpretation finds support in the tables: in Table VI, 6 results are significant at 1 percent level, 3 results at 5 percent level, and 2 results at 10 percent level; 7 results are not statistically significant; for Table VII, the respective numbers are 3, 6, 2 and 7.

[333] Djankov et al., *supra* note 11, at 506. But note that "latitude" exerts an effect on "law and order" which is statistically significant at 1 percent level.

a negative [...] influence" on judicial quality.[334] For the formalism index, the Study finds a negative impact on most judicial quality measures.

Without exhibiting a table and without incorporating the data in the Dataset, the Study claims to have analyzed the effect of the regulation of entry by new firms on duration and the other determinants of the quality of adjudication. As source of the data on the regulation of entry, the Study cites the homonymous study of the same authors.[335] The Study's findings are that such regulation indeed predicts longer duration and lower judicial quality, but with considerably less explanatory power than procedural formalism.[336]

Table VIII[337] can be described as based on an amended version of Table VI. It also exhibits the ordinary least square regressions and uses the same judicial quality measures as Table VI, but adds to the potential judicial quality determinants the variables concerning incentives: "index of mandatory time limits", "quota litis prohibited", and "loser pays rule". The data for the other determinants, which are included in the regressions, are not displayed. The Study finds no significant influence of the incentives variables on duration and the other judicial quality measures. On the other hand, it observes that the formalism index keeps its statistical significance even after inclusion of the three incentives variables in the regressions.

2. *The Study's Interpretation*

In the face of the collected data on duration, the authors of the Study take the position that on average, it takes too long to pursue the two model cases in court. In their eyes, "[w]ith all the other costs, this number suggests why individuals in most countries choose not to use the formal legal system to resolve their disputes."[338] No doubt excessive duration can be an important incentive for individuals not to pursue their rights in courts. However, "this number" – or rather these numbers – concern hypotheticals for which another way, at least another *legal* way, of resolving the dispute is hard to imagine. How else than by the enforcement of a court order could you make the party, who is obligated to pay a claim arising from a

---

[334] *Id.* Note that the statistical data only permits predictions, but does not prove causation, as the Study purports by using the expression "exerts a negative influence".

[335] Simeon Djankov, Rafael La Porta, Florencio Lopez-de-Silanes & Andrei Shleifer, *The Regulation of Entry*, 117 QUARTERLY JOURNAL OF ECONOMICS 1–37 (2002) (country data on p. 18–21).

[336] Djankov et al., *supra* note 11, at 506.

[337] *Id.*, at 508–509 (reprinted *infra* Appendix 9).

[338] *Id.*, at 501. *See also id.*, at 511 (noting that "the evidence points to extremely long expected duration of dispute resolution, suggesting that courts are not an attractive venue for resolving disputes.").

check, pay or make the residential tenant leave her current home? Absent special circumstances, check collection and eviction cases appear not to be very suitable for arbitration, mediation or any other form of ADR.[339] Moreover, the Study does not collect itself data on the importance of extra-judicial forms of dispute resolution. Neither does it refer to any existing data. To the contrary, the authors explain elsewhere that these forms of dispute resolution are out of the focus of their study on procedural formalism.[340] Nevertheless, in the interpretation they suddenly point to ADR, without providing any source, be it numerical data or traditional legal literature. In view of the lack of reflection on whether the model cases could be resolved by ADR and the lack of any support for their statement, the reference to the attractiveness of courts as a venue of dispute resolution seems somewhat misplaced.

The Study's interpretation of the results with regard to the development hypothesis is ambiguous. When considering the lack of effect of the development measures – per capita income and average years of schooling as well as ethnic fractionalization and latitude – on duration, the Study takes a clear position: It sees this result as "*inconsistent* with the development hypothesis."[341] However, unlike what one might have expected, it does not reject the development hypothesis because of this one result. Rather, having noted the significant influence of the formalism index on duration, it attenuates its position by suggesting that "legal structure, rather than the level of development, shapes this crucial dimension of judicial efficiency."[342] Finally, the Study interprets the effect of per capita income on judicial quality, which is highly significant, the counter-intuitive effect of schooling on judicial quality and the unclear influence of ethnic fractionalization and latitude as "mixed" evidence.[343].

Having found that "expected duration is highly correlated with procedural formalism", the Study asks the "crucial question", that is, whether "procedural formalism, at the cost of longer proceedings, secure[s] better justice". The Study's authors believe that Table VI suggests the answer to be "no", for "nearly all survey measures suggest that higher formalism is

[339] On eviction cases, cf. Tina Drake Zimmerman, *Representation in ADR and Access To Justice for Legal Services Clients*, 10 GEO. J. ON POVERTY L. & POL'Y 181, 189–190, 192, 194 (2003) and the very special cases reported in Dorothy Wright Nelson, *ADR in the Federal Courts – One Judge's Perspective: Issues and Challenges Facing Judges, Lawyers, Court Administrators, and the Public*, 17 OHIO ST. J. ON DISP. RESOL. 1, 14 (2001).

[340] Djankov et al., *supra* note 11, at 461.

[341] *Id.*, at 501 (emphasis added).

[342] *Id.*, at 501, 506.

[343] *Id.*, at 506.

associated with inferior justice."[344] Therefore, Table VI is described as containing the "basic bottom line" of the Study, according to which "at least for simple disputes, higher formalism is associated not only with the expected higher duration of dispute resolution, but also with lower quality justice as perceived by the participants."[345] While up to this point the Study's language was quite cautious, only speaking of "suggestions" and results that are "associated" with each other, the tone becomes sharper when interpreting Table VII: This table is said to "*confirm* that formalism *has adverse effects on* both the expected duration and other aspects of the quality of the legal system."[346]

From a purely statistical standpoint, the results of the regressions may propose a causal link between formalism on the one hand and duration and judicial quality on the other. However, we have identified several problems concerning the formalism index, and recognized quite a few concerns as to the duration variable and the "judicial quality measures". At this point, only one thing with regard to duration should be added: Good and speedy justice does not only depend on the characteristics of the procedural law, but also on other, "external" circumstances, like the question whether there is a sufficient number of qualified judges.[347] It could be that duration is as, or even more highly, correlated with the number of judges than with formalism. This would suggest other conclusions. To corroborate its interpretation, the Study could have included as a control a variable covering the number of judges.[348] Without such a control, the Study's interpretation is not as convincing as it seems.

---

[344] *Id.*

[345] *Id.*, at 507.

[346] *Id.* (emphasis added).

[347] *See only* Sutter-Somm, *supra* note 134, at 13 and Varano, *supra* note 16, at 673 (describing the delay caused by the severely understaffed office of the examining judges at the Tribunale di Prato). *Cf. also* Marco Fabri & Philip M. Langbroek, *Delay in judicial proceedings: a preliminary inquiry into the relation between the demands of the reasonable time requirements of article 6, 1 ECHR and their consequences for judges and judicial administration in the civil, criminal and administrative justice chains* 8, Preliminary Draft Report, Working Party N° 2 of the European Commission for the Efficiency of Justice (CEPEJ-GT2), *available at* <http://www.coe.int/t/e/legal_affairs/legal_co%2D operation/operation_of_justice/efficiency_of_justice/documents/20%202003%20E%20re port%20Fabri%20Langbroek%20rev%20nov2003.pdf> (last visited July 17, 2006) (mentioning research evidence according to which *criminal* court delay cannot be explained by a shortage of capacity, but stressing that "below a certain threshold, court resources are certainly an issue that effect court performance, and then court delay...").

[348] Such a variable would have to measure the ratio of judges to a country's population or another ratio like the number of files per judge to account for the different size of the countries. *See*, as an example, tables 9–14 *in* European Commission for the Efficiency of Justice, *supra* note 218, at 30–37.

The Study's purely technical interpretation leaves no room for such doubts. To the contrary, it – intentionally or not – exploits the reader's preconceptions: Obviously, the reader is ready to believe that formalism *causes* longer duration. Insofar, she will see no reason to question the Study's interpretation. By combining in the very sentence the statement on duration with a statement about "other aspects of quality of the legal system", the reader might instinctively be led to uncritically accept that this second causal link also exists. This is not to deny that there may indeed be a causal link between formalism and judicial quality, however defined. Yet the reader should be aware that both the formalism data and the judicial quality data used by the Study for proving such causal link are not beyond all doubt.

The Study employs a similar pattern when addressing the related question of whether some countries have deliberately chosen a higher level of formalism in an attempt to prevent arbitrariness, thereby following the idea vividly put in Rudolf von Jhering's famous exclamation[349] cited elsewhere in the Study.[350] According to the Study, the fact that many countries' legal system is at least in part the result of exogenous circumstances[351] "suggests that it is unlikely to be the case that countries with a worse law and order environment *choose* heavier formalism."[352] It is certainly true that legal origin and tradition are significant factors for the current state of a country's law. On the other hand, the current state of a country's law is not the product of one single decision in the past. To the contrary, the legislature is free to change the law if it deems her appropriate. Thus, even if it may be difficult to imagine that nowadays a country's legislature would say: "Let us increase procedural formalism to enhance our law and order environment!" the fact that it does not reduce existing formalism can also be understood as a form of choice. And a country's legislature may very well not dare to reduce existing and inherited formal requirements for fear that the "law and order requirement" or the quality of adjudication could suf-

---

[349] RUDOLF VON JHERING, GEIST DES RÖMISCHEN RECHTS AUF DEN VERSCHIEDENEN STUFEN SEINER ENTWICKLUNG Vol. 2/2 471 (5th ed., 1898) ("Die Form ist die geschworene Feindin der Willkür, die Schwester der Freiheit.").

[350] Djankov et al., *supra* note 11, at 458.

[351] It should be mentioned that these exogenous circumstances are by no means only "conquest and colonization", as the Study presents it (*id.*, at 458: "These legal families ... were transplanted to many countries by conquest and colonization (by France, Germany, and Spain in the case of civil law, and England in the case of common law)."). To the contrary, historic coincidences with which a legal system was identified or considerations of quality also were significant. As to the German legal system, conquest and colonization hardly played any role. *See* Stürner, *supra* note 273, at 292–295.

[352] Djankov et al., *supra* note 11, at 507 (emphasis in original).

fer.[353] The Study does not make such considerations. It contents itself with the statement that a choice of heavier formalism seems unlikely – a statement that at first sight has its appeal – and, making the reader thus well-disposed to what follows, goes on by proposing just the contrary: In the Study's interpretation, the results from Table VII "suggest the opposite direction of causality: countries that have inherited legal systems with heavily formalized dispute resolution *end up with* lower quality legal systems, at least for simple disputes."[354] Although causation is presented here as a suggestion and not a conclusion, the formulation is such that the reader might miss the weaknesses of the suggestion. Not only could other empirical methods better support an alleged causal relationship, like for example a comparison of judicial quality data before and after an amendment of a country's procedural law either increasing or lowering the degree of formalism, but also can we only speculate what the judicial quality data would look like if the civil procedure in one and the same country at one and the same moment in history had shown more or less formalism. Basing the suggested causality only on the observed influence of the formalism index on the variables on judicial quality from the sample of countries at one moment in time therefore embraces a good amount of speculation. Here again, the Study could easily have employed a more conservative language.

Interestingly and contrary to what one might expect after the criticism expressed in the preceding paragraphs of this book, the Study *does* acknowledge that higher formalism is not necessarily the only reason for lower quality of dispute resolution. However, the scope of this concession is limited as to the legal origin and, more importantly, as to other potential causes for the observed quality of dispute resolution: The only legal origin for which the possibility of another cause is discussed is French legal origin, and the only "channel other than formalism" which is discussed is "general state interventionism".[355] It is in this context that the Lex Mundi Study presents the results of its running the regressions of Tables VI and VII with data from the same authors' study on the regulation of entry. It would go too far to engage in a discussion of that other study here. Suffice it to remark that the number of countries in that study (85) differs from the number of countries in the Lex Mundi Study (109) and that one can have doubts about how good an indicator of general state interventionism the regulation of entry is. Having found less explanatory power of the regula-

[353] Of course, there can be various reasons for a country's not alleviating existing formal requirements. Nevertheless, one could assume that over time unnecessary formal requirements would be eliminated.

[354] Djankov et al., *supra* note 11, at 507 (emphasis added).

[355] *Id.*, at 507.

tion of entry, the Study concludes that procedural formalism "explains much more than a generic measure of interventionism."[356] Whether the differences in explanatory power – 4 to 5 percent of the regulation of entry, compared with 18 to 20 percent of formalism – are really so meaningful, taking into account that the regulation of entry is certainly not a perfect measure of state interventionism, is an open question.

The Study's interpretation of Table VIII, which includes the Study's three variables on incentives, is relatively short and cautious. Having found no clear numerical relationship between these incentives and duration or judicial quality, and noting the formalism index's retaining effect and statistical significance, the Study concludes that "[t]he results on the incentive theory are negative, but must be interpreted with caution, since we might not have the most appropriate measures of incentives facing the participants in a dispute."[357] Indeed, as indicated above, much must be said about the incentives variables, in particular the two concerning lawyer compensation and cost allocation:[358] It is not clear why just contingency fee and the loser-pays rule are incentives; it is questionable what type of incentives they create; and the Study fails to include other relevant circumstances like legal aid or litigation expense insurance. What is to be added at this place is that, as with any other hypothesis of causation, the Study does not and obviously cannot compare the situation in one and the same country at one and the same moment in time with and without a particular legal characteristic – be it a formal requirement or a rule creating an incentive in a certain direction. In addition, the Study does not collect data before and after the introduction or abolition of a particular legal characteristic, a method that would offer more reliable information on which a hypothesis of causation might be based.

Finally, the Study confronts its interpretation with the three theories of what determines court performance, theories it had presented at the outset:[359] the 'incentive' theory, the 'development' theory, and the 'formalism' theory. In addition to the negative result for the incentive theory and the Study's express caveat discussed just before, it concludes that "[t]he results on the development theory are mixed"[360] as there is an influence of the wealth of a population on judicial quality, but not of a country's level of education – a conclusion that is beclouded by our doubts pertaining to the Study's data on education.[361] Not surprisingly, the Study finds that the

---

[356] *Id.*, at 509.

[357] *Id.*

[358] *See supra* II.C.1 and III.C.2.

[359] Djankov et al., *supra* note 11, at 454–455.

[360] *Id.*, at 509.

[361] *See supra* sub VI.B.4.

data support its theory of procedural formalism, according to which "countries with heavier procedural formalism have both more slow and lower quality systems of dispute resolution, at least when one focuses on simple disputes."[362] Presented this way, the formalism theory is the clear and only "winner", and with this impression the reader reaches the Study's part VI, the "Conclusion".

3. Additional Observations

In its discussion of Table V, which is dedicated to duration, the Study makes just two substantial statements, the first concerning the comparison of duration by legal origin, the second the comparison of the two cases for German legal origin. Both statements deserve some comments.

According to the Study, "[t]he comparison by legal origin for eviction puts common law and Scandinavian legal origin countries on top (shortest duration) and socialist and French legal origin countries at the bottom."[363] Undeniably, it follows from the data in Table V that, with only few exceptions, duration is shortest for countries with Scandinavian and English legal origin.[364] However, to say that French and socialist legal origin are at the bottom without disclosing that in the eviction case, duration in countries with German legal origin typically was found to be among the longest, draws a much distorted picture of the collected data.[365] Maybe the Study meant check collection instead of eviction.[366]

While the Study omits to mention German legal origin in its description of the relationship between legal origins and duration in the eviction case,

---

[362] Djankov et al., *supra* note 11, at 510.

[363] *Id.*, at 501.

[364] Scandinavian legal origin takes the first place for total duration (mean and median) and duration until completion of service of process (mean) and shares the first place for duration of enforcement (median) with English legal origin. It is second for duration until completion of service of process (median) and duration of trial (mean). It is only fourth for duration of trial (median).

English legal origin is first for duration of trial (mean and median) and duration until completion of service of process (median) and shares the first place with Scandinavian legal origin for duration of enforcement (median). It is second for total duration (mean and median) and for duration of enforcement (mean). It is only third for duration until completion of service of process (mean).

[365] German legal origin is longest for total duration (mean and median) and duration of trial (mean and median) and fourth for duration until completion of service of process (median) and duration of enforcement (mean and median). It is second for duration until completion of service of process (mean).

[366] According to the collected data for the check collection case, means and medians for French and Socialist legal origin are the longest, except for two "third places" by median: French legal origin for duration until completion of service of process and Socialist legal origin for duration of trial.

it devotes the next sentence to German legal origin. More precisely, it comments the finding that duration for countries of German legal origin is considerably shorter in the check collection case by absolute numbers as well as by rank within the legal origins[367] by saying that "German legal origin countries are comparatively more *efficient* at check collection than at eviction."[368] This is found to be consistent with an earlier study on creditor rights.[369] Both this interpretation – if it is one – and the reference are quite vague: First of all, it is not clear what is meant by "efficient" in this particular context. Does efficiency equal short duration? Or does it – as it should – include some aspect of judicial, economic or social quality?[370] Second, as discussed earlier, the eviction of a residential tenant in many countries involves special procedural features, intended to ensure that the law justly and equitably balance the interest of the tenant threatened to lose her home and the interest of the owner or lessor in receiving the rent agreed upon. It goes without saying that such special procedural features tend to increase duration. If a society, represented by its legislature and courts, deliberately provides for such procedural safeguards, this does not necessarily say anything about that legal system's *efficiency*.[371] Third, the reference to the earlier study, which is entitled "Legal Determinants of External Finance", is anything but obvious. That study in itself says nothing about differences concerning creditor rights in check collection and eviction cases.[372] It tries to establish a relationship between investor protection and the size of capital markets. As for data on creditor rights

---

[367] For check collection, German legal origin ranks second (median) or third (mean) as to total duration, third as to duration of enforcement (mean and median), first as to duration until completion of service of process (mean) and duration of trial (median), second as to duration of trial (mean) and fourth as to duration until completion of service of process (median).

[368] Djankov et al., *supra* note 11, at 501 (emphasis added).

[369] *Id.*, referring to Rafael La Porta, Florencio Lopez-de-Silanes, Andrei Shleifer & Robert Vishny, *Legal Determinants of External Finance*, 52 THE JOURNAL OF FINANCE 1131–1150 (1997).

[370] *Cf.* Rolf Stürner, *Gründe und Ursachen des Problems der Ineffizienz von Verfahren – ein historischer Überblick, German National Report for the VIIIth World Conference on Procedural Law in Utrecht 1987*, *in* EFFIZIENTE RECHTSVERFOLGUNG/ EFFICIENCY IN THE PURSUIT OF JUSTICE 1, 28 (Peter Gilles, ed., 1987). *See also* James et al., *supra* note 57, at § 6.7, 381–383 (noting on the one hand that "if the American system of civil justice were designed for maximum efficiency in deciding cases, presumably it would be patterned after the English system," but that as a system of compulsory bargaining, it "can be considered very efficient.").

[371] If efficiency is what maximizes social welfare, the positive effects of procedural safeguards may very well outweigh the negative effects of a potentially longer duration.

[372] Maybe the authors wanted to point to their statement in the earlier study according to which "German civil law countries are somewhat of a mystery". *See* La Porta et al., *supra* note 369, at 1139.

generally, it refers to another study of the same authors,[373] which collects data about countries' commercial and bankruptcy laws' rules on restrictions for going into reorganization, automatic stay, creditors' rank, and management's staying in reorganization – aspects that have little to do with the two model cases, and even less with the different results for German legal origin countries as to duration in these two cases.

Apart from these two substantial statements, the Study limits itself to deploring the "extraordinary length" and to illustrating the "tremendous variation in the estimated duration". A closer look at the table reveals some interesting aspects. First, within all five legal origins identified by the Study, there are some outliers, mostly toward higher duration.[374] Therefore, it would have been preferable if the table had also exhibited the medians in addition to the means for the different legal origins.[375] Mean and median deviate in particular for the variable "duration of trial",[376] the stage of the proceedings to which many if not most of the formalism variables pertain. A comparison of the legal origins based on the medians instead of the means has a remarkable influence on the results: the discrepancies between the legal origins become less striking,[377] and often even the order of the legal origins changes.[378] Second and even more interesting, if one con-

[373] La Porta et al., *supra* note 255.

[374] *Compare* the following numbers for the total duration of eviction cases: English legal origin: mean 199/median 180, Sri Lanka 730, Thailand 630; Socialist legal origin: mean 347/median 248, Bulgaria 660, Poland 1080, Slovenia 1003; French legal origin: mean 266/median 206, Lebanon 973, Malta 730, Morocco 745, Tunisia 33; German legal origin: mean 357/median 331, Austria 547; Scandinavian legal origin: mean 187/median 160, Norway 365.

[375] The Study provides the median only in the text when discussing the period of time the cases take and only for the total duration; *see* Djankov et al., *supra* note 11, at 501. This is the only occasion when the Study uses the median at all.

[376] Eviction (mean/median): all countries (151/97), English legal origin (112/82), Socialist legal origin (187/98), French legal origin (167/94), German legal origin (230/186), Scandinavian legal origin (139/135).

Check collection (mean/median): all countries (122/90), English legal origin (88/67), Socialist legal origin (167/98), French legal origin (147/110), German legal origin (92/60), Scandinavian legal origin (101/105).

[377] *E.g.*, the medians for total duration of a check collection case for French (221) and Socialist (224) legal origin differ only by 3, whereas the means – 272 and 327, respectively – differ by 55.

[378] Eviction (mean/median): French (27/20) and German (19/23) legal origin as to duration until completion of service of process; Socialist (113/90) and German (107/102) legal origin as to duration of enforcement.

Check collection (mean/median): German (25.75/24.5), English (26.18/14) and Scandinavian (26.8/15) legal origin as to duration until completion of service; English (88/67) and German (92/61) and Socialist (169/98), French (147/110) and Scandinavian (101/105) legal origin as to duration of trial; Socialist (116/90) and French (90/90) as to

fronts the formalism index values for the five legal origins from Table II with the total duration values for the five legal origins from Table V, one would not necessarily assume that there is any strong relationship between formalism and duration. For the aggregate data for the five legal origins – mean of formalism index and mean of total duration – do not exactly go hand in hand, and the same is true if one takes the median instead of the mean.[379] This first impression finds support in the tests of means exhibited at the end of Table V:[380] Only four of the 80 results are significant at 1 percent level, ten are significant at 5 percent level, eight are significant at 10 percent level, and the remaining 58 results are not significant at all. The Study does not hide these results, but it does not discuss them either. To the contrary, it goes straight to the regressions involving the individual countries' formalism index and duration data in Table VI, which show indeed results that are significant at 1 percent level in both the eviction and the check collection case.

The Study's discussion of duration ends with the following literal quotation from "an Indonesian legal scholar":[381] "[I]n connection with the nature of judicial process itself and considering formal, punctual, and rather complicated manners and usages upheld by courts according to the Law of Procedure (especially for laymen), it could be said that correct judgment cannot be performed in a short time."[382] This statement has been made at a conference on court congestion in a country paper on Indonesia. In the paragraph before, its author points out that "trial and adjudication of cases

---

duration of enforcement; English (176/126), German (193/182) and Scandinavian (170/190) as to total duration.

[379] In the eviction case, the order of the legal origins as to formalism on one hand and duration on the other remains the same regardless of whether the mean or the median is used. But the two orders do not exactly match: For duration (mean/median), the list reads as follows: Scandinavian (187/160), English (199/180), French (266/206), Socialist (347/248) and German (357/330) legal origin; for the formalism index (mean/median), it is English (3.01/3.10), Scandinavian (3.32/3.47), German (3.57/3.67), Socialist (3.83/3.73) and French (4.38/4.33).

In the check collection case, the orders do not match either, but they match better if one takes the medians instead of the means. Duration (mean/median; list according to median): English (176/126), German (193/182), Scandinavian (170/190), French (272/221), Socialist (327/224) legal origin; formalism index (mean/median, list according to median): English (2.76/2.63), Scandinavian (3.15/2.98), German (3.15/3.25), Socialist (3.93/3.99), French (4.29/4.10) legal origin.

[380] Djankov et al., *supra* note 11, at 499–500.

[381] *Id.*, at 501.

[382] Purwoto Gandasubrata, *Indonesia*, *in* ADMINISTRATION OF JUSTICE: PROCEDURAL REFORMS ON COURT CONGESTION, 1980 ASEAN COMPARATIVE LAW SERIES, VOL. 2, 1, 7 (Purificacion Valera-Quisumbing, volume ed., 1982).

before the court should not be exercised in a hurry and carelessly, because into the hands of the court, the rights, duties and fate of people are entrusted" and explains the necessity for judges to "thoroughly consider all aspects of law and justice in each particular case because once a judgment has been pronounced and comes into force [...] it is binding and must be executed."[383] In the original text, the quoted phrase is linked to that explanation with the conjunction "thus". This context is not visible for the reader of the Study. To the contrary, it is not at all clear what the authors of the Study want to express by including this statement. Do they see this quotation as support for their preceding sentence, presenting "the higher expected duration in civil law countries" as the "bottom line of Table V"? This is suggested by the Study's introduction of the quotation: "In the words of an Indonesian legal scholar ..." Or is it meant to be a general observation about pursuing claims in courts? This would respect its original meaning, except for the fact that originally it has been made as a positive justification for longer duration, while in the context of the Study, longer duration is presented as something inherently negative. Finally, what is "a short time"? Not only seems the quoted statement, separated from its context as it is in the Study, rather trivial, but also it raises so many questions that the Study had done better to omit it.

Contrary to what one might think with regard to a seemingly neutral variable like duration,[384] not only the collection but also the interpretation of the data on duration invites a fair amount of comments. This confirms our impression that the variable on duration is all but plain sailing.

C. The Study's Conclusion

After a summary of its method and findings, the Study offers two conflicting, and more general, interpretations of this evidence,[385] the sketches of which it had already proposed earlier.[386] The first interpretation views

---

[383] *Id.* (also noting that "[c]ourt decisions are expected to be as satisfactory as possible for the parties concerned and in harmony with the sense of justice of the people.").

[384] *But see, e.g.,* Robert G. Bone, *Mapping the Boundaries of the Dispute: Conceptions of Ideal Lawsuit Structure from the Field Code to the Federal Rules*, 89 COLUM. L. REV. 1, 4 (1989) (answering the question why there is a periodic recurrence of complaints about cost and delay as follows: "Cost and delay are relative concepts. Cost becomes 'excessive' and delay 'unreasonable' only relative to some norm. The recurrence of complaints about excessive cost and delay seems odd only if one assumes that normative beliefs about procedure have not changed, that each generation of critics has meant the same thing by the rhetoric it has used. But that assumption is wrong.")

[385] Djankov et al., *supra* note 11, at 510–511.

[386] *Id.*, at 459.

"greater" procedural formalism as a necessary and therefore efficient form of regulation, guaranteeing a fair judicial process that would otherwise not exist. The second proposed interpretation sees procedural formalism in developing countries as a product of their colonial history, rejects a presumption of efficiency, and suggests that some formal requirements may be superfluous. According to the Study, its data – in particular the data on duration, the fact that the data reflect no benefits of formalism, and the observed connection between legal origin and judicial quality which suggests to rebut the idea of formalism as "part of an efficient design" – "support[] the second theory".

At closer look, this analysis is not very convincing. First of all, what is proposed as the first "broad view" obviously is not only a possible explanation for "*greater* formalism" and "*heavily* formalized adjudication", as the Study presents it,[387] but a potential justification of *any* formal requirement in (procedural) law.[388] In the latter way the Study presents this idea elsewhere,[389] and it would be absurd to reject this idea completely, because then hardly any legitimate reason for procedural formalism (and formalism in general) would remain at all.[390] In order to be able to present the basic idea of this first interpretation as one of two mutually exclusive alternatives and to reject it later, the Study had to confine it to a justification for "*greater* formalism" and "*heavily* formalized adjudication", of course without defining more precisely when formalism is "greater" or "heavy". This way of skewing the general concept of formal requirements in the law does not leave a good impression.

Second, the alternative "broad view" is not really an alternative. It is presented as only concerning "developing countries" which according to the Study inherited procedural formalism as a result of "the transplantation of their legal system from their colonizers." However, one should not oversee that in our post-colonial times a country's legislature at least in principle is free to abolish inherited formal rules if it deems her fit. Numerical data may suggest that such amendments occur only slowly and rarely, but they do not tell us why this is so – it could be the result of deliberate choice as well as the consequence of successful lobbying by

---

[387] Emphasis added.

[388] In a certain sense, procedural law is inherently "formal" law, what legal terminology in other languages reveals by sometimes using the expression "formal law" as a synonym for "procedural law".

[389] Djankov et al., *supra* note 11, at 458. *See also* Djankov et al., *supra* note 1, at 602 (noting that „[a] common way of protecting judges from influence is to formalize law and procedures through codes so as to minimize judicial discretion and the potential for subversion.").

[390] It is assumed that equal treatment before courts is one aspect of a "fair judicial process" that is to be secured by procedural formalism.

groups like lawyers who might benefit from formalism, the consequence of political instability or just the legislature's inattention. Furthermore, legal transplants did and do not only happen through the involuntary channels of "conquest and colonization". A country considering the adoption of (parts of) a foreign legal system may prefer an abstract, systematic and complete codification instead of a system based on precedents which were decided under factual circumstances completely different from those prevalent in that country.[391] Taking this into account, it is very plausible that even if the adoption of the codified system involved a relatively higher level of formalism – what is, as exhibited above, not necessarily so – the decision to adopt this system may very well be an efficient choice. Thus, the two allegedly alternative "broad views" do by no means exclude each other.[392]

Maybe intended as a distinctive feature of the second interpretation, but quite ambiguous is the statement that "[a]lthough *heavy* procedural formalism has theoretically plausible reasons for its existence, the reality it brings is extreme costs and delays, unwillingness by potential participants to use courts, and ultimately injustice."[393] Once more, it is first and foremost the understanding of the word "heavy" that causes difficulty.[394] Finally, that "some of the burdens of formalism may […] be unnecessary, and could be relieved through reform,"[395] is as a matter of fact certainly true under both possible interpretations, because legal change typically does not fully coincide with changes in the determinants of a society.

---

[391] *Cf.* Peter L. Murray, *The American Legal System in the Global Legal Order: The Influence of American Law and Legal Institutions in the Modern World*, 9 ZZPINT 245, 247 (2004) (describing the difficulties in exporting a case-law system).

[392] *Cf.* the somewhat more cautious wording at the end of the Study's Introduction (Djankov et al., *supra* note 11, at 457, noting that the paper "supports the hypothesis that transplantation is *in part* responsible for the structure and quality of the existing institutions"; emphasis added) and in Djankov et al., *supra* note 1, at 609 ("Although some institutional diversity can be explained by focusing on efficient choices, transplantation is a dramatic deviation from this approach.").

[393] Djankov et al., *supra* note 11, at 511 (emphasis added).

[394] If "heavy" is interpreted case-by-case or country-by-country, that is, if "heavy formalism" is formalism not necessary to secure fair justice in a particular country, this sentence would also hold under the first interpretation, unless that interpretation is read in the idealistic way that actual formalism always fully reflects what is necessary in one country. If "heavy" is understood as an absolute measure, this would clearly be opposed to the first interpretation's idea of formalism as being determined by one country's particular circumstances. However, at which point would "heavy" formalism begin?

Note also that the Study deplores "extreme costs", but did not collect data on the actual costs in the two model cases; it only relies on the perception data from the WBES "legal system is affordable".

[395] Djankov et al., *supra* note 11, at 511.

Third, the way the Study frames the evidence for the second interpretation in the conclusion reflects some of the Study's problematic interpretations mentioned above. Even "extremely long expected duration", suggesting to create a lack of attractiveness of dispute resolution by courts, does not per se support either of the two interpretations: It can reflect general problems of the judicial system in a country and suggest that the degree of formalism is still the best solution, or it can be the product of disadvantageous legal rules (substantive and procedural) and insufficient financing of the judicial system, or any combination of both. That the Study finds "no offsetting benefits of formalism" is equally inconclusive: The Study only provides a comparison between countries at one moment in time and therefore cannot take into account how different levels of formalism would affect judicial quality in one and the same country, all other things equal. Whether the observed significance of legal origin for judicial quality really suggests "that formalism is unlikely to be part of an efficient design" is a question which one is only constraint to answer under the Study's dichotomy of two conflicting "broad views". In the light of the ambiguity of the two interpretations' definitions, one might wonder if such question deserves a prominent place in the conclusion.

The Study's last paragraph starts with statements which are not really related to procedural formalism. Hardly anyone would disagree that "the systems of dispute resolution in many countries *may* be inefficient,"[396] but the relevant evidence in the Study for this statement can rather be found in the "judicial quality measures" than in the formalism index. And nobody will be surprised to read that "one cannot presume [...] that property and contract are secured by courts."[397] By these two statements to which everybody can agree, the Study prepares its reader to accept the "two implications" of the conclusion. The first implication is that the deficiencies of courts may explain the importance of "alternative strategies of securing property and contract" in developing countries – as indicated above, taking into account the rest of the Study, this implication is rather a by-product. The second implication is not really an implication of what preceded in this very paragraph: Although expressly introduced as the "second" implication, it is not only an implication of the statements about suggested court inefficiency and doubts as to whether courts secure property and contract. To the contrary, at the same time it embraces the whole Study by referring to "our results". Not surprisingly for any reader knowing the authors' writings and the Study's sponsor, this second "implication" proposes that the Study's "results suggest a practical strategy of judicial reform, at least with respect to simple disputes, namely the reduction of procedural formal-

[396] *Id.* (emphasis added).

[397] *Id.*

ism."[398] Note that although the Study has been relatively cautious as to the question of causation when interpreting the results of the individual tables, this recommendation clearly rests on the assumption that procedural formalism is the *cause* of inefficiencies and lower quality of adjudication.

In sum, the Study's conclusion is not fully backed by the Study's findings, but contains its own arguments. The reasoning, which seems not to be completely consequential, is based on the conviction that higher formalism causes lower court performance. Thus, the final recommendation cannot other than suggest that formalism be reduced.

[398] *Id.*

Part VIII

Brief Thoughts about the Implication of the Study's Conclusion

One who failed to read the star-footnote, where the World Bank is listed as having funded the Study in cooperation with the now defunct[399] International Institute of Corporate Governance at Yale School of Management, or who missed the hints suggesting that the authors' main concern is not so much about civil procedure as such, but about "the security of property and the enforcement of contracts [which] are essential for investment, trade, and ultimately economic growth to come about"[400], should at least be alerted by the Study's last sentence – the suggestion to reduce procedural formalism – that this study pursues a purpose which is not purely academic.

Indeed, it is an open secret that such studies sponsored by the World Bank serve as a basis for recommendations to developing countries or, even more directly, as a basis for specific requirements and conditions on how a country has to reform its legal system. Such recommendations and conditions are most notably set up in connection with a developing country's application for financial and technical assistance of one of the international development institutions or lenders like the World Bank or the IMF, its affiliates or services.[401] Moreover, governments eager to improve

---

[399] *See, e.g.,* Steve Higgins, *Eminent Group Gathers at Yale*, New Haven Register.com, September 10, 2005, <http://www.yale.edu/opa/download/newsYale/eminent Group_nhReg_091005.pdf> (last visited July 17, 2006).

[400] Djankov et al., *supra* note 11, at 453 (reference immediately following the quotation omitted); *see also* the reference to property and contract in the last paragraph of the Study, *id.*, at 511.

[401] For the World Bank, see World Bank, *OP 8.60 – Development Policy Lending*, THE WORLD BANK OPERATIONAL MANUAL, August 2004, <http://web.worldbank.org/WBSITE/EXTERNAL/PROJECTS/EXTPOLICIES/EXTOPMANUAL/0,,contentMDK:20240031~pagePK:64141683~piPK:64141620~theSitePK:502184,00.html> (last visited July 17, 2006) and JAMES M. CYPHER & JAMES L. DIETZ, THE PROCESS OF ECONOMIC DEVELOPMENT 517 (2nd ed., 2004); for the IMF, see IMF, *Guidelines on Conditionality*, September 25, 2002, <http://www.imf.org/External/np/pdr/cond/2002/eng/guid/092302.pdf> and *Policy Statement on IMF Technical Assistance*, April 1, 2001, <http://www.imf.org/external/pubs/ft/psta/index.htm> (last visited July 17, 2006); *see generally* Namita Wahi, *Human Rights Accountability of the IMF and the World Bank: A*

the economic situation of their country may rely on such studies when deciding on a reform program. Last but not least, policymakers might well seek the advice of the authors of such studies.[402] Therefore, the practical importance of these studies can hardly be overestimated.[403]

The recommendation that procedural formalism be reduced is, of course, much too unspecific to be directly included as a condition in a lending agreement or to be applied as a precise guide for legal reform. Constructed reasonably, the recommendation does not mean that any formalism whatsoever is bad – in other words, that the neighbor model constitutes the ideal form of dispute resolution. Rather, what is to be reduced is only that "amount" of formalism that is excessive. The "beneficial fraction" of formalism is to be preserved.[404]

But it is not only for the purpose of determining of the correct level of formalism that the recommendation needs to be refined. The level of procedural formalism as defined by the Study is the result of an aggregation of various variables. Reducing the level of formalism can only be done by changing the value of these variables, and there are many different possible combinations which result in one and the same level of formalism. Presumably, what matters is not merely the level of formalism, but also the correct combination.

The drafter of a clause in an international lending agreement or the policymaker who are aware of this would like to have more specific guidance than just the recommendation "reduce!" In this situation, what is easier than to look to the preceding pages of the Study in order to find a country whose legal system can serve as a model? Our drafter or policymaker who cannot invest too much time and effort in a thorough comparative research will probably exclude those countries which, according to the Study, belong to one of the legal families with the "worst" outcomes, and from the

---

Critique of Existing Mechanisms and Articulation of a Theory of Horizontal Accountability, 12 U.C. DAVIS J. INT'L L. & POL'Y 331, 339–350 (2006); Murray, *supra* note 391, at 251–252.

[402] *Cf.* David McClintick, *How Harvard Lost Russia*, InstitutionalInvestor.com, January 13, 2006, <http://www.institutionalinvestor.com/default.asp?page=1&ISS=21210&SID=606917&PUB=24> (last visited April 7, 2006) (describing Andrei Shleifer's position at the Harvard advisory program in Russia in the mid-1990s).

[403] *Cf.* Jordan, *supra* note 269, at 1023–1024 (suggesting that cumulative voting provisions, which "are fossils trapped in the bedrock of U.S. corporate statutes", might nevertheless have gained "international prominence" because of the studies of La Porta et al.).

[404] *See generally* Baur, *supra* note 77, at 100/118/1687 et seq. (describing the dichotomy between powerful judge and formal procedure). This problem can also be interpreted as a variety of what has been described elsewhere as "[a] fundamental problem of institutional design [, namely] the conflict between the twin goals of controlling disorder and dictatorship." *See* Djankov et al. *supra* note 1, at 597.

remaining group choose a country she considers "successful". In other words, the Lex Mundi Study – and the same appears to be true for the numerous other studies of this group of authors – might have the power to promote a tendency, in legal development, away from civil law, in particular French legal origin, and towards English legal origin, in particular English and U.S. common law.[405] Thereby, policymakers risk losing sight of alternative models for reform in the field of procedural law, models developed by distinguished scholars from different legal cultures under the auspices of important organizations that appear to us much more balanced and promising.[406]

---

[405] Obviously, a byproduct of a possible harmonization in this direction is that it may facilitate expansion for firms based in these countries by reducing barriers of divergent regulation and create a bigger market for common law-trained lawyers – *honi soit qui mal y pense*? *See also* Rolf Stürner, *Schlussbetrachtung und Ausblick*, *in* 41 JAHRBUCH BITBURGER GESPRÄCHE 143, 150 (2003) (mentioning differences between the Anglo-American and the Continental European attitude towards law marketing); Stürner, *supra* note 54, at 1086 (noting that "international litigation is a new and perhaps growing market [for American lawyers,] especially if the procedural role and position of the lawyers will be the same as in national proceedings"); Goldstein, *supra* note 54, at 7 (noting "the remarkable American emotional attachment to the systemic aspects of its procedural system; an attachment which goes beyond any rational analysis. And, again, such an emotional attachment is a cultural fact which must be considered in any comparative analysis aimed at improving a given system by implanting systemic aspects of a radically different one") and Langbein, *supra* note 13, at 551, 554 (describing the "Cult of the Common Law", a "powerful ideology of celebration", and noting that "[American jurists] operate on the assumption that the foreigners have nothing to teach.").

[406] *See*, in particular, the ALI/UNIDROIT Principles of Transnational Civil Procedure. On their potential as a model for reforms, see Stürner, *supra* note 20, at 210–211.

Part IX

Some General Comments on the Study

A. The Study's Approach – "Numerical Comparative Law"

After a relatively long period of silence, legal scholars have started commenting on the surging "new wave"[407] of quantitative studies by economists comparing the efficiency of legal systems in the world with the help of statistical tools. A new and more precise labeling, "numerical comparative law"[408] in place of "new comparative economics,"[409] may help to attract the attention of more legal scholars to this field.

Thus far, probably the most basic analysis and evaluation of this new method has been provided by Mathias M. Siems.[410] Unlike previous comments, his article does not focus on specific points of critique concerning particular studies, but asks whether the methodology as such, "numerical comparative law", "can be (or has to be) criticized or supported."[411] He assembles several "arguments against numerical comparative law" and confronts them with counter-arguments: Is it feasible to reduce complex legal phenomena to numbers? Is law extraordinary and therefore not a proper object of statistics? Is "numerical comparative law" too much focused on legal rules? And finally, is statistical analysis an acceptable method in the field of comparative law? He concludes that "[his] results are mixed" and proposes "guidelines"[412] which cover the following topics: "necessity", "methodical awareness", "transparency", "comparability", "functional equivalents", and "reflections".

In our view, this article indeed addresses the most important problems faced by the use of statistical methods in comparative law. Despite the various lines of criticism, it seems not justified from a conceptual point of view to categorically reject any statistical analysis in this field. However, it is extremely intricate to design a viable study. The fact that the use of em-

---

[407] Vagts, *supra* note 221, at 595.

[408] Mathias M. Siems, *Numerical Comparative Law: Do We Need Statistical Evidence in Law in Order to Reduce Complexity?*, 13 CARDOZO J. INT'L & COMP. L. 521 (2005).

[409] Djankov et al., *supra* note 1.

[410] *Supra* note 408.

[411] *Id.*, at 522, 528.

[412] *Id.*, at 538.

pirical research combined with statistical analysis is more or less widely accepted not only in natural sciences, but also in psychology, sociology, political science and, last not least, economics, of course suggests that it should also work in law. And indeed the collection and interpretation of statistical information on legal issues is by no means a sensational novelty. On the contrary, the use of statistical material before and after a law reform has become increasingly popular with national and supra-national lawmakers. What distinguishes these studies from the new comparative economists' "numerical comparative law" is not so much that they usually do not cover more than one country, because for some regions, like the European Union, there are also truly comparative studies. What is special about the new wave of "numerical comparative law" studies is, first, that they use more sophisticated statistical methods to interpret the collected data; second, that they claim to provide answers which hold true for the whole world, not only a country or a region with a relatively similar economic and cultural environment; and third, that they are authored not by unknown experts or private institutes hired by the state, a governmental agency or international organization, but by famous academics from some of the most highly esteemed academic institutions in the world who appear to be neutral and therefore have a high credibility.

But there *is* a difference between natural sciences, psychology, sociology, political science and economics on one hand and law on the other: Law can neither be understood merely by observing what happens in the real world, nor merely by looking into the books. It is the combination of social reality and a uniquely sophisticated theoretical framework that makes (comparative) law so challenging, and grasping this difficulty with the tools of statistics is even more difficult. It is crucial that researchers as well as their audience be aware of this extra level of complexity. This implies that researchers should ask themselves whether what they want to measure can reasonably be expressed in numbers. It further requires them to take into account functional equivalents as well as the respective social, cultural and economic environment. And it strongly suggests that they disclose to the reader the exact methods applied and that they openly discuss the strengths and weaknesses of their research.[413]

Neither the Lex Mundi Study nor any other of the "numerical comparative law" studies that have been published to date actually satisfies these requirements. Whether the publication of a perfect or at least convincing study is just a matter of time, or whether we will wait for such a study eternally, is still an open question. "Numerical comparative law" may develop into a serious scholarly approach, but may also burst like a bubble

[413] *Cf.* no. 2–5 of the Siems guidelines. *Id.*, at 539–40.

when the euphoria of these years (and the generosity of the institutions financing these studies) is over.

B. The Study's Understanding of Legal History and the "Transplantation Hypothesis"

It is always interesting to read what scholars of other disciplines than law think about legal history. The authors of the Study follow a version similar to what three of them with another co-author have also published elsewhere.[414] According to them, civil law countries' procedural codes are a product of the French "revolutionaries and Napoleon [who] did not trust the judges, and codified judicial procedures in order to control judicial discretion", whereas the English and the U.S. judiciary could preserve "a great deal more judicial independence" because "lawyers and judges were on the 'right' side of the revolutions." They argue that for this reason, and because of the supplemental nature of codes in the common law tradition, "less formalism is required in the judicial procedure."[415]

The history of codification in continental Europe and in those states for which continental European codes served as a model is, of course, much more complicated, and although the French Revolution and Napoleon played an important role, the Study's restriction on this part of the story must raise some criticism.[416] Suffice it to say that codification did not start

---

[414] *See, e.g.,* La Porta et al., *supra* note 255, at 4 et seq. (NBER Working Paper) = 1115 et seq. (106 J. Pol. Econ.). *See also* Djankov et al., *supra* note 1, at 609 (suggesting that the French system was "exported" by Napoleon to Spain and Portugal and transplanted from there to Latin America by their colonial conquests); similarly Thorsten Beck, Asli Demirgüç-Kunt & Ross Levine, *Law, Endowments, and Finance*, 70 J. ECON. FIN. 137, 138 (2003). This sounds a bit surprising, given that Spain's and Portugal's conquests occurred long before Napoleon was born. The prevailing view is that the influence of the Code Napoléon on 19th century codifications in the newly independent Latin American countries was due to its reputation as a "modern" – and probably also its flavor of a "liberal" or even "revolutionary" – code. *See, e.g.*, PEDRO FERNÁNDEZ DE CÓRDOVA, ESTUDIOS DE DERECHO COMPARADO 100 (1997); JULIO AYASTA GONZALEZ, EL DERECHO COMPARADO Y LOS JURÍDICOS CONTEMPORANEOS 186 (1991); Zweigert & Kötz, *supra* note 111, at 113–115. In the field of civil procedure, some countries have been influenced by French procedural law via French-speaking cantons of Switzerland; *see* Stürner, *supra* note 274, at 24. Today, it is rather Italian than French law and legal literature that still play an important role in Latin American countries; *cf.* Stürner, *supra* note 273, at 290. For an overview on the studies' understanding of legal history, see Siems, *supra* note 256, at 4–6.

[415] Djankov et al., *supra* note 11, at 458.

[416] Note that the revolutionaries' concerns were only in part identical with those of the rather restaurationist emperor Napoleon. *See also* Damaška, *supra* note 14, at 208 (noting

with Napoleon.[417] But more important for our purposes is the question of whether the codification of procedural law in continental Europe actually is linked to the alleged higher level of formalism in civil law countries.[418] On one hand, codified rules facilitate the postulating and controlling of formal requirements. On the other hand, though, these codifications not only clarified the formal requirements, but also unified them throughout most types of claims, so that pre-existing procedural rules, which may have differed for different causes of action and before different courts, were harmonized or aligned.[419] As a consequence, the total number of rules presumably was reduced.[420] As regards common law, we already mentioned the extremely formalistic procedural rules which existed even in (or because of) the absence of any codification. Therefore, the evidence from the codification story is at least mixed. Moreover, it somewhat contradicts

---

that "old forms of civil procedure survived the upheavals of the French Revolution with fewer changes than the administration of criminal justice") and *generally* RENÉ DAVID, FRENCH LAW 12 (Michael Kindred, trans., 1972) (explaining, for the French Code civil, that the draftsmen were lawyers and judges of the pre-Revolutionary era who "could not be expected to forget their education, experience, and preconceptions.").

[417] Talking of France, a prior, although somewhat incomplete codification was the 1667 ordinance by Louis XIV (Ordonnance de Saint-Germain-en-Laye), called "Code Louis" (Ordonnance civile touchant la réformation de la justice), prepared by Jean-Baptiste Colbert; *see* Guinchard & Ferrand, *supra* note 97, at 69, ¶ 37. On earlier codifications in Germany, see Rosenberg, *supra* note 156, at 9–11.

[418] Note that New York – apparently the place chosen by the Study to represent U.S. law – had a Code of Civil Procedure as early as the mid 19th century; *see* Stephen N. Subrin, *David Dudley Field and the Field Code: A Historical Analysis of an Earlier Procedural Vision*, 6 LAW & HIST. REV. 311 (1988); David S. Clark, *The Civil Law Influence on David Dudley Field's Code of Civil Procedure*, *in* THE RECEPTION OF CONTINENTAL IDEAS IN THE COMMON LAW WORLD 1820–1920 63 (Mathias Reimann, ed., 1993). Although what this code codified was not common law procedure (Bone, *supra* note 384, at 5–78), and although the perhaps most influential event for the creation of a – compared to what existed – modern and less formalistic civil procedural law in the U.S. and its States was the promulgation in 1938 of the Federal Rules of Civil Procedure (*cf.* Carrington, *supra* note 152, at 323–325), one might argue that these "codifications" stood in the tradition of the English legal origin. Yet this argument is ambiguous: If so, codification as such has no influence on the level of formalism.

[419] *See, e.g.*, the quotation in Bone, *supra* note 384, at 3, of the New York Commissioners on Practice and Pleadings, 1849, REPORT TO THE NEW YORK LEGISLATURE OF 1850, at v (Albany 1850): "The purpose of the constitutional provision and of the statute under which [the New York Field Code of Procedure] is prepared, was to make legal proceedings more intelligible, more certain, more speedy, and less expensive."

[420] One can also hypothesize that due to the continental understanding of codes in the hierarchy of norms and the reluctance to accept judgments as a source of law, codification limited the power of judges to introduce new formal requirements. *See also* Leubsdorf, *supra* note 222, at 63–65 (doubting that codification results in any significant changes).

the Study's argument that "procedural differences between common and civil law actually go back to the twelfth and thirteenth centuries"[421] – that is, long before the French Revolution and Napoleon, and even long before most other great and influential codifications we know today, apart of course from Justinian's *corpus iuris civilis*.[422]

The latter argument, which explains higher formalism in French law with the less peaceful situation in France as compared to England, continues by proposing that the differences in the law and order requirements entailed different approaches to legal procedure that were transplanted to most other countries "through conquest and colonization." Apart from the fact that the Study's focus on involuntary forms of transplant is disturbing, the idea of legal transplants is widely accepted and can draw on important writings in the field. Yet in spite of legal scholar's centuries-old familiarity with the concept of legal transplants, there is still no distinct definition or uniform use of this term. Furthermore, what is required as evidence of a legal transplant is quite unclear, even more so if one concentrates on the field of civil procedure.[423] A look in the general literature on comparative law is a good starting point, but not the finish. It has already been explained that blind reliance on what "macro-comparison" tells us can lead astray in an analysis pertaining to civil procedure.[424] Admittedly, the Study cannot be expected to make a substantial theoretical contribution on these issues. Nevertheless, the ease with which it keeps quiet about all these fundamental questions is remarkable.

---

[421] Djankov et al., *supra* note 11, at 458.

[422] It is another question whether this second historical argument put forward by the Study is a complete explanation. Common law scholars often emphasize with much pride that their legal system is the result of a completely independent and autochthonous development. This thesis has been challenged, though; for an overview on these relatively new insights, see Stürner, *supra* note 18, at 15–17.

[423] For an instructive discussion of both problems (with further references), see, e.g., Kohler, *supra* note 14, at 9–22.

[424] *See supra* VI.B.2. Note in addition that by focusing, on one hand, on the 12th and 13th century, and on codification on the other, the Study's historical sketch leaves uncovered crucial periods for the development of French and German procedural law, for example the "positive" influence of French civil procedure's principle of orality on the pre-20th century German procedural law, where a complex and cumbersome procedure based on writing prevailed (*see* Murray & Stürner, *supra* note 16, at 26–29). Today, of course, mandatory oral hearings may be seen as formalistic, and legal systems which expressly follow a principle of orality typically provide for exceptions (*e.g.*, Germany: §§ 128(2)–(4), 495a ZPO). Yet at the time orality was clearly beneficial.

In addition, both "original/genuine"[425] and transplanted legal systems are in a constant and never-ending process of development.[426] During the last decades, one important direction of this development has been the reduction of regulation and formalism in nearly all fields of the law. The Study is not only static in that it merely collects data for one moment in time, but also in that it does not consider differences in the pace at which this development has occurred in the various countries. Couldn't it be that differences in the development towards less formalism have an impact on the results on procedural formalism? Let us assume that, for the legal origins at issue,[427] what has been transplanted was more or less the legal system as it existed in the "transplanting" country at the time of the transplant and that this transplant was initially not completely unsuccessful.[428] Then, if the pace at which the development towards less formalism occurred did not matter, we should expect similar levels of formalism for the transplanting country and the "recipient" countries – always presupposing that the Study's numbers are correct. But in particular for French and English legal origin – for which "conquest and colonization" may be most relevant – this is not true: The U.K. exhibits a formalism index value of 2.22, well below mean (3.02) and median (3.10) of the English legal origin countries; France exhibits a formalism index value of 3.60 which also lies well below mean (4.38) and median (4.33) of the French legal origin countries. An analog phenomenon has also been observed for a similar study.[429] Consequently, the Study's own data indicate that differences in the pace of legal development in a country are one factor influencing differences in the level of formalism. And indeed in many countries, reforms with important consequences for the structure of civil proceedings have been undertaken just in the 20th century, that is, a long time after most of the discussed legal

[425] But note that it is debatable to what degree those legal systems that are commonly regarded as "original" or "genuine" have themselves borrowed elsewhere; *see*, e.g., *supra* note 424 (mentioning the influence of French on German civil procedure).

[426] *See, e.g.*, Ugo Mattei, *Three Patterns of Law: Taxonomy and Change in the World's Legal Systems*, 45 AM. J. COMP. L. 5, 14 (1997) (summarizing comparative law writings with the words "legal systems never are. They always become.").

[427] This specification intends to exclude from the assumption the "reception" of Roman law in continental Europe.

[428] For the purpose of proposing a weakness of the "transplantation hypothesis", this assumption must be regarded as admissible, because it is at the core of this hypothesis; but note the opposed view of the "endowment theory", Beck et al., *supra* note 414, at 139–141.

[429] Vagts, *supra* note 221, at 599, discussing La Porta et al., *supra* note 255 (noting that "[t]he most French of the French-origin legal systems is, after all, France and its level of concentration (.34) is far below the average of the group (.54).").

transplants have taken place.[430] We can only speculate whether the pace of legal development in French legal origin countries might have been slower for reasons other than the legal origin as such. Think about, e.g., the local concentration of French legal origin countries in Latin America with its eventful history,[431] which might have prevented continuous reform, or the presumably stronger and persistent links between the U.K. and its sphere of influence in the rest of the world,[432] which might have facilitated the communication of reform ideas from more developed to less developed countries. Needless to say that these and other similar "soft" factors are difficult to determine, require thorough and country-specific research and will in part always be subjective. Furthermore, it would be very challenging to develop a numerical representation of such factors. This should not discourage those who believe in "numerical comparative law" in their search for results that correctly map correlations and causal relationships in the real world. However, if it is true that the pace and direction of legal development play a role, an approach and interpretation like the Study's which exclusively focuses on a "transplantation hypothesis" should not be used uncritically.[433]

Finally, the new "legal origins" literature pertaining to corporate governance and financial markets, which promotes the same "transplantation

---

[430] *Generally* Stürner, *supra* note 18, at 12–18; Stürner, *supra* note 204, at 776–778; on the relatively recent development of the "main hearing model" Stürner, *supra* note 20, at 224–225.

[431] *Cf.* Beck et al., *supra* note 414, at 139–140 (proposing that the type of colonization strategy had an influence on shaping the institutional development, distinguishing between "settler colonies" and "extractive colonies" and classifying "much of Latin America" as extractive colonies).

[432] Note that the vast majority of the surveyed countries with English legal origin are among the 53 current members of the British Commonwealth of Nations.

[433] *See also* Raghuram G. Rajan & Luigi Zingales, *The Great Reversals: The Politics of Financial Development in the 20th Century*, NBER Working Paper No. 8178 (2002), <http://papers.nber.org/papers/w8178.pdf> (last visited July 17, 2006). They find that "in contrast to the findings of La Porta et al., (1997) for the 1990s, [...] countries with Common Law systems were not more financially developed in 1913" and that "the main countries of Continental Europe were more developed financially in 1913 than the United States" (id., at 3), while by 1980, France's stick market capitalization by GDP, almost twice than the U.S. in 1913, amounted to less than one fourth, with convergence in 1999 (*id.*, at 3). Their interpretation is that there is no "inherent superiority" of one or the other legal origin, but that legal origins matter "because Civil Law systems may have more exaggerated reactions to changes in private interests", as only the legislator has to be influenced (*id.*, at 37–39). *See also* Stürner, *supra* note 20, at 223–224 (describing the "main hearing model" of Germany, England and Spain and noting that "[m]ost Anglo-Americans attribute th[e model of the Romance legal family] with its sequence of hearings to all civil law systems without accurate differentiation.").

hypothesis", has received important criticism. It has been argued, and correctly so, that not only legal families, but also political structures, history, and culture matter and that the focus on legal origins does not sufficiently cover these aspects.[434] As far as it is general or can be generalized, this criticism is also valid for the Lex Mundi Study.[435] In sum, there appears to be much evidence that the "transplantation hypothesis" is at least incomplete.[436] By pointing out that an inclusion in the regressions of relatively unspecific "controls" like latitude and ethnic fractionalization shows no significant results, the Study suggests a somewhat illusive completeness.

C. The Recommendation

Outsiders' recommendations, it is often said, are the most valuable ones. One expects outsiders not to be influenced by traditions or blinded by routine, but to be open and ready to question even those aspects which insiders wrongly think are immovable. The Study's authors are outsiders in two respects: First, they are economists and not legal scholars, let alone proceduralists. Second, the recommendation appears to be based on no particular legal system, but on objective numbers, so that it can readily be applied to

---

[434] *See, e.g.*, Amir N. Licht, Chanan Goldschmidt & Shalom H. Schwartz, *Culture, Law, and Corporate Governance*, 25 INT'L REV. L. & ECON. 229, 231 et seq. (2005) (finding that the legal origins classification in La Porta et al., *supra* note 255, "provides only a partial depiction of the universe of corporate governance regimes" and concluding that "analyses of corporate governance regimes should combine the legal with the cultural approach." *Id.*, at 232); Carrington, *supra* note 58, at 79, 88-94 (suggesting that the right to jury trial is indispensable within the constitutional scheme of the U.S.); Beck et al., *supra* note 414; Chase, *supra* note 268. But note that the relationship between a nation's culture and its procedural law remains controversial: Langbein, *The German Advantage...*, *supra* note 14, at 855 (admitting that "[c]ultural differences surely do explain something of why institutional and procedural differences arise in different legal systems", but continuing that "[t]he important question for present purposes is what weight to attach to this factor, and my answer is, 'Not much.'"); Jackson, *supra* note 83.

[435] Legal scholars have emphasized that national characteristics of procedural law depend even more on the sociological environment and the historical and political situation than do questions of substantive law. *See, e.g.*, Stürner & Stadler, *supra* note 30, at 279 et seq. For general remarks on culture and law from a legal scholar's perspective, *see, e.g.*, Chase, *supra* note 83; Chase, *supra* note 268; BERNHARD GROSSFELD, THE STRENGTH AND WEAKNESS OF COMPARATIVE LAW 41–49 (Tony Weir, trans., 1990). On the relationship between (legal) culture and civil procedure, see Goldstein, *supra* note 62, at 388–392; Oscar G. Chase, *Some Observations on the Cultural Dimension in Civil Procedure Reform*, 45 AM. J. COMP. L. 861 (1997); Taruffo, *supra* note 83, at 623–624, 632–635 (1996); Gottwald, *supra* note 14, at 231.

[436] *Cf.* Rajan & Zingales, *supra* note 433, at 4 ("All this is not to suggest that structural theories are incorrect, but that they are incomplete.").

each and any country. But outsiders' recommendations also risk being inappropriate just because outsiders lack knowledge of how things are really like and therefore start from false or at least skewed assumptions.

Apart form our discussions of the Study's input – which mention some points where, from the perspective of legal scholars somewhat familiar with comparative civil procedure, the Study seems to miss the crucial point – the recommendation raises a more general concern: To what extent can such statistical analysis provide a basis for practical strategies of reform? The Study's recommendation is based on an observed negative effect of procedural formalism on judicial quality. This rests on the assumption that results from a comparison of a big enough number of countries not only can be generalized, but also can be translated into practical advice for any specific country regardless of this country's particular situation. Of course, the call for a reduction of procedural formalism is not very specific and may often be justified at least to a certain degree. Moreover, the authors' reading of their "transplantation hypothesis", which makes the transplant of unsuitable rules responsible for inefficiencies, shows that they do not believe a rule has the same effects in all countries.[437] Nevertheless, deriving practical strategies from a statistical analysis of a sample of countries can hardly get rid of the flavor of suggesting that what works in many countries or in the most successful countries must also work in one particular country.[438] Among legal scholars, this belief has since long been identified as flawed, and its revival would be a step back – at least in today's world where regional differences in history and culture sill play a role.

---

[437] *See also* Djankov et al., *supra* note 1, at 598 ("An institution that respects the delicate tradeoff between dictatorship and disorder in the origin country may not remain efficient once transplanted to a colony."), 604 ("Ultimately, efficient institutional design depends on specific characteristics of countries and sectors, which can only be ascertained empirically."), 609 ("The general point is that economic and social change in each country should be considered in light of its own institutional possibilities, rather than some idealized view of a rich capitalist democracy."), 610 ("A legal and regulatory system that is perfectly suitable to France may yield inefficiently high levels of regulation and state ownership when transplanted to countries with lower civic capital. Likewise, a system of independent courts that works in Australia or the US may fail in Malaysia or Zimbabwe."), 614 ("Now economic analysis can move further by recognizing that different institutions are appropriate in different circumstances.").

[438] The belief that one can objectively determine "what works" is perfectly illustrated by the title of the papers of Barth et al., *supra* note 6, and Rafael La Porta, Florencio Lopez-de-Silanes & Andrei Shleifer, *What Works in Securities Laws?*, 61 THE JOURNAL OF FINANCE 1–31 (2006) (earlier draft *available at* <http://papers.nber.org/papers/w9882.pdf>; last visited July 17, 2006).

Part X

About this Book

In the preceding discussion of the Lex Mundi Study, this book has identified various points of criticism and many open questions. A common reply of statisticians to such critique, especially insofar as it concerns the correctness of the input, is that if such deficiencies really were meaningful, the statistical analysis would not yield any reasonable result, and in particular not a result that is consistent with what has been expected beforehand. This defense also works for the Lex Mundi Study: Its results appear to be significant, their interpretation consistent, and the Study seems to confirm much of the traditional wisdom of comparative law. Is our critique therefore unjustified and futile? We do not think so.

First, the argument that the results are meaningful may be persuasive as to errors in individual answers for this or that country to this or that question. Yet it does not help much if the question as such misses the crucial point, if the available answers are limited to a few predetermined options and do not completely reproduce reality, if the classification or coding – the transformation of the answers into numerical values – is defective, or if the aggregation of the data is questionable. In these cases, errors potentially have consequences throughout the whole sample of countries. Therefore, the variables may still yield a statistically significant result, although this result might be without any value because it does not correctly reflect the real world. Such a systematic error, which does not necessarily lead to an obvious insignificance of the results, is favored if the research is based on a simple theoretical model or conducted against the background of a certain (legal) system. As indicated at the beginning, the focus of this book was not on the individual answers for individual countries – the book does not provide a re-coding. Therefore, the defense with the alleged significance of the results should not affect our criticism.

Second, the question of whether the results correspond to what one could expect to find may be a useful control. However, it faces the objection that these expected results, this "general wisdom", to which the defendants of statistical studies resort as support for the correctness of their work, are just what should be proven by the research. Even if one takes into consideration that there exist usually good reasons for the expectation of certain results, this argument cannot be taken as so strong a defense that all criticism would be irrelevant, once the expected and the found results coincide. Moreover, as far as the Lex Mundi Study is concerned, it is, at a closer look, not so obvious that the results are in line with the "traditional wisdom of comparative law", although the Study is repeating this assertion conspicuously often.[439] Again, what matters is the level of comparison – comparative law in general, comparative civil procedure, comparison of specific procedural institutions – , and the definition of what can be called the "traditional wisdom" of comparisons limited to the field of procedural law, is at best ambiguous.[440]

It shall be acknowledged that the book criticizes a lot the lack of caveats and qualifications and therefore may be seen as an example of orthodox comparative lawyering, so amusingly described by Professor Vagts.[441] Nevertheless, we think that such a study – that is, a study that can be expected, by its aim to give a recommendation and the World Bank's attention to this recommendation, to have much more practical influence than open-ended, purely academic research – *must* disclose its weaknesses and make clear on which points it enters the area of subjective evaluations or even speculation. This is not only a matter of scientific candor and fairness. It also helps the authors themselves to fully and thoroughly contemplate their methods and conclusions. Last not least, the persuasiveness of a study is increased if its authors enter in an open dialogue with the readers, allowing them to better understand why, in the frequent case of alternatives, the authors preferred one over another.

---

[439] Djankov et al., *supra* note 11, at 456, 477, 491, 510.

[440] *See supra* sub VI.B.2; as examples for distinguished scholars whose statements on procedural formalism are diametrically opposed to what according to the Study is the position of comparative law literature, *see, e.g.* René David, *De l'importance d'études comparatives relatives à la procédure*, *in* ESTUDIOS JURIDICOS EN MEMORIA DE EDUARDO J. COUTURE 929, 933 (1957) (describing the common law as formalistic with the words "il subsiste dans les droits anglais et américain du Nord, dans bien des matières, et en ce qui concerne en particulier le droit et l'administration de la preuve, des règles souvent désuètes, un formalisme qui laisse trop de place à des abus de la technique juridique."); Baur, *supra* note 77, at 101/119/1688 (classifying English civil procedure as rather formalistic on the basis of his dichotomy between powerful judge and formalist procedure). *See also* Cammack, *supra* note 57, at 789 (noting that "[i]f formality and repetition is the hallmark of ritual, the judicial trial must be counted as among the most decidedly ritualistic institutions of our society. Few if any features of modern life are as imbued with formality as jury trials.").

[441] Vagts, *supra* note 221, at 604, after calling La Porta et al, *supra* note 255, a "ground-breaking endeavor": "Orthodox comparative lawyers would have shrunk back from such an ambitious endeavor and if they had attempted, it would have wound up with a tome of 2000 pages and 6000 footnotes filled with caveats and qualifications that would have rendered it unreadable."

This publication faces two other reproaches. First, it does no statistical research of its own and rarely suggests one clear alternative to the Study's approach. Second, it applies a relatively high standard for its criticism, while itself it would probably not be up to that standard either. However, a study which could have an essential impact on what procedural law will look like in some decades and which is authored by such eminent and influential researchers, explicitly backed by the credit of Harvard University, Yale University and the World Bank, and financed to an important part by the money of the World Bank's member countries' taxpayers, must meet the highest expectations. It therefore must be allowed also for attentive scholars who do not enjoy the same possibilities, means and skills the Study's authors have, to express well-founded concerns and criticism. Any rejoinder mitigating our concerns and refuting our criticism or pointing out its weaknesses will enrich and advance the debate and shall hereby expressly be encouraged.

Part XI

Conclusion

Comparative law has been enriched by a new methodology: the statistical analysis of various countries' legal solutions to specific social and economic problems. On the theoretical level, where the debate has been relatively limited to date, decisive conceptual arguments against the use of statistics in this field have not yet been put forward. However, the present state of this surging field of research is in its infancy, and it remains to be seen whether the approach will prove successful in the long run.

A particularly impressive example for the current state of this approach is the Lex Mundi Study on formalism in civil procedural law. First, civil procedure is not as simple a field as it might appear to economists who have taken courage producing studies in the field of corporate governance and business law. Selecting appropriate model cases, asking the right questions and evaluating correctly their relative significance requires a good deal of knowledge about the legal diversities in this specific field. Second, measuring a whole process, here civil procedure, against a broad concept like "formalism" involves intricate questions of how this concept is to be interpreted at each stage of the proceedings. Abstract answers risk to miss the meaning and implications of certain structural elements like judicial review. Third, offering only binary answers for the various legal solutions is often unsatisfactory. In today's legal systems we rarely find solutions at one extreme of the spectrum. Rather, the solutions mostly do not differ so much in practice. Binary answers therefore tend to overstate differences. A certain degree of simplification is of course inevitable in comparative law. However, things can also be oversimplified. Fourth, unlike in other fields of the law where more objective measures for evaluating the effect of particular legal solutions may exist,[442] objective measures for an evaluation of a country's civil procedural law are rare. Indeed, duration seems to be the only relevant variable that is inherently numerical; any other measures of judicial quality are based on highly subjective assessments. Fifth, applying classifications of legal origins used elsewhere on the particular field of civil procedure and finding corroborated a "transplantation hypothesis"

[442] For example, characteristics of the capital markets in the various countries which can easily be expressed in numbers and collective from statistical sources other than to subjective "perceptions data".

which in itself is not free of doubt raises serious questions rather than adding to the persuasiveness of the study.

This abstract of our above discussion may suffice to explain our conclusion that in sum, the Study leaves a mixed impression. Unfortunately, it mostly refrains from disclosing potential problems or weaknesses. In any event, it is far from "finding objective measures of institutional structure". Taking into account the above discussion and the many open questions, it seems doubtful whether the Study's results really justify suggesting any practical strategy, and be it only the broad recommendation to reduce procedural formalism, even more so as the Study's future impact on the development of procedural law can be very important. Moreover, given that a probable implication of the Study's broad recommendation is the use as a model of the procedural law in a successful country of English legal origin,[443] the Study is not above suspicion of hidden benchmarking.

The Study has the undeniable merit of introducing the method of large-scale statistical analysis to the field of comparative civil procedural law. Its Dataset, results and conclusions can be the starting point for fruitful further research. The future of "numerical comparative law" is hard to predict. New studies intending "to investigate and constructively challenge" the findings of the studies by professors La Porta, Lopez-de-Silanes, Shleifer and their collaborators are on the way.[444] These second-generation studies might prove decisive not only for an evaluation of the studies of the first generation, but also for the future of the statistical approach, "numerical comparative law", itself.

It remains to be hoped that the World Bank – whose role in the promotion of these studies certainly deserves respect, but which at the same moment is responsible for the somewhat unfortunate entanglement of unreviewed pioneering research and powerful proposals for legal reform – closely observes the starting discussion. The World Bank and the other international development organizations must not limit their attention to the studies of the first generation which received their personal and financial support. This is even more important as many of these first-generation studies were undertaken more or less by one and the same group of persons. It is our wish that this book helps encouraging scholars and institutions to more thoroughly discuss the strengths and weaknesses of the statistical approach to comparative (procedural) law.

---

[443] *See supra* part VIII (note 405 and accompanying text).

[444] *See, e.g.,* the project "Law, Finance, and Development" of the Centre for Business Research at the University of Cambridge (U.K.), <http://www.cbr.cam.ac.uk/research/programme2/project2-20.htm> (last visited July 17, 2006).

Appendix 1

Table I

DESCRIPTION OF THE VARIABLES

This table describes the variables in the paper. Unless otherwise specified, the source for the variables is the survey of law firms and the laws of each country. All the data for each country can be found at http://iicg.som.yale.edu/.

Variable	Description
	Professionals versus laymen
General jurisdiction court	The variable measures whether a court of general or of limited jurisdiction would be chosen or assigned to hear the case under normal circumstances. We define a court of general jurisdiction as a state institution, recognized by the law as part of the regular court system, generally competent to hear and decide regular civil or criminal cases. A limited jurisdiction court would hear and decide only some types of civil cases. Specialized debt-collection or housing courts, small-claims courts, and arbitrators or justices of the peace are examples. Equals one for a court of general jurisdiction, and zero for a court of limited jurisdiction.
Professional versus nonprofessional judge	The variable measures whether the judge, or the members of the court or tribunal, could be considered as professional. A professional judge is one who has undergone a complete professional training as required by law, and whose primary activity is to act as judge or member of a court. A nonprofessional judge is an arbitrator, administrative officer, practicing attorney, merchant, or any other layperson who may be authorized to hear and decide the case. Equals one for a professional judge, and zero for a nonprofessional judge.
Legal representation is mandatory	The variable measures whether the law requires the intervention of a licensed attorney. The variable equals one when legal representation is mandatory, and zero when legal representation is not mandatory.

Table I (continued)

Variable	Description
Index: professionals versus laymen	The index measures whether the resolution of the case relies on the work of professional judges and attorneys, as opposed to other types of adjudicators and lay people. The index is the normalized sum of (i) general jurisdiction court, (ii) professional versus nonprofessional judge, and (iii) legal representation is mandatory. The index ranges from zero to one, where higher values mean more participation by professionals.
	Written Versus Oral
Filing	Equals one if the complaint is normally submitted in written form to the court, and zero if it can be presented orally.
Service of process	Equals one if the defendant's first official notice of the complaint is most likely received in writing, and zero otherwise.
Opposition	Equals one if under normal circumstances the defendant's answer to the complaint should be submitted in writing, and zero if it may be presented orally to court.
Evidence	Equals one if evidence is mostly submitted to the court in written form, in the form of attachments, affidavits, or otherwise, and zero if most of the evidence, including documentary evidence, is presented at oral hearings before the judge.
Final arguments	Equals one if final arguments on the case are normally submitted in writing, and zero if they are normally presented orally in court before the judge.
Judgment	Equals one if the judge issues the final decision in the case in written form, and zero if he issues it orally in an open court hearing attended by the parties. The defining factor is whether the judge normally decides the case at a hearing. If the judge simply reads out a previously made written decision, the variable equals one. Conversely, for an orally pronounced judgment that is later transposed into writing for enforcement purposes, the variable equals zero.

Table I (continued)

Variable	Description
Notification of judgment	Equals one if normally the parties receive their first notice of the final decision in written form, by notice mailed to them, publication in a court board or gazette, or through any other written means. The variable equals zero if they receive their first notice in an open court hearing attended by them.
Enforcement of judgment	Equals one if the enforcement procedure is mostly carried out through the written court orders or written acts by the enforcement authority, and zero otherwise.
Index: Written versus oral elements	The index measures the written or oral nature of the actions involved in the procedure, from the filing of the complaint until the actual enforcement. The index is calculated as the number of stages carried out mostly in written form over the total number of applicable stages, and it ranges from zero to one, where higher values mean higher prevalence of written elements.
	Legal justification
Complaint must be legally justified	The variable measures whether the complaint is required, by law or court regulation, to include references to the applicable laws, legal reasoning, or formalities that would normally require legal training. Equals one for a legally justified complaint, and zero when the complaint does not require legal justification (specific articles of the law or case-law).
Judgment must be legally justified	The variable measures whether the judgment must expressly state the legal justification (articles of the law or case-law) for the decision. Equals one for a legally justified judgment, and zero otherwise.
Judgment must be on law (not on equity)	The variable measures whether the judgment may be motivated on general equity grounds, or if it must be founded on the law. Equals one when judgment must be on law only, and zero when judgment may be based on equity grounds.

Table I (continued)

Variable	Description
Index: legal justification	The index measures the level of legal justification required in the process. The index is formed by the normalized sum of (i) complaint must be legally justified, (ii) judgment must be legally justified, and (iii) judgment must be on law (not on equity). The index ranges from zero to one, where higher values mean a higher use of legal language or justification.
	Statutory regulation of evidence
Judge cannot introduce evidence	Equals one if, by law, the judge cannot freely request or take evidence that has not been requested, offered, or introduced by the parties, and zero otherwise.
Judge cannot reject irrelevant evidence	Equals one if, by law, the judge cannot refuse to collect or admit evidence requested by the parties, even if she deems it irrelevant to the case, and zero otherwise.
Out-of-court statements are inadmissible	Equals one if statements of fact that were not directly known or perceived by the witness, but only heard from a third person, may not be admitted as evidence. The variable equals zero otherwise.
Mandatory prequalification of questions	Equals one if, by law, the judge must prequalify the questions before they are asked.
Oral interrogation only by judge	Equals one if parties and witnesses can only be orally interrogated by the judge, and zero if they can be orally interrogated by the judge and the opposing party.
Only original documents and certified copies are admissible	Equals one if only original documents and "authenthic" or "certified" copies are admissible documentary evidence, and zero if simple or uncertified copies are admissible evidence as well.
Authenticity and weight of evidence defined by law	Equals one if the authenticity and probative value of documentary evidence is specifically defined by the law, and zero if all admissible documentary evidence is freely weighted by the judge.
Mandatory recording of evidence	Equals one if, by law, there must be a written or magnetic record of all evidence introduced at trial, and zero otherwise.

Table I (continued)

Variable	Description
Index: statutory regulation of evidence	The index measures the level of statutory control or intervention of the administration, admissibility, evaluation, and recording of evidence. The index is formed by the normalized sum of the following variables: (i) judge cannot introduce evidence, (ii) judge cannot reject irrelevant evidence, (iii) out-of-court statements are inadmissible, (iv) mandatory prequalification of questions, (v) oral interrogation only by judge, (vi) only original documents and certified copies are admissible, (vii) authenticity and weight of evidence defined by law, and (viii) mandatory recording of evidence. The index ranges from zero to one, where higher values mean a higher statutory control or intervention.
	Control of superior review
Enforcement of judgment is automatically suspended until resolution of appeal	Equals one if the enforcement of judgment is automatically suspended until resolution of the appeal when a request for appeal is granted. Equals zero if the suspension of the enforcement of judgment is not automatic, or if the judgment cannot be appealed at all.
Comprehensive review in appeal	Equals one if issues of both law and fact (evidence) can be reviewed by the appellate court. Equals zero if only new evidence or issues of law can be reviewed in appeal, or if judgment cannot be appealed.
Interlocutory appeals are allowed	Equals one if interlocutory appeals are allowed, and zero if they are always prohibited. Interlocutory appeals are defined as appeals against interlocutory or interim judicial decisions made during the course of a judicial proceeding in first instance and before the final ruling on the entire case.
Index: control of superior review	The index measures the level of control or intervention of the appellate court's review of the first-instance judgment. The index is formed by the normalized sum of the following variables: (i) enforcement of judgment is automatically suspended until resolution of appeal, (ii) comprehensive review in appeal, and (iii) interlocutory appeals are allowed. The index ranges from zero to one, where higher values mean higher control or intervention.

Table I (continued)

Variable	Description
Engagement formalities	
Mandatory pretrial conciliation	Equals one if the law requires plaintiff to attempt a pretrial conciliation or mediation before filing the lawsuit, and zero otherwise.
Service of process by judicial officer required	Equals one if the law requires the complaint to be served to the defendant through the intervention of a judicial officer, and zero if service of process may be accomplished by other means.
Notification of judgment by judicial officer required	Equals one if the law requires the judgment to be notified to the defendant through the intervention of a judicial officer, and zero if notification of judgment may be accomplished by other means.
Index: engagement formalities	The index measures the formalities required to engage someone in the procedure or to hold him/her accountable of the judgment. The index is formed by the normalized sum of the following variables: (i) mandatory pretrial conciliation, (ii) service of process by judicial officer required, and (iii) notification of judgment by judicial officer required. The index ranges from zero to one, where higher values mean a higher statutory control or intervention in the judicial process.
Independent procedural actions	
Filing and service	The total minimum number of independent procedural actions required to complete filing, admission, attachment, and service.
Trial and judgment	The total minimum number of independent procedural actions required to complete opposition to the complaint, hearing or trial, evidence, final arguments, and judgment.
Enforcement	The total minimum number of independent procedural actions required to complete notification and enforcement of judgment.

Table I (continued)

Variable	Description
Index: independent procedural actions	An independent procedural action is defined as a step of the procedure, mandated by law or court regulation, that demands interaction between the parties or between them and the judge or court officer (e.g., filing a motion, attending a hearing, mailing a letter, or seizing some goods). We also count as an independent procedural action every judicial or administrative writ or resolution (e.g., issuing judgment or entering a writ of execution) which is legally required to advance the proceedings until the enforcement of judgment. Actions are always assumed to be simultaneous if possible, so procedural events that may be fulfilled in the same day and place are only counted as one action. To form the index, we (1) add the minimum number of independent procedural actions required to complete all the stages of the process (from filing of lawsuit to enforcement of judgment); and (2) normalize this number to fall between zero and one using the minimum and the maximum number of independent procedural actions among the countries in the sample. The index takes a value of zero for the country with the minimum number of independent procedural actions, and a value of one for the country with the maximum number of independent procedural actions.
	Formalism index
Formalism index	The index measures substantive and procedural statutory intervention in judicial cases at lower-level civil trial courts, and is formed by adding up the following indices: (i) professionals versus laymen, (ii) written versus oral elements, (iii) legal justification, (iv) statutory regulation of evidence, (v) control of superior review, (vi) engagement formalities, and (vii) independent procedural actions. The index ranges from zero to seven where seven means a higher level of control or intervention in the judicial process.
	Incentives of parties
Mandatory time limit for admission	Equals one if the judge is required by law to admit or reject the lawsuit within a certain period of time, and zero otherwise.

Table I (continued)

Variable	Description
Mandatory time limit to present evidence	Equals one if the period in which the parties may collect or present evidence is fixed by law to a certain number of days after service or number of days before hearing, and zero otherwise.
Mandatory time limit to present defense	Equals one if the defendant is required by law to file the opposition within certain time limit, either in terms of number of days from service or number of days before the hearing. The variable equals zero otherwise.
Mandatory time limit for judgment	Equals one if the judge is required by law to enter judgment within a specified period of time after the conclusion of the hearing or the final pleadings, and zero otherwise.
Mandatory time limit for notification of judgment	Equals one if the court is required by law to notify the parties within a specified period of time after judgment is entered, and zero otherwise.
Index: mandatory time limits	The presence of mandatory time limits in the procedure. The index is calculated as the average of (i) term for admission, (ii) term to present evidence, (iii) term to present defense, (iv) term for judgment, (v) term for compliance, (vi) term for notification of judgment. The index ranges from zero to one, where higher values mean more mandatory deadlines.
Quota litis prohibited	The variable equals one if quota litis or contingent fee agreements are prohibited by law in all cases, and zero otherwise.
Loser pays rule	The variable equals one if the loser is required to pay all the costs of the dispute, and zero otherwise.
	Duration in practice
Duration until completion of service of process	Estimated duration, in calendar days, between the moment the plaintiff files the complaint until the moment of service of process to the defendant.
Duration of trial	Estimated duration, in calendar days, between the moment of service of process and the moment the judgment is issued.

Table I (continued)

Variable	Description
Duration of enforcement	Estimated duration, in calendar days, between the moment of issuance of judgment and the moment the landlord repossesses the property (for the eviction case) or the creditor obtains payment (for the check collection case).
Total duration	The total estimated duration in calendar days of the procedure under the factual and procedural assumptions provided. It equals the sum of (i) duration until completion of service of process, (ii) duration of trial, and (iii) duration of enforcement.
	Other judicial quality measures
Enforceability of contracts	"The relative degree to which contractual agreements are honored and complications presented by language and mentality differences." Scale for 0 to 10, with higher scores indicating higher enforceability. *Source: Business Environmental Risk intelligence.* Exact definition in *Knack and Keefer [1995].*
Legal system is fair and impartial	"In resolving business disputes, do you believe your country's court system to be fair and impartial?" The scale ranges from 1 to 6, where higher scores mean a fairer and more impartial legal system. *Source: World Business Environment Survey [2000, 2002].*
Legal system is honest or uncorrupt	"In resolving business disputes, do you believe your country's court system to be honest/uncorrupt?" The scale ranges from 1 to 6, where a higher score signals a more honest and uncorrupt system. *Source: World Business Environment Survey.*
Legal system is affordable	"In resolving business disputes, do you believe your country's court system to be affordable?" The scale ranges from 1 to 6, where a higher score means a more affordable legal system. *Source: World Business Environment Survey.*
Legal system is consistent	"In resolving business disputes, do you believe your country's court system to be consistent?" The scale ranges from 1 to 6, where a higher score means a more consistent legal system. *Source: World Business Environment Survey.*

Table I (continued)

Variable	Description
Confidence in legal system	The questionnaire asks the managers the degree to which they believe the system will uphold contracts and property rights in a business dispute. The scale ranges from 1 to 6, where a higher score means a higher degree of confidence in the system. *Source: World Business Environment Survey.*
Corruption	A composite index for the year 2000 that draws on fourteen data sources from seven institutions: the World Economic Forum, the World Business Environment Survey of the World Bank, the Institute of Management Development (in Lausanne), PricewaterhouseCoopers, the Political and Economic Risk Consultancy (in Hong Kong), the Economist Intelligence Unit and Freedom House's Nations in Transit. The score ranges between 10 (highly clean) and 0 (highly corrupt). *Source: Transparency International (www.transparency.org).*
Law and order	Integrity of legal system in 2000. This component is based on the Political Risk Component 1 (Law and Order) from the PRS Group's International Country Risk Guide (various issues). Rankings are modified to a ten-point scale. *Source: Economic Freedom of the World [Gwartney, Lawson, and Block 2001].*
Log of GNP per capita	Logarithm of GNP per capita in 1999, Atlas method, expressed in current US dollars. When 1999 income data in US dollars were not available, the latest number available was used (1996 for Kuwait, 1997 for Cayman Islands, Gibraltar, Turks and Caicos Island, 1998 for Anguilla, Bahrain, Netherlands Antilles, United Arab Emirates). Income for Anguilla, the British Virgin Islands, the Cayman Islands, Gibraltar, Monaco, the Netherlands Antilles, and the Turks and Caicos Islands is GDP per capita (PPP) from the CIA World Factbook. *Source: World Development Indicators [2001].*
Legal origin	Identifies the legal origin of the company law or commercial code of each country (English, French, Socialist, German, Scandinavian). *Source: La Porta et al. [1999].*
Latitude	The absolute value of the latitude of the capital of the country, scaled to take values between zero and one. *Source: CIA Factbook.*

Table I (continued)

Variable	Description
Average years of schooling	Average number of years of schooling received per person aged 25 and over in 1992 (last available). *Source: Human Development Report [1994].*
Ethnic fractionalization	Ethnic fractionalization is computed as one minus the Herfindahl index of ethnic group shares. This calculation considers the probability that two persons, randomly chosen, from a population belong to different groups. *Source: Alesina et al. [2003].*

Source: Djankov et al., *supra* note 11, at 463–473.

Appendix 2

Table IIa

EVICTION OF TENANT

This table classifies countries by legal origin and shows the professionals versus laymen, written versus oral elements, legal justification, statutory regulation of evidence, control of superior review, and engagement formalities indices, and the normalized number of independent procedural actions for the case of eviction of a tenant. All variables are described in Table I, and the data can be found at http://iicg.som.yale.edu/.

	Professionals versus laymen	Written versus oral elements	Legal justification	Statutory regulation of evidence	Control of superior review	Engagement formalities	Independent procedural actions	**Formalism index**
English legal origin								
Anguilla	0.67	0.88	0.67	0.13	1.00	0.67	0.28	**4.28**
Australia	0.00	0.57	0.33	0.25	0.67	0.00	0.17	**1.99**
Bahrain	0.33	0.63	1.00	0.38	1.00	0.33	0.25	**3.92**
Bangladesh	0.33	0.63	0.67	0.13	1.00	0.33	0.28	**3.36**
Barbados	0.67	0.50	0.00	0.25	0.67	0.00	0.25	**2.33**
Belize	0.00	0.38	0.67	0.38	0.67	0.00	0.00	**2.08**
Bermuda	0.33	0.38	0.00	0.25	0.33	0.00	0.03	**1.32**
Botswana	0.67	0.75	0.67	0.38	0.67	0.67	0.28	**4.07**
BVI	0.67	0.50	0.33	0.38	0.67	0.00	0.33	**2.88**
Canada	0.00	0.75	0.33	0.38	0.33	0.33	0.19	**2.32**
Cayman	0.67	0.63	0.67	0.25	0.67	0.33	0.39	**3.60**
Cyprus	0.67	0.63	0.67	0.38	0.67	0.33	0.17	**3.50**
Ghana	0.67	0.50	0.00	0.50	0.33	0.33	0.36	**2.69**
Gibraltar	0.67	0.75	0.33	0.13	0.33	0.00	0.31	**2.51**
Grenada	0.33	0.38	0.67	0.38	0.67	0.33	0.11	**2.86**
Hong Kong	0.33	0.75	1.00	0.13	0.67	0.00	0.25	**3.13**
India	0.33	0.75	1.00	0.38	0.33	0.33	0.39	**3.51**
Ireland	0.67	0.71	0.33	0.13	1.00	0.00	0.36	**3.20**
Israel	0.67	0.88	1.00	0.50	0.67	0.00	0.19	**3.90**
Jamaica	0.67	0.38	0.33	0.25	0.67	0.00	0.08	**2.38**
Kenya	0.33	0.75	0.33	0.38	0.67	0.00	0.39	**2.85**
Malawi	0.33	0.63	0.67	0.38	0.67	0.33	0.14	**3.14**
Malaysia	0.67	0.63	0.33	0.50	0.67	0.00	0.42	**3.21**
Namibia	0.67	0.63	0.67	0.38	1.00	0.33	0.19	**3.86**
New Zealand	0.00	0.50	0.33	0.00	0.33	0.00	0.08	**1.25**
Nigeria	0.33	0.63	0.33	0.38	1.00	0.00	0.42	**3.08**
Pakistan	0.67	0.63	0.67	0.25	1.00	0.00	0.53	**3.74**
Singapore	0.67	0.63	0.33	0.38	0.67	0.00	0.44	**3.11**
South Africa	0.67	0.50	0.67	0.38	1.00	0.33	0.14	**3.68**
Sri Lanka	0.67	0.63	1.00	0.38	1.00	0.00	0.22	**3.89**
St. Vincent	0.67	0.50	0.67	0.38	0.67	0.67	0.31	**3.85**
Swaziland	0.67	0.63	1.00	0.25	1.00	0.00	0.19	**3.74**
Tanzania	0.33	0.63	0.33	0.50	0.67	0.33	0.11	**2.90**
Thailand	0.67	0.88	1.00	0.38	0.67	0.33	0.33	**4.25**
Trinidad and Tobago	0.67	0.63	0.00	0.25	0.33	0.00	0.28	**2.15**
Turks and Caicos	0.67	0.63	0.00	0.38	0.67	0.00	0.47	**2.81**

Table IIa (continued)

	Professionals versus laymen	Written versus oral elements	Legal justification	Statutory regulation of evidence	Control of superior review	Engagement formalities	Independent procedural actions	**Formalism index**
UAE	0.00	0.50	0.33	0.00	0.00	0.33	0.28	**1.44**
Uganda	0.00	1.00	0.33	0.38	0.67	0.00	0.14	**2.51**
United Kingdom	0.67	0.75	0.33	0.00	0.33	0.00	0.14	**2.22**
USA	0.33	0.63	1.00	0.13	0.67	0.00	0.22	**2.97**
Zambia	0.67	0.50	0.33	0.38	0.67	0.33	0.19	**3.07**
Zimbabwe	0.33	0.63	0.67	0.38	0.67	0.33	0.11	**3.11**
Mean	**0.48**	**0.63**	**0.52**	**0.30**	**0.67**	**0.17**	**0.25**	**3.02**
Socialist legal origin								
Bulgaria	0.67	0.88	1.00	0.25	1.00	0.33	0.39	**4.51**
China	0.67	0.75	0.33	0.38	1.00	0.00	0.28	**3.40**
Croatia	0.67	0.63	1.00	0.25	0.67	0.00	0.22	**3.43**
Czech Republic	0.67	0.38	1.00	0.25	1.00	0.00	0.25	**3.54**
Estonia	0.67	0.75	1.00	0.38	1.00	0.67	0.28	**4.74**
Georgia	0.67	0.63	0.67	0.25	1.00	0.00	0.31	**3.51**
Hungary	0.67	0.75	1.00	0.13	0.67	0.00	0.25	**3.46**
Kazakhstan	0.67	0.63	0.67	0.38	1.00	0.00	0.67	**4.00**
Latvia	0.67	0.63	1.00	0.38	1.00	0.00	0.19	**3.86**
Lithuania	0.67	0.75	1.00	0.38	1.00	0.00	0.42	**4.21**
Poland	0.67	0.75	1.00	0.50	1.00	0.00	0.17	**4.08**
Romania	0.67	0.75	1.00	0.50	1.00	0.00	0.56	**4.47**
Russia	0.67	0.50	0.67	0.38	1.00	0.00	0.11	**3.32**
Slovenia	0.67	0.75	1.00	0.38	1.00	0.00	0.47	**4.26**
Ukraine	0.67	0.75	0.33	0.63	1.00	0.00	0.22	**3.60**
Vietnam	0.67	0.50	0.00	0.25	1.00	0.00	0.42	**2.83**
Mean	**0.67**	**0.67**	**0.79**	**0.35**	**0.96**	**0.06**	**0.32**	**3.83**
French legal origin								
Argentina	1.00	1.00	1.00	0.13	1.00	0.67	0.69	**5.49**
Belgium	0.67	0.75	0.33	0.25	0.67	0.33	0.17	**3.17**
Bolivia	1.00	1.00	0.67	0.25	1.00	0.67	0.53	**5.11**
Brazil	1.00	0.63	1.00	0.38	0.67	0.00	0.17	**3.83**
Chile	1.00	0.88	0.67	0.50	0.67	0.67	0.42	**4.79**
Colombia	0.67	1.00	1.00	0.25	0.00	0.33	0.69	**3.94**
Costa Rica	0.67	0.86	1.00	0.50	1.00	0.67	0.36	**5.05**
Cote d'Ivoire	0.67	0.50	0.67	0.25	0.67	0.67	0.22	**3.64**
Dominican Republic	0.33	0.63	1.00	0.38	1.00	0.67	0.36	**4.36**
Ecuador	0.67	0.88	1.00	0.63	0.67	0.33	0.47	**4.64**
Egypt	0.67	0.63	1.00	0.50	0.33	0.33	0.14	**3.60**
El Salvador	0.33	1.00	0.67	0.75	0.67	0.67	0.17	**4.25**
France	0.33	0.75	1.00	0.13	0.67	0.67	0.06	**3.60**
Greece	1.00	1.00	1.00	0.50	0.00	0.67	0.14	**4.31**
Guatemala	1.00	1.00	1.00	0.75	1.00	0.67	0.36	**5.78**
Honduras	0.67	1.00	1.00	0.63	0.67	0.33	0.39	**4.68**
Indonesia	0.33	0.88	0.67	0.50	0.67	0.33	0.50	**3.88**
Italy	1.00	1.00	0.67	0.13	0.67	0.67	0.11	**4.24**
Jordan	0.67	0.63	0.67	0.50	0.00	0.33	0.58	**3.38**
Kuwait	0.33	0.88	1.00	0.25	1.00	1.00	0.14	**4.69**
Lebanon	1.00	0.88	1.00	0.50	1.00	0.67	0.53	**5.57**
Luxembourg	0.33	0.86	0.67	0.50	1.00	0.00	0.31	**3.66**
Malta	0.67	0.63	0.67	0.38	0.67	0.33	0.08	**3.42**
Mexico	0.33	0.88	1.00	0.50	0.67	0.67	0.78	**4.82**
Monaco	0.33	0.63	0.67	0.25	0.33	0.67	0.06	**2.93**
Morocco	0.67	1.00	0.67	0.63	1.00	0.67	0.17	**4.79**
Mozambique	1.00	0.75	1.00	0.38	1.00	0.67	0.36	**5.15**

Table IIa (continued)

	Professio-nals versus laymen	Written versus oral elements	Legal justifi-cation	Statutory regulation of evi-dence	Control of supe-rior review	Engage-ment formali-ties	Independent procedural actions	**Forma-lism index**
Netherlands	0.33	0.63	0.67	0.13	0.67	0.33	0.25	**3.00**
Netherlands Antilles	0.67	0.63	0.33	0.25	0.67	0.67	0.42	**3.63**
Panama	1.00	1.00	1.00	0.25	1.00	0.67	1.00	**5.92**
Paraguay	0.67	0.86	1.00	0.63	0.67	0.67	0.61	**5.09**
Peru	1.00	0.88	1.00	0.38	1.00	0.67	0.50	**5.42**
Philippines	1.00	1.00	1.00	0.50	0.33	0.67	0.50	**5.00**
Portugal	1.00	0.75	1.00	0.38	1.00	0.00	0.42	**4.54**
Senegal	0.67	0.63	0.33	0.63	0.67	0.67	0.31	**3.89**
Spain	0.67	0.88	1.00	0.63	0.67	0.67	0.31	**4.81**
Tunisia	0.67	0.75	0.67	0.25	0.67	0.67	0.22	**3.89**
Turkey	0.67	0.63	1.00	0.75	0.00	0.00	0.44	**3.49**
Uruguay	1.00	0.50	0.67	0.13	0.67	0.33	0.69	**3.99**
Venezuela	1.00	1.00	1.00	0.50	1.00	0.67	0.64	**5.81**
Mean	**0.72**	**0.81**	**0.83**	**0.42**	**0.69**	**0.53**	**0.38**	**4.38**
German legal origin								
Austria	0.67	0.86	1.00	0.13	0.67	0.00	0.31	**3.62**
Germany	0.33	0.88	1.00	0.50	0.67	0.00	0.39	**3.76**
Japan	0.67	1.00	1.00	0.25	0.67	0.00	0.14	**3.72**
Korea	0.67	0.88	0.33	0.13	0.67	0.33	0.33	**3.33**
Switzerland	0.67	0.63	1.00	0.25	1.00	0.33	0.08	**3.96**
Taiwan	0.67	0.50	0.67	0.38	0.67	0.00	0.17	**3.04**
Mean	**0.61**	**0.79**	**0.83**	**0.27**	**0.72**	**0.11**	**0.24**	**3.57**
Scandinavian legal origin								
Denmark	0.67	0.75	0.67	0.13	1.00	0.00	0.39	**3.60**
Finland	0.33	0.50	0.67	0.25	0.67	0.00	0.11	**2.53**
Iceland	0.67	0.38	1.00	0.38	0.67	0.33	0.06	**3.47**
Norway	0.67	0.75	0.67	0.13	1.00	0.33	0.17	**3.71**
Sweden	0.67	0.75	0.33	0.25	1.00	0.00	0.31	**3.31**
Mean	**0.60**	**0.63**	**0.67**	**0.23**	**0.87**	**0.13**	**0.21**	**3.32**
Mean for all countries	**0.58**	**0.71**	**0.68**	**0.33**	**0.71**	**0.27**	**0.30**	**3.58**
				Test of means (t-stats)				
English versus Socialist	-3.08a	-1.13	-2.89a	-1.31	-4.57a	1.87c	-1.98c	**-3.87a**
English versus French	-4.34a	-5.61a	-5.20a	-3.21a	-0.41	-7.07a	-3.38a	**-7.77a**
English versus German	-1.31	-2.53b	-2.29b	0.50	-0.54	0.70	0.22	**-1.74c**
English versus Scandinavian	-1.10	0.01	-0.98	1.20	-1.77c	0.42	0.72	**-0.86**
Socialist versus French	-0.78	-3.14a	-0.57	-1.27	3.38a	-7.00a	-0.94	**-2.49b**
Socialist versus German	1.71	-1.68	-0.28	1.31	4.12a	-0.57	1.29	**1.10**
Socialist versus Scandinavian	1.90c	0.65	0.80	2.07c	1.36	-0.76	1.57	**1.93c**
French versus German	0.98	0.35	0.00	1.81c	-0.24	4.09a	1.56	**2.37b**
French versus Scandinavian	0.99	2.44b	1.63	2.23b	-1.25	3.55a	1.72c	**2.82a**
German versus Scandinavian	0.13	1.48	1.06	0.59	-1.51	-0.21	0.39	**1.04**

a = significant at 1 percent level; b = significant at 5 percent level; c = significant at 10 percent level.

Source: Djankov et al., *supra* note 11, at 478–483.

Appendix 3

Table IIb

COLLECTION OF A CHECK

This table classifies countries by legal origin and shows the professionals versus laymen, written versus oral elements, legal justification, statutory regulation of evidence, control of superior review, and engagement formalities indices, and the normalized number of independent procedural actions for the case of collection of a check. All variables are described in Table I, and the data can be found at http://iicg.som.yale.edu/.

	Professionals versus laymen	Written versus oral elements	Legal justification	Statutory regulation of evidence	Control of superior review	Engagement formalities	Independent procedural actions	**Formalism index**
English legal origin								
Anguilla	0.00	0.38	0.33	0.13	1.00	0.00	0.13	**1.96**
Australia	0.00	0.50	0.33	0.25	0.67	0.00	0.05	**1.80**
Bahrain	0.33	0.75	1.00	0.75	1.00	0.33	0.24	**4.40**
Bangladesh	0.67	0.63	0.67	0.13	1.00	0.00	0.16	**3.24**
Barbados	0.33	0.38	0.33	0.25	0.67	0.33	0.08	**2.37**
Belize	0.00	0.38	0.00	0.38	0.67	0.00	0.00	**1.42**
Bermuda	0.33	0.38	0.00	0.25	0.33	0.33	0.16	**1.78**
Botswana	0.67	0.75	0.67	0.38	0.67	0.67	0.29	**4.08**
BVI	0.33	0.38	0.00	0.38	1.00	0.33	0.11	**2.52**
Canada	0.33	0.50	0.00	0.38	0.67	0.00	0.21	**2.09**
Cayman	0.67	0.63	0.33	0.25	0.67	0.00	0.21	**2.75**
Cyprus	0.67	0.63	0.67	0.38	0.67	0.33	0.34	**3.68**
Ghana	0.67	0.50	0.00	0.50	0.33	0.33	0.32	**2.65**
Gibraltar	0.67	0.75	0.33	0.13	0.33	0.00	0.18	**2.39**
Grenada	0.33	0.38	0.67	0.38	0.67	0.33	0.05	**2.80**
Hong Kong	0.00	0.63	0.00	0.00	0.00	0.00	0.11	**0.73**
India	0.67	0.63	1.00	0.38	0.33	0.00	0.34	**3.34**
Ireland	0.67	0.57	0.33	0.13	0.67	0.00	0.26	**2.63**
Israel	0.33	0.88	0.67	0.50	0.67	0.00	0.26	**3.30**
Jamaica	0.67	0.38	0.33	0.25	0.67	0.00	0.05	**2.34**
Kenya	0.67	0.63	0.33	0.38	0.67	0.00	0.42	**3.09**
Malawi	0.67	0.63	0.33	0.25	0.67	0.33	0.08	**2.95**
Malaysia	0.33	0.50	0.00	0.50	0.67	0.00	0.34	**2.34**
Namibia	0.67	0.63	0.67	0.38	1.00	0.33	0.16	**3.82**
New Zealand	0.00	0.50	0.33	0.00	0.67	0.00	0.08	**1.58**
Nigeria	0.33	0.63	0.33	0.38	0.67	0.33	0.53	**3.19**
Pakistan	0.67	0.63	0.67	0.25	1.00	0.00	0.55	**3.76**
Singapore	0.33	0.38	0.00	0.50	0.67	0.33	0.29	**2.50**
South Africa	0.00	0.38	0.33	0.25	0.67	0.00	0.05	**1.68**
Sri Lanka	0.67	0.86	0.67	0.38	1.00	0.00	0.21	**3.78**
St. Vincent	1.00	0.43	0.67	0.38	0.67	0.33	0.16	**3.63**
Swaziland	0.67	0.63	1.00	0.25	1.00	0.00	0.16	**3.70**
Tanzania	0.67	0.86	0.67	0.50	0.67	0.33	0.13	**3.82**
Thailand	0.33	0.50	0.67	0.38	0.67	0.33	0.26	**3.14**
Trinidad and Tobago	0.33	0.63	0.00	0.25	0.33	0.00	0.26	**1.80**
Turks and Caicos	0.00	0.25	0.00	0.38	1.00	0.00	0.24	**1.86**

Table IIb (continued)

	Professionals versus laymen	Written versus oral elements	Legal justification	Statutory regulation of evidence	Control of superior review	Engagement formalities	Independent procedural actions	**Formalism index**
UAE	1.00	0.88	1.00	0.13	0.33	0.00	0.47	**3.81**
Uganda	0.00	0.71	0.67	0.38	0.67	0.00	0.18	**2.61**
United Kingdom	0.67	0.71	0.33	0.13	0.67	0.00	0.08	**2.58**
USA	0.33	0.75	0.33	0.13	1.00	0.00	0.08	**2.62**
Zambia	0.00	0.57	0.33	0.38	0.67	0.00	0.18	**2.13**
Zimbabwe	0.33	0.63	0.67	0.38	0.67	0.33	0.11	**3.11**
Mean	**0.43**	**0.58**	**0.42**	**0.31**	**0.68**	**0.13**	**0.20**	**2.76**
Socialist legal origin								
Bulgaria	0.67	0.88	1.00	0.25	1.00	0.33	0.45	**4.57**
China	0.67	0.75	0.33	0.38	1.00	0.00	0.29	**3.41**
Croatia	0.67	0.75	1.00	0.25	0.67	0.00	0.29	**3.62**
Czech Republic	0.67	0.83	1.00	0.38	1.00	0.00	0.18	**4.06**
Estonia	0.67	0.75	1.00	0.38	1.00	0.33	0.24	**4.36**
Georgia	0.67	0.63	0.67	0.25	0.67	0.00	0.21	**3.09**
Hungary	0.67	0.75	0.67	0.13	1.00	0.00	0.21	**3.42**
Kazakhstan	0.67	0.75	0.67	0.50	1.00	0.33	0.84	**4.76**
Latvia	0.67	0.63	1.00	0.38	1.00	0.00	0.26	**3.93**
Lithuania	0.67	0.75	1.00	0.50	1.00	0.00	0.55	**4.47**
Poland	0.67	0.88	1.00	0.38	1.00	0.00	0.24	**4.15**
Romania	0.67	0.75	1.00	0.50	1.00	0.00	0.50	**4.42**
Russia	0.67	0.50	0.67	0.38	1.00	0.00	0.18	**3.39**
Slovenia	0.67	0.75	1.00	0.50	1.00	0.00	0.34	**4.26**
Ukraine	0.67	0.75	0.33	0.63	1.00	0.00	0.29	**3.66**
Vietnam	0.67	0.50	0.33	0.25	1.00	0.00	0.50	**3.25**
Mean	**0.67**	**0.72**	**0.79**	**0.38**	**0.96**	**0.06**	**0.35**	**3.93**
French legal origin								
Argentina	1.00	1.00	1.00	0.13	1.00	0.67	0.61	**5.40**
Belgium	0.33	0.75	0.33	0.13	0.67	0.33	0.18	**2.73**
Bolivia	1.00	1.00	0.67	0.38	1.00	1.00	0.71	**5.75**
Brazil	0.33	0.50	1.00	0.38	0.67	0.00	0.18	**3.06**
Chile	1.00	0.75	0.67	0.50	0.67	0.67	0.32	**4.57**
Colombia	0.67	1.00	1.00	0.38	0.00	0.33	0.74	**4.11**
Costa Rica	1.00	1.00	1.00	0.50	1.00	0.67	0.32	**5.48**
Cote d'Ivoire	0.67	0.63	0.67	0.13	0.67	0.67	0.24	**3.65**
Dominican Republic	0.33	0.75	0.67	0.38	1.00	0.67	0.29	**4.08**
Ecuador	1.00	1.00	0.67	0.63	0.67	0.33	0.63	**4.92**
Egypt	1.00	0.75	1.00	0.50	0.00	0.33	0.21	**3.79**
El Salvador	0.33	0.88	1.00	0.88	0.67	0.67	0.18	**4.60**
France	0.33	0.75	1.00	0.13	0.33	0.67	0.03	**3.23**
Greece	0.67	1.00	1.00	0.50	0.00	0.67	0.16	**3.99**
Guatemala	1.00	1.00	1.00	0.75	1.00	0.67	0.26	**5.68**
Honduras	0.67	1.00	1.00	0.63	0.67	0.33	0.61	**4.90**
Indonesia	0.33	0.88	0.67	0.50	0.67	0.33	0.53	**3.90**
Italy	0.67	0.86	1.00	0.00	0.67	0.67	0.18	**4.04**
Jordan	0.67	0.75	0.67	0.50	0.00	0.33	0.61	**3.52**
Kuwait	0.67	0.88	0.67	0.13	0.67	0.67	0.21	**3.88**
Lebanon	1.00	0.75	0.67	0.63	1.00	0.33	0.47	**4.85**
Luxembourg	0.33	0.71	0.67	0.50	1.00	0.00	0.34	**3.56**
Malta	0.00	0.63	0.33	0.38	0.67	0.33	0.11	**2.44**
Mexico	0.33	0.88	1.00	0.50	0.67	0.33	1.00	**4.71**
Monaco	0.33	0.71	0.33	0.25	0.33	0.67	0.11	**2.74**
Morocco	1.00	1.00	0.67	0.50	0.67	0.67	0.21	**4.71**
Mozambique	0.67	0.75	1.00	0.50	0.67	0.67	0.24	**4.49**

Table IIb (continued)

	Professionals versus laymen	Written versus oral elements	Legal justification	Statutory regulation of evidence	Control of superior review	Engagement formalities	Independent procedural actions	**Formalism index**
Netherlands	0.33	0.63	0.67	0.13	0.67	0.33	0.32	**3.07**
Netherlands Antilles	0.67	0.88	0.33	0.25	0.33	0.00	0.39	**2.85**
Panama	1.00	1.00	1.00	0.25	1.00	0.67	0.92	**5.84**
Paraguay	1.00	1.00	1.00	0.63	0.67	0.67	0.95	**5.91**
Peru	1.00	0.88	1.00	0.38	1.00	0.67	0.68	**5.60**
Philippines	1.00	1.00	1.00	0.50	0.33	0.67	0.50	**5.00**
Portugal	0.67	0.75	1.00	0.50	0.67	0.00	0.34	**3.93**
Senegal	0.67	0.88	0.67	0.63	0.67	0.67	0.55	**4.72**
Spain	1.00	1.00	1.00	0.63	0.67	0.67	0.29	**5.25**
Tunisia	0.67	1.00	0.67	0.25	0.67	0.67	0.13	**4.05**
Turkey	0.00	1.00	0.67	0.63	0.00	0.00	0.24	**2.53**
Uruguay	1.00	0.50	0.67	0.13	0.67	0.33	0.76	**4.05**
Venezuela	1.00	1.00	1.00	0.50	1.00	0.67	0.84	**6.01**
Mean	**0.68**	**0.85**	**0.80**	**0.42**	**0.63**	**0.49**	**0.41**	**4.29**
German legal origin								
Austria	0.67	0.86	1.00	0.38	0.33	0.00	0.29	**3.52**
Germany	0.33	0.88	1.00	0.50	0.67	0.00	0.13	**3.51**
Japan	0.33	0.88	0.67	0.25	0.67	0.00	0.18	**2.98**
Korea	0.67	0.88	0.33	0.13	0.67	0.33	0.37	**3.37**
Switzerland	0.67	0.63	0.67	0.38	0.33	0.33	0.13	**3.13**
Taiwan	0.33	0.50	0.67	0.38	0.33	0.00	0.16	**2.37**
Mean	**0.50**	**0.77**	**0.72**	**0.33**	**0.50**	**0.11**	**0.21**	**3.15**
Scandinavian legal origin								
Denmark	0.33	0.63	0.00	0.13	1.00	0.33	0.13	**2.55**
Finland	0.67	0.63	0.67	0.25	0.67	0.00	0.26	**3.14**
Iceland	0.67	0.63	1.00	0.38	1.00	0.33	0.13	**4.13**
Norway	0.33	0.75	0.67	0.13	1.00	0.00	0.08	**2.95**
Sweden	0.67	0.75	0.33	0.25	0.67	0.00	0.32	**2.98**
Mean	0.53	0.68	0.53	0.23	0.87	0.13	0.18	**3.15**
Mean for all countries	**0.57**	**0.71**	**0.64**	**0.36**	**0.70**	**0.25**	**0.30**	**3.53**
				Test of means (t-stats)				
English versus Socialist	-3.29a	-3.38a	-4.19a	-1.55	-4.53a	1.45	-3.38a	**-5.24a**
English versus French	-3.85a	-7.97a	-6.29a	-2.71a	0.82	-7.42a	-4.63a	**-7.52a**
English versus German	-0.59	-2.73a	-2.25b	-0.37	1.84c	0.30	-0.11	**-1.12**
English versus Scandinavian	-0.79	-1.35	-0.75	1.22	-1.70c	0.02	0.33	**-1.03**
Socialist versus French	-0.21	-3.05a	-0.12	-0.74	4.07a	-6.47a	-0.92	**-1.36**
Socialist versus German	3.81a	-0.73	0.55	0.67	7.13a	-0.70	1.78c	**3.23a**
Socialist versus Scandinavian	3.11a	0.93	1.71	2.35b	1.36	-0.95	1.95c	**2.81b**
French versus German	1.40	1.24	0.78	0.96	1.02	3.58a	1.88c	**2.72a**
French versus Scandinavian	1.05	2.55b	2.32b	2.05b	-1.64	3.09a	1.94c	**2.45b**
German versus Scandinavian	-0.30	1.17	0.99	1.51	-3.32a	-0.21	0.44	**-0.02**

a = significant at 1 percent level; b = significant at 5 percent level; c = significant at 10 percent level.

Source: Djankov et al., *supra* note 11, at 484–489.

Appendix 4

Table III

CORRELATIONS OF FORMALISM INDEX AND ITS COMPONENTS

Indices	Formalism index	Professionals versus laymen	Written versus oral elements	Legal justification	Statutory regulation of evidence	Control of superior review	Engagement formalities	Independent procedural actions
Panel A: Eviction								
Professionals v. laymen	0.6420a	1.0000						
Written v. oral elements	0.6614a	0.3073c	1.0000					
Legal justification	0.6840a	0.2598	0.3976a	1.0000				
Stat. reg. of evidence	0.4161a	0.1471	0.2390	0.2049	1.0000			
Control of superior rev.	0.4573a	0.2342	0.1009	0.2121	0.0090	1.0000		
Engagement formalities	0.5988a	0.2349	0.4041a	0.2795	0.1995	0.0037	1.0000	
Ind. procedural actions	0.5353a	0.3952a	0.3858a	0.1799	0.1546	0.1110	0.1713	1.0000
Panel B: Check								
Professionals v. laymen	0.7625a	1.0000						
Written v. oral elements	0.7305a	0.5090a	1.0000					
Legal justification	0.7573a	0.4921a	0.6083a	1.0000				
Stat. reg. of evidence	0.4800a	0.1845	0.3052c	0.3184b	1.0000			
Control of superior rev.	0.3264b	0.1255	-0.0439	0.1051	0.0316	1.0000		
Engagement formalities	0.6125a	0.4082a	0.4391a	0.2977c	0.2296	-0.0296	1.0000	
Ind. procedural actions	0.6517a	0.4836a	0.4538a	0.3406b	0.2869	0.0957	0.2909c	1.0000
Panel C: Correlations between eviction and check indices								
Formalism index	0.8257a							
Professionals v. laymen		0.5229a						
Written v. oral elements			0.7054a					
Legal justification				0.7502a				
Stat. reg. of evidence					0.9086a			
Control of superior rev.						0.7866a		
Engagement formalities							0.8126a	
Ind. procedural actions								0.8575a

a = significant at 1 percent level; b = significant at 5 percent level; c = significant at 10 percent level.

Source: Djankov et al., *supra* note 11, at 490.

Appendix 5

Table IV

INDICES REGRESSIONS

Ordinary least squares regressions of the cross section of countries. The dependent variables are the indices of formalism and their component. Robust standard errors are in parentheses. All variables are described in Table I, and the data can be found at http://iicg.som.yale.edu/.

	Independent variables:						
Dependent variables:	Log GNP per capita	Socialist legal origin	French legal origin	German legal origin	Scandinavian legal origin	Constant	N [R^2]
			Panel A: Eviction of a tenant				
Formalism index	-0.1254b	0.7437a	1.3681a	0.7842a	0.5729b	4.0386a	109
	(0.0489)	(0.1791)	(0.1712)	(0.2257)	(0.2677)	(0.3789)	[0.44]
Professionals versus	-0.0115	0.1843a	0.2410a	0.1556b	0.1482c	0.5697a	109
laymen	(0.0180)	(0.0387)	(0.0562)	(0.0744)	(0.0851)	(0.1469)	[0.20]
Written versus oral	-0.0047	0.0435	0.1887a	0.1714b	0.0092	0.6644a	109
elements	(0.0102)	(0.0395)	(0.0342)	(0.0774)	(0.0790)	(0.0865)	[0.26]
Legal justification	0.0057	0.2710a	0.3092a	0.2991b	0.1306	0.4769a	109
	(0.0216)	(0.0902)	(0.0602)	(0.1273)	(0.1203)	(0.1776)	[0.22]
Statutory regulation	-0.0435a	0.0274	0.1171a	0.0489	0.0169	0.6557a	109
of evidence	(0.0102)	(0.0357)	(0.0333)	(0.0660)	(0.0524)	(0.0808)	[0.26]
Control of superior	-0.0276	0.2768a	0.0263	0.1053	0.2585a	0.8914a	109
review	(0.0171)	(0.0464)	(0.0617)	(0.0736)	(0.0931)	(0.1410)	[0.17]
Engagement	-0.0218	-0.1239b	0.3514a	-0.0242	0.0049	0.3520a	109
formalities	(0.0141)	(0.0571)	(0.0497)	(0.0772)	(0.0876)	(0.1190)	[0.46]
Independent	-0.0221b	0.0647	0.1343a	0.0281	0.0045	0.4285a	109
procedural actions	(0.0107)	(0.0424)	(0.0398)	(0.0520)	(0.0640)	(0.0909)	[0.17]
			Panel B: Check collection				
Formalism index	-0.2072a	1.0579a	1.5422a	0.7622a	0.8339a	4.4465a	109
	(0.0501)	(0.1915)	(0.1922)	(0.2464)	(0.2977)	(0.4042)	[0.48]
Professionals versus	-0.0420b	0.2154a	0.2568a	0.1473	0.1939b	0.7712a	109
laymen	(0.0185)	(0.0462)	(0.0656)	(0.0899)	(0.0952)	(0.1555)	[0.21]
Written versus oral	-0.0162	0.1386a	0.2751a	0.2207a	0.1330a	0.7090a	109
elements	(0.0099)	(0.0373)	(0.0343)	(0.0726)	(0.0467)	(0.0767)	[0.42]
Legal justification	-0.0328c	0.3533a	0.3809a	0.3609a	0.1824	0.6884a	109
	(0.0193)	(0.0852)	(0.0586)	(0.1191)	(0.1684)	(0.1615)	[0.32]
Statutory regulation	-0.0402a	0.0437	0.1080a	0.0965	0.0009	0.63 76a	109
of evidence	(0.0115)	(0.0398)	(0.0372)	(0.0656)	(0.0557)	(0.0915)	[0.20]
Control of superior	-0.0131	0.2687a	-0.0486	-0.1589c	0.2119b	0.7893a	109
review	(0.0169)	(0.0456)	(0.0615)	(0.0864)	(0.0940)	(0.1357)	[0.21]
Engagement	-0.0262c	-0.0866c	0.3580a	0.0235	0.0540	0.3485a	109
formalities	(0.0138)	(0.0446)	(0.0482)	(0.0745)	(0.0852)	(0.1175)	[0.47]
Independent	-0.0366a	0.1247b	0.2120a	0.0723c	0.0576	0.5025a	109
procedural actions	(0.0120)	(0.0478)	(0.0453)	(0.0429)	(0.0495)	(0.1039)	[0.26]

a = significant at 1 percent level; b = significant at 5 percent level; c = significant at 10 percent level.

Appendix 6

Table V

DURATION IN PRACTICE

This table classifies countries by legal origin and shows the duration in practice for both eviction and check collection. All variables are described in Table I, and the data can be found at http://iicg.som.yale.edu/.

	Eviction of a tenant				Check collection			
By legal origin	Duration until completion of service of process	Duration of trial	Duration of enforcement	Total duration	Duration until completion of service of process	Duration of trial	Duration of enforcement	Total duration
English legal origin								
Anguilla	1	60	30	91	1	30	7	38
Australia	3	35	6	44	25	160	135	320
Bahrain	41	120	224	385	54	114	200	368
Bangladesh	30	180	180	390	30	180	60	270
Barbados	4	67	21	92	2	49	60	111
Belize	30	15	14	59	30	15	15	60
Bermuda	4	25	21	50	4	100	21	125
Botswana	14	42	7	63	14	42	21	77
BVI	2	42	14	58	42	21	120	183
Canada	5	21	17	43	21	250	150	421
Cayman	30	136	14	180	30	60	30	120
Cyprus	60	120	180	360	60	120	180	360
Ghana	20	140	90	250	20	52	18	90
Gibraltar	160	50	14	224	160	50	14	224
Grenada	15	90	75	180	8	90	30	128
Hong Kong	7	35	150	192	7	40	14	61
India	142	24	46	212	7	53	46	106
Ireland	11	60	50	121	11	60	60	130
Israel	3	272	135	410	60	120	135	315
Jamaica	45	46	14	105	45	87	70	202
Kenya	12	122	121	255	12	122	121	255
Malawi	3	30	2	35	3	90	15	108
Malaysia	60	90	120	270	15	15	60	90
Namibia	11	25	83	118	11	25	83	118
New Zealand	10	40	30	80	10	30	20	60
Nigeria	32	126	208	366	81	100	60	241
Pakistan	60	245	60	365	60	185	120	365
Singapore	9	40	11	60	11	18	19	47
South Africa	10	189	10	209	10	60	14	84
Sri Lanka	90	440	200	730	60	200	180	440
St. Vincent	3	302	30	335	3	22	10	35
Swaziland	5	28	7	40	5	28	7	40
Tanzania	7	180	30	217	7	90	30	127
Thailand	30	510	90	630	30	90	90	210
Trinidad and	54	103	35	192	51	101	42	194
Turks and Caicos	14	100	60	174	14	30	30	74
UAE	14	180	90	285	14	365	180	559

Table V (continued)

By legal origin	Eviction of a tenant: Duration until completion of service of process	Eviction of a tenant: Duration of trial	Eviction of a tenant: Duration of enforcement	Eviction of a tenant: Total duration	Check collection: Duration until completion of service of process	Check collection: Duration of trial	Check collection: Duration of enforcement	Check collection: Total duration
Uganda	1	7	21	29	14	40	45	99
United Kingdom	14	73	28	115	14	73	14	101
USA	6	33	10	49	23	17	14	54
Zambia	14	90	7	111	14	120	54	188
Zimbabwe	8	180	9	197	8	180	9	197
Mean	**26**	**112**	**61**	**199**	**26**	**88**	**62**	**176**
Socialist legal origin								
Bulgaria	60	450	150	660	10	250	150	410
China	15	105	60	180	15	120	45	180
Croatia	60	180	90	330	60	180	90	330
Czech Republic	60	90	180	330	30	60	180	270
Estonia	59	136	110	305	59	136	110	305
Georgia	30	60	90	180	30	60	90	180
Hungary	90	185	90	365	90	185	90	365
Kazakhstan	10	50	60	120	10	50	60	120
Latvia	27	41	11	79	28	41	120	189
Lithuania	30	90	30	150	30	60	60	150
Poland	90	720	270	1080	90	730	180	1000
Romania	30	140	103	273	30	105	90	225
Russia	10	90	30	130	10	90	60	160
Slovenia	133	510	360	1003	133	510	360	1003
Ukraine	14	90	120	224	14	90	120	224
Vietnam	35	55	60	150	35	35	50	120
Mean	**47**	**187**	**113**	**347**	**42**	**169**	**116**	**327**
French legal origin								
Argentina	60	300	80	440	20	200	80	300
Belgium	3	60	57	120	0	20	100	120
Bolivia	14	60	20	94	14	360	90	464
Brazil	30	60	30	120	30	90	60	180
Chile	15	200	25	240	15	140	45	200
Colombia	139	279	82	500	165	216	146	527
Costa Rica	20	90	30	140	10	180	180	370
Cote d'Ivoire	8	120	2	130	8	82	60	150
Dominican Republic	30	90	90	210	35	90	90	215
Ecuador	38	40	30	108	38	235	60	333
Egypt	7	180	45	232	7	150	45	202
El Salvador	45	60	45	150	25	15	20	60
France	16	75	135	226	16	75	90	181
Greece	32	35	180	247	180	45	90	315
Guatemala	10	180	90	280	10	120	90	220
Honduras	15	30	30	75	30	90	105	225
Indonesia	30	165	30	225	30	165	30	225
Italy	0	450	180	630	0	415	230	645
Jordan	7	100	30	137	7	100	40	147
Kuwait	3	65	25	93	7	240	110	357
Lebanon	1	912	60	973	1	540	180	721
Luxembourg	20	120	240	380	15	45	150	210
Malta	30	610	90	730	30	365	150	545
Mexico	20	60	100	180	33	99	151	283
Monaco	17	86	16	119	24	26	16	66
Morocco	15	365	365	745	15	135	42	192
Mozambique	30	450	60	540	30	300	210	540

Table V (continued)

By legal origin	Eviction of a tenant: Duration until completion of service of process	Eviction of a tenant: Duration of trial	Eviction of a tenant: Duration of enforcement	Eviction of a tenant: Total duration	Check collection: Duration until completion of service of process	Check collection: Duration of trial	Check collection: Duration of enforcement	Check collection: Total duration
Netherlands	17	7	28	52	20	36	37	93
Netherl. Antilles	15	70	20	105	20	36	37	93
Panama	36	50	48	134	76	86	35	197
Paraguay	12	50	140	202	25	32	165	222
Peru	41	135	70	246	81	135	165	441
Philippines	42	97	25	164	42	97	25	164
Portugal	20	280	30	330	20	280	120	420
Senegal	5	60	90	155	5	150	180	335
Spain	60	55	68	183	49	69	29	147
Tunisia	3	28	2	33	3	1	3	7
Turkey	30	180	90	300	30	30	45	105
Uruguay	120	120	90	330	150	120	90	360
Venezuela	30	300	30	360	30	300	30	360
Mean	**27**	**167**	**72**	**266**	**34**	**147**	**90**	**272**
German legal origin								
Austria	7	360	180	547	14	270	150	434
Germany	29	191	111	331	29	61	64	154
Japan	3	350	10	363	3	47	10	60
Korea	30	180	93	303	20	40	15	75
Switzerland	16	180	70	266	59	75	90	224
Taiwan	30	120	180	330	30	60	120	210
Mean	**19**	**230**	**107**	**357**	**26**	**92**	**75**	**193**
Scandinavian legal Origin								
Denmark	20	180	25	225	15	40	28	83
Finland	15	70	35	120	35	145	60	240
Iceland	22	12	30	64	71	105	75	251
Norway	7	300	58	365	7	50	30	87
Sweden	6	135	19	160	6	165	19	190
Mean	**14**	**139**	**33**	**187**	**27**	**101**	**42**	**170**
Mean all countries	**29**	**151**	**74**	**254**	**31**	**122**	**80**	**234**
Tests of means(t-stats)								
Engl. v. Socialist	-2.05b	-1.84c	-2.46b	-2.42b	-1.74c	-2.37b	-2.91a	-2.85a
English v. French	-0.16	-1.66	-0.77	-1.64	-0.93	-2.66a	-2.16b	-2.94a
Engl. v. German	0.47	-2.49b	-1.65	-2.36b	0.03	-0.13	-0.52	-0.30
English v. Scandinavian	0.76	-0.52	0.95	0.17	-0.05	-0.39	0.76	0.10
Socialist v. French	2.23b	0.37	1.80c	1.14	0.71	0.51	1.33	0.91
Socialist v. German	1.90c	-0.51	0.15	-0.07	1.06	0.94	1.18	1.12
Socialist v. Scandinavian	2.08c	0.51	1.91c	1.14	0.88	0.78	2.05c	1.23
French v. German	0.68	-0.83	-1.14	-1.03	0.45	1.04	0.57	1.10
French v. Scandinavian	1.03	0.33	1.23	0.83	0.35	0.82	1.72c	1.33
German v. Scandinavian	0.82	1.43	2.44b	2.63b	-0.08	-0.19	1.19	0.32

a = significant at 1 percent level; b = significant at 5 percent level; c = significant at 10 percent level.

Source: Djankov et al., *supra* note 11, at 492–500.

Appendix 7

Table VI

OUTCOMES AND THE FORMALISM INDEX (OLS REGRESSIONS)

Ordinary least squares regressions of the cross section of countries. Robust standard errors are in parentheses. All variables are described in Table I, and the data can be found at http://iicg.som.yale.edu/.

Dependent variables:	Independent variables: Log GNP per capita	Formalism index	Ethnic fractionalization	Average years of schooling	Latitude	Constant	N $[R^2]$
	Panel A: Eviction of a tenant						
Log of duration	-0.0736	0.3012a	-0.2202	0.0305	0.1635	4.5593a	91
	(0.0937)	(0.0812)	(0.4766)	(0.0556)	(0.5432)	(0.7183)	[0.15]
Enforceability of contracts	0.7728a	-0.5648a	1.7036a	0.0755	0.7046	0.1959	50
	(0.1237)	(0.0863)	(0.4907)	(0.0612)	(0.5646)	(0.9043)	[0.85]
Legal system is fair and impartial	0.3501a	-0.5032a	-0.8773c	-0.1729a	0.0481	4.0479a	60
	(0.1094)	(0.0827)	(0.5192)	(0.0514)	(0.6593)	(0.9578)	[0.49]
Legal system is honest or uncorrupt	0.5087a	-0.4637a	-0.9113c	-0.1938a	0.2377	2.6552a	60
	(0.1050)	(0.0703)	(0.4679)	(0.0491)	(0.5956)	(0.8661)	[0.54]
Legal system is affordable	-0.0344	-0.1374b	-0.7111b	-0.0953b	0.3681	4.6225a	60
	(0.0918)	(0.0663)	(0.3528)	(0.0377)	(0.4174)	(0.6865)	[0.26]
Legal system is consistent	0.3379a	-0.2847a	-0.6666	-0.1621a	0.3352	2.7261a	60
	(0.1060)	(0.0774)	(0.4376)	(0.0466)	(0.5306)	(0.8494)	[0.41]
Confidence in legal system	0.3250a	-0.1289c	-0.4663	-0.0781c	-0.7303	2.6542a	60
	(0.0999)	(0.0758)	(0.4223)	(0.0411)	(0.4862)	(0.8153)	[0.29]
Corruption	1.5238a	-0.6393a	-0.2640	-0.0998	0.5314	-4.5186a	76
	(0.1365)	(0.1189)	(0.5182)	(0.0632)	(0.7226)	(0.9537)	[0.87]
Law and Order	0.9416a	-0.3594c	-0.0867	-0.1632	4.4505a	0.1644	82
	(0.2245)	(0.2107)	(0.7624)	(0.1048)	(1.2861)	(1.9529)	[0.57]
	Panel B: Check collection						
Log of duration	-0.0377	0.3038a	0.7677	0.0693	0.0866	3.6403a	91
	(0.0826)	(0.0598)	(0.4969)	(0.0599)	(0.4612)	(0.6473)	[0.20]
Enforceability of contracts	0.6013a	-0.5041a	1.6713a	0.1304b	0.8437	0.8848	50
	(0.1310)	(0.0684)	(0.4586)	(0.0618)	(0.5685)	(0.8835)	[0.86]
Legal system is fair and impartial	0.2567b	-0.4415a	-1.0089b	-0.1522a	0.0171	4.4417a	60
	(0.1080)	(0.0582)	(0.4777)	(0.0524)	(0.5951)	(0.8833)	[0.52]
Legal system is honest or uncorrupt	0.4258a	-0.3950a	-1.0105b	-0.1756a	0.2284	2.9389a	60
	(0.1076)	(0.0568)	(0.4347)	(0.0522)	(0.5504)	(0.8239)	[0.55]
Legal system is affordable	-0.0564	-0.1074b	-0.7225b	-0.0906b	0.3811	4.6416a	60
	(0.0940)	(0.0497)	(0.3493)	(0.0388)	(0.4141)	(0.6895)	[0.25]
Legal system is consistent	0.2814b	-0.2637a	-0.7670c	-0.1493a	0.2951	3.0424a	60
	(0.1071)	(0.0539)	(0.4261)	(0.0485)	(0.4998)	(0.8246)	[0.44]
Confidence in legal system	0.2943a	-0.1393b	-0.5487	-0.0707c	-0.7808	2.9304a	60
	(0.0996)	(0.0530)	(0.4193)	(0.0411)	(0.4766)	(0.8039)	[0.31]
Corruption	1.4255a	-0.4528a	-0.2994	-0.0761	0.7321	-4.6737a	76
	(0.1494)	(0.1077)	(0.5308)	(0.0707)	(0.7556)	(1.0804)	[0.85]
Law and Order	0.9261a	-0.2647	-0.0359	-0.1615	4.5262a	-0.1441	82
	(0.2160)	(0.1915)	(0.7375)	(0.1063)	(1.2763)	(1.7720)	[0.57]

a = significant at 1 percent level; b = significant at 5 percent level; c = significant at 10 percent level.

Appendix 8

Table VII

OUTCOMES AND THE FORMALISM INDEX (INSTRUMENTAL VARIABLES REGRESSIONS)

Instrumental variables regressions of the cross section of countries using legal origins dummies as instruments for formalism. Standard errors are in parentheses. All variables are described in Table I.

	Independent variables:						
Dependent variables:	Log GNP per capita	Formalism index	Ethnic fractionalization	Average years of schooling	Latitude	Constant	N
			Panel A: Eviction of a tenant				
Log of duration	-0.0766	0.2486c	-0.2583	0.0276	0.1544	4.8183a	91
	(0.0935)	(0.1299)	(0.4826)	(0.0551)	(0.5485)	(0.9317)	
Enforceability of contracts	0.7854a	-0.7656a	1.6159a	0.0605	0.5138	1.0620	50
	(0.1243)	(0.1586)	(0.5441)	(0.0625)	(0.6369)	(1.1726)	
Legal system is fair and impartial	0.3358a	-0.8331a	-1.3299b	-0.1634a	-0.4026	5.7299a	60
	(0.1101)	(0.1363)	(0.5368)	(0.0547)	(0.7484)	(0.0021)	
Legal system is honest or uncorrupt	0.4954a	-0.7735a	-1.3363a	-0.1849a	-0.1856	4.2348a	60
	(0.1067)	(0.1334)	(0.4782)	(0.0523)	(0.6876)	(0.9426)	
Legal system is affordable	-0.0367	-0.1920	-0.7859b	-0.0937b	0.2936	4.9006a	60
	(0.0899)	(0.1149)	(0.3867)	(0.0374)	(0.4227)	(0.8735)	
Legal system is consistent	0.3277a	-0.5218a	-0.9919b	-0.1553a	0.0113	3.9350a	60
	(0.981)	(0.1314)	(0.4379)	(0.0470)	(0.5824)	(0.9125)	
Confidence in legal system	0.3170a	-0.3149b	-0.7214	-0.0728c	-0.9843c	3.6022a	60
	(0.0995)	(0.1212)	(0.4395)	(0.0422)	(0.5335)	(1.0189)	
Corruption	1.5277a	-0.9139a	-0.4378	-0.1108c	0.3227	-3.2976a	76
	(0.1356)	(0.1565)	(0.5586)	(0.0648)	(0.8019)	(1.1151)	
Law and Order	0.8983a	-0.8432b	-0.5352	-0.1710	4.0787a	2.7075	82
	(0.2321)	(0.3192)	(0.7586)	(0.1080)	(1.2767)	(2.3042)	
			Panel B: Check collection				
Log of duration	-0.0365	0.3117a	0.7746	0.0697	0.0881	3.5959a	91
	(0.0862)	(0.1034)	(0.4707)	(0.0587)	(0.4660)	(0.7668)	
Enforceability of contracts	0.5637a	-0.6438a	1.5940a	0.1339b	0.7335	1.7504	50
	(0.1366)	(0.1353)	(0.4977)	(0.0642)	(0.6396)	(1.1637)	
Legal system is fair and impartial	0.1905c	-0.6955a	-1.4818a	-0.1319b	-0.3962	6.1443a	60
	(0.1100)	(0.1076)	(0.4962)	(0.0571)	(0.6871)	(0.9813)	
Legal system is honest or uncorrupt	0.3610a	-0.6436a	-1.4733a	-0.1558b	-0.1761	4.6052a	60
	(0.1137)	(0.1118)	(0.4611)	(0.0580)	(0.6635)	(1.0004)	
Legal system is affordable	-0.0718	-0.1664c	-0.8323b	-0.0859b	0.2851	5.0370a	60
	(0.0966)	(0.0950)	(0.4009)	(0.0393)	(0.4301)	(0.9297)	
Legal system is consistent	0.2354b	-0.4403a	-1.0957b	-0.1352b	0.0077	4.2260a	60
	(0.1027)	(0.1021)	(0.4338)	(0.0503)	(0.5451)	(0.9241)	
Confidence in legal system	0.2616b	-0.2644a	-0.7816c	-0.0607	-0.9843c	3.7688a	60
	(0.1067)	(0.0953)	(0.4375)	(0.0436)	(0.5010)	(1.0289)	
Corruption	1.3683a	-0.7426a	-0.5811	-0.0775	0.5495	-2.9536b	76
	(0.1565)	(0.1527)	(0.5755)	(0.0761)	(0.8372)	(1.3086)	
Law and Order	0.8290a	-0.8054b	-0.6128	-0.1701	4.1170a	3.0842	82
	(0.2209)	(0.3159)	(0.8051)	(0.1097)	(1.3400)	(2.4298)	

a = significant at 1 percent level; b = significant at 5 percent level; c = significant at 10 percent level.

Appendix 9

Table VIII

OUTCOMES AND INCENTIVES (OLS REGRESSIONS)

Ordinary least squares regressions of the cross section of countries. The regressions also include log of GNP per capita, ethnic fractionalization, average years of schooling, latitude, and a constant term. Robust standard errors are in parentheses. All variables are described in Table I, and the data can be found at http://iicg.som.yale.edu/.

	Selected independent variables:				
Dependent variables:	Formalism index	Index of mandatory time limits	Quota litis prohibited	Loser pays rule	N [R^2]
	Panel A: Eviction of a tenant				
Log of duration	0.4303a	-0.6335	0.3162c	0.0383	91
	(0.1030)	(0.3931)	(0.1768)	(0.1722)	[0.21]
Enforceability of	-0.5465a	-0.4260	-0.0642	0.1393	50
contracts	(0.0965)	(0.4977)	(0.2147)	(0.2278)	[0.86]
Legal system is fair	-0.4019a	-0.4282	0.0520	-0.2147	60
and impartial	(0.1135)	(0.3504)	(0.1550)	(0.1574)	[0.52]
Legal system is	-0.3557a	-0.5440	-0.0751	-0.2704	60
honest or uncorrupt	(0.1024)	(0.3527)	(0.1650)	(0.1694)	[0.58]
Legal system is	-0.2077b	0.2588	-0.2991c	-0.1124	60
affordable	(0.1019)	(0.3326)	(0.1652)	(0.1432)	[0.33]
Legal system is	-0.1820c	-0.4575	-0.0045	-0.2557c	60
consistent	(0.0951)	(0.2974)	(0.1423)	(0.1404)	[0.47]
Confidence in legal	-0.0234	-0.4047	-0.0717	-0.4249a	60
system	(0.0882)	(0.3114)	(0.1365)	(0.1386)	[0.43]
Corruption	-0.5351a	-0.4128	0.0527	-0.1617	76
	(0.1670)	(0.6082)	(0.2273)	(0.2230)	[0.87]
Law and order	-0.0543	-1.2233	1.1384a	0.3560	82
	(0.2562)	(0.7414)	(0.3702)	(0.3745)	[0.64]
	Panel B: Check collection				
Log of duration	0.3239a	-0.1918	0.1040	0.1054	91
	(0.0850)	(0.3328)	(0.1930)	(0.1544)	[0.20]
Enforceability of	-0.4557a	-0.2515	-0.0242	-0.0785	50
contracts	(0.0967)	(0.4798)	(0.2259)	(0.2032)	[0.86]
Legal system is fair	-0.2930a	-0.8371a	0.0897	-0.3587b	60
and impartial	(0.0735)	(0.2968)	(0.1440)	(0.1490)	[0.61]
Legal system is	-0.2870a	-0.5676	-0.0619	-0.4496a	60
honest or uncorrupt	(0.0799)	(0.3458)	(0.1654)	(0.1666)	[0.62]
Legal system is	-0.1394c	0.1677	-0.2870c	-0.1541	60
affordable	(0.0755)	(0.3198)	(0.1649)	(0.1392)	[0.31
Legal system is	-0.1683b	-0.5283c	-0.0081	-0.3085b	60
consistent	(0.0714)	(0.2909)	(0.1535)	(0.1384)	[0.51]

Table VIII (continued)

Dependent variables:	Formalism index	Index of mandatory time limits	Quota litis prohibited	Loser pays rule	N [R^2]
	Selected independent variables:				
Confidence in legal system	-0.0866	-0.1780	-0.1018	-0.4514a	60
	(0.0710)	(0.3231)	(0.1502)	(0.1277)	[0.43]
Corruption	-0.2762b	-0.6330	0.1550	-0.5330b	76
	(0.1243)	(0.4452)	(0.2436)	(0.2175)	[0.86]
Law and order	0.1890	-2.3986a	1.3469a	0.1304	82
	(0.2369)	(0.7659)	(0.3783)	(0.3639)	[0.67]

a = significant at 1 percent level; b = significant at 5 percent level; c = significant at 10 percent level.

Source: Djankov et al., *supra* note 11, at 508–509.

Bibliography

Acomb, Robert B., Jr.: *Foreign Depositions: The Problems, Pitfalls and Procedures*, 14 THE FORUM 440–458 (1978/1979)

ADLER, STEPHEN J.: THE JURY, New York 1995

Alesina, Alberto & Eliana La Ferrara: *Ethnic Diversity and Ethnic Performance*, 43 JOURNAL OF ECONOMIC LITERATURE 762–800 (2005) = NBER Working Paper 10313 (2004), <http://www.nber.org/papers/w10313.pdf> (last visited July 17, 2006)

Alesina, Alberto, Arnaud Devleeschauwer, William Easterly, Sergio Kurlat & Romain Wacziarg: *Fractionalization*, NBER Working Paper 9411 (2002), <http://www.nber.org/papers/w9411.pdf> (last visited July 17, 2006)

ALI/UNIDROIT: PRINCIPLES OF TRANSNATIONAL CIVIL PROCEDURE, Cambridge, New York 2006

—: Principles of Transnational Civil Procedure, IX UNIF. L. REV. NS 749–809 (2004-4), English version *available at* <http://www.unidroit.org/english/principles/civilprocedure/ali-unidroitprinciples-e.pdf> (last visited July 17, 2006)

Allen, Ronald J.: *Idealization and Caricature in Comparative Scholarship*, 82 NW. U. L. REV. 785–807 (1988)

Allen, Ronald J., Stefan Köck, Kurt Riecherberg & D. Toby Rosen: *The German Advantage in Civil Procedure: A Plea for More Details and Fewer Generalities in Comparative Scholarship*, 82 NW. U. L. REV. 705–762 (1988)

Amir N. Licht, Chanan Goldschmidt & Shalom H. Schwartz: *Culture, Law, and Corporate Governance*, 25 INT'L REV. L. & ECON. 229–255 (2005)

ANDENAS, MADS, NEIL ANDREWS & RENATO NAZZINI, EDS.: THE FUTURE OF TRANSNATIONAL CIVIL LITIGATION, London 2004

ANDREWS, NEIL: ENGLISH CIVIL PROCEDURE, Oxford, New York 2003

AYASTA GONZALEZ, JULIO: EL DERECHO COMPARADO Y LOS JURÍDICOS CONTEMPORANEOS, Lima 1991

Barth, James R., Gerard Caprio Jr. & Ross Levine: *Bank regulation and supervision: what works best?*, 13 JOURNAL OF FINANCIAL INTERMEDIATION 205–248 (2004)

Baudenbacher, Carl: *Some Remarks on the Method of Civil Law*, 34 TEX. INT'L L.J. 333–360 (1999)

Baur, Fritz: *Richtermacht und Formalismus im Verfahrensrecht*, *in* SUMMUM IUS SUMA INIURIA 97–116 (Tübingen 1963) = FRITZ BAUR, BEITRÄGE ZUR GERICHTSVERFASSUNG UND ZUM ZIVILPROZESSRECHT 115–134 (Tübingen 1983), Italian translation: Fritz Baur, *Potere giudiziale e formalismo nel diritto processuale*, 19 RIVISTA TRIMESTRALE DI DIRITTO E PROCEDURA CIVILE 1683–1704 (1965)

Beck, Thorsten, Asli Demirgüç-Kunt & Ross Levine: *Law, Endowments, and Finance*, 70 J. ECON. FIN. 137–181 (2003)

Bentham, Jeremy: *Principles of Judicial Procedure, with the outlines of a Procedure Code*, *in* THE WORKS OF JEREMY BENTHAM, Reprod. of the Bowring ed. of 1838 – 1843, vol. 2, New York 1962

BERI S.A.: *Historical Ratings Research Package User Guide*

Beys, Kostas E.: *Die Ausstrahlung des deutschen zivilprozessualen Denkens auf das griechische Recht der Privatrechtsstreitigkeiten*, *in* DAS DEUTSCHE ZIVILPROZESSRECHT UND SEINE AUSSTRAHLUNG AUF ANDERE RECHTSORDNUNGEN 300–332 (Walther J. Habscheid, ed., Bielefeld 1991)

BÖHM, ULRIKE: AMERIKANISCHES ZIVILPROZESSRECHT, Cologne 2005

Bone, Robert G.: *Mapping the Boundaries of the Dispute: Conceptions of Ideal Lawsuit Structure from the Field Code to the Federal Rules*, 89 COLUM. L. REV. 1–118 (1989)

Borel, Jacques & Stephen M. Boyd: *Opportunities for and Obstacles to Obtaining Evidence in France for Use in the United States*, 13 INT'L LAW. 35–45 (1979)

Botero, Juan, Simeon Djankov, Rafael La Porta, Florencio Lopez-de-Silanes & Andrei Shleifer: *The Regulation of Labor*, 119 THE QUARTERLY JOURNAL OF ECONOMICS 1339–1382 (2004), first published as NBER Working Paper 9756 (2003), <http://papers.nber.org/papers/w9756.pdf> (last visited July 17, 2006)

Brada, Josef C.: *What Is Comparative Economics, and What Ought It Be?*, 31 COMPARATIVE ECONOMIC STUDIES 16–23 (1989)

Braeutigam, Ronald, Bruce Owen & John Panzar: *An Economic Analysis of Alternative Fee Shifting Systems*, 47 LAW AND CONTEMPORARY PROBLEMS 173–185 (1984)

BREYER, MICHAEL: KOSTENORIENTIERTE STEUERUNG DES ZIVILPROZESSES, Tübingen 2006

Broun, Kenneth S.: *Giving Codification a Second Chance – Testimonial Privileges and the Federal Rules of Evidence*, 53 HASTINGS L.J. 769–815 (2002)

Bruns, Alexander: *Das Verbot der quota litis und die erfolgshonorierte Prozeßfinanzierung*, 55 JZ 232–241 (2000)

Bryan, Bradley: *Justice and Advantage in Civil Procedure: Langbein's Conception of Comparative Law and Procedural Justice in Question*, 11 TULSA J. COMP. & INT'L L. 521–555 (2004)

Cammack, Mark: *Evidence Rules and the Ritual Functions of Trials: "Saying Something of Something"*, 25 LOY. L.A. L. REV. 783–796 (1992)

Cappelletti, Mauro & Bryant G. Garth: *Introduction – Policies, Trends and Ideas in Civil Procedure*, *in* INTERNATIONAL ENCYCLOPEDIA OF COMPARATIVE LAW, VOL. XVI, CIVIL PROCEDURE, CH. 1 (Mauro Cappelletti, chief ed., Tübingen 1987)

CAPPELLETTI, MAURO & JOSEPH M. PERILLO: CIVIL PROCEDURE IN ITALY, The Hague 1965

Cappelletti, Mauro: *An Open Letter to Professor Hans Schima about the Need, Difficulties and Purposes of Comparative Civil Procedure*, *in* FESTSCHRIFT FÜR HANS SCHIMA ZUM 75. GEBURTSTAG 125–131 (Hans W. Fasching & Winfried Kralik, eds., Vienna 1969)

Carrington, Paul D.: *The Seventh Amendment: Some Bicentennial Reflections*, 1990 U. CHI. L. F. 33–86

—: *Virtual Civil Litigation: A Visit to John Bunyan's Celestial City*, 98 COLUM. L. REV. 1516, 1533–1534 (1998)

—: *Teaching Civil Procedure: A Retrospective View*, 49 J. LEGAL EDUC. 311–332 (1999)

—: *The Civil Jury and American Democracy*, 13 DUKE J. COMP. & INT'L L. 79–94 (2003)

Chase, Oscar G.: *Legal Processes and National Culture*, 5 CARDOZO J. INT'L & COMP. L. 1–24 (1997)

—: *Some Observations on the Cultural Dimension in Civil Procedure Reform*, 45 AM. J. COMP. L. 861–870 (1997)

—: LAW, CULTURE AND RITUAL, New York 2005

Chemlíček, Petr: *Einführung in das Tschechische Zivilprozessrecht*, 7 ZEITSCHRIFT FÜR ZIVILPROZESS INTERNATIONAL [ZZPINT] 429–450 (2002)

Chodosh, Hiram E.: *Reforming Judicial Reform Inspired by U.S. Models*, 52 DEPAUL L. REV. 351–381 (2002)

—: *Emergence from the Dilemmas of Justice Reform*, 38 TEX. INT'L L.J. 587–620 (2003)

CIA: CIA World Factbook 2000, *available at* <https://www.cia.gov/cia/download 2000.html> (last visited July 17, 2006, formerly <http://odci.gov/cia/download.html>)

Clark, David S.: *The Civil Law Influence on David Dudley Field's Code of Civil Procedure*, *in* THE RECEPTION OF CONTINENTAL IDEAS IN THE COMMON LAW WORLD 1820–1920 63–97 (Mathias Reimann, ed., Berlin 1993)

Coase, Ronald H.: *The Problem of Social Cost*, 3 JOURNAL OF LAW AND ECONOMICS 1–44 (1960)

COESTER-WALTJEN, DAGMAR: INTERNATIONALES BEWEISRECHT, Ebelsbach 1983

CYPHER, JAMES M. & JAMES L. DIETZ: THE PROCESS OF ECONOMIC DEVELOPMENT, 2nd ed., London 2004

DAMAŠKA, MIRJAN R.: EVIDENCE LAW ADRIFT, New Haven 1997

—: THE FACES OF JUSTICE AND STATE AUTHORITY: A COMPARATIVE APPROACH TO THE LEGAL PROCESS, New Haven 1986

Damle, Sarang Vijay: *Specialize the Judge, Not the Court: A Lesson From the German Constitutional Court*, 91 VA. L. REV. 1267–1311 (2005)

David, René: *De l'importance d'études comparatives relatives à la procedure*, *in* ESTUDIOS JURIDICOS EN MEMORIA DE EDUARDO J. COUTURE 929–938 (Montevideo 1957)

—: FRENCH LAW: ITS STRUCTURE, SOURCES, AND METHODOLOGY (Michael Kindred, transl.,) Baton Rouge 1972

DAVIS, JOSEPH W.S.: DISPUTE RESOLUTION IN JAPAN, The Hague 1996

Davis, Kevin E.: *What can the rule of law variable tell us about rule of law reforms?*, 26 MICH. J. INT'L L. 141–161 (2004)

DE LEVAL, GEORGES: ÉLÉMENTS DE PROCÉDURE CIVILE, Bruxelles 2003

DELEBECQUE, PHILIPPE & MICHEL GERMAIN: 2 TRAITÉ DE DROIT COMMERCIAL, 17th ed., Paris 2004

Department of Justice: *Number of Federal Tort Trials Fell by Almost 80 Percent from 1985 through 2003*, Press Release of August 17, 2005, *available at* <http://www.ojp.usdoj.gov/newsroom/2005/fttv03pr.htm> (last visited July 17, 2006)

Dickopf, Karl: *Friedrich Thiersch und Georg Ludwig von Maurer – Zwei Konzeptionen zum Neubau eines griechischen Staates in den Jahren 1833/1834*, 56 ZEITSCHRIFT FÜR BAYERISCHE LANDESGESCHICHTE [ZBLG] 165–174 (1993)

—: GEORG LUDWIG VON MAURER 1790–1872 – EINE BIOGRAPHIE, Kallmünz 1960

Djankov, Simeon, Caralee McLiesh & Andrei Shleifer: *Private Credit in 129 Countries*, NBER Working Paper 11078 (2005), <http://papers.nber.org/papers/w11078.pdf> (last visited July 17, 2006)

Djankov, Simeon, Caralee McLiesh, Tatiana Nenova & Andrei Shleifer: *Who Owns the Media?*, 46 JOURNAL OF LAW AND ECONOMICS 341–381 (2003), first published as NBER Working Paper 8288 (2001), <http://papers.nber.org/papers/w8288.pdf> (last visited July 17, 2006)

Djankov, Simeon, Edward L. Glaeser, Rafael La Porta, Florencio Lopez-de-Silanes &Andrei Shleifer: *The New Comparative Economics*, 31 JOURNAL OF COMPARATIVE ECONOMICS 595–619 (2003), first published as NBER Working Paper 9608 (2003), <http://papers.nber.org/papers/w9608.pdf> (last visited July 17, 2006)

Djankov, Simeon, Rafael La Porta, Florencio Lopez-de-Silanes & Andrei Shleifer: *The Regulation of Entry*, 117 QUARTERLY JOURNAL OF ECONOMICS 1–37 (2002), first published as NBER Working Paper 7892 (2001), <http://papers.nber.org/papers/w7892.pdf> (last visited July 17, 2006)

—: *Courts*, 118 QUARTERLY JOURNAL OF ECONOMICS 453–517 (2003), first published with the title *Courts: The Lex Mundi Project* as NBER Working Paper 8890 (2002), <http://papers.nber.org/papers/w8890.pdf> (last visited July 17, 2006)

—: *The Law and Economics of Self-Dealing*, NBER Working Paper 11883 (2005) <http://papers.nber.org/papers/w11883.pdf> (last visited July 17, 2006)

—: *The Regulation of Entry*, 117 QUARTERLY JOURNAL OF ECONOMICS 1–37 (2002)

DWORKIN, RONALD M.: A MATTER OF PRINCIPLE 72–103, Cambridge, Mass. 1985

Easton, Stephen D.: *Cashing in Your Credibility During Final Argument*, 46-APR FED. LAW. 30–34 (1999)

EBRD & World Bank: Business Environment and Enterprise Performance Survey Screener Questionnaire, <http://info.worldbank.org/governance/beeps2002/beeps2_questions.pdf> (last visited July 17, 2006)

EBRD & World Bank: World Business Environment Survey Screener Questionnaire, <http://www.worldbank.org/wbi/governance/pdf/beeps_questions.pdf> (last visited July 17, 2006)

Ehricke, Ulrich: *Art. 12 I (ex 6 I) EG-Vertrag und das nationale Zivilprozessrecht – Bilanz und Perspektiven*, 19 PRAXIS DES INTERNATIONALEN PRIVAT- UND VERFAHRENSRECHTS [IPRAX] 311–323 (1999)

Ekeløf, Per Olof: *Schweden und das deutsche Zivilprozeßrecht*, *in* DAS DEUTSCHE ZIVILPROZESSRECHT UND SEINE AUSSTRAHLUNG AUF ANDERE RECHTSORDNUNGEN 214–218 (Walther J. Habscheid, ed., Bielefeld 1991)

EUROPEAN COMMISSION FOR THE EFFICIENCY OF JUSTICE: EUROPEAN JUDICIAL SYSTEMS 2002 (2005), *available at* <http://www.coe.int/t/e/legal_affairs/legal_co%2Doperation/operation_of_justice/efficiency_of_justice/systeme%20judiciaire%20A.pdf> (last visited July 17, 2006)

Fabri, Marco & Philip M. Langbroek: *Delay in judicial proceedings : a preliminary inquiry into the relation between the demands of the reasonable time requirements of article 6, 1 ECHR and their consequences for judges and judicial administration in the civil, criminal and administrative justice chains* 8, Preliminary Draft Report, Working Party N° 2 of the European Commission for the Efficiency of Justice (CEPEJ-GT2), *available at* <http://www.coe.int/t/e/legal_affairs/legal_co%2Doperation/operation_of_justice/efficiency_of_justice/documents/20%202003%20E%20report%20Fabri%20Langbroek%20rev%20nov2003.pdf> (last visited July 17, 2006)

Farina, Cynthia R.: *Conceiving Due Process*, 3 YALE J.L. & FEMINISM 189–279 (1991)

FAZZALARI, ELIO & PIERRE FORTIN (EDS.): CIVIL JUSTICE IN THE COUNTRIES OF THE EUROPEAN UNION, Padova 1998

FERNANDEZ DE CORDOVA, PEDRO: ESTUDIOS DE DERECHO COMPARADO, Quito 1997

FERRAND, FRÉDÉRIQUE, ED.: LA PROCÉDURE CIVILE MONDIALE MODÉLISÉE, Paris 2004

Fiss, Owen M.: *Against Settlement*, 93 YALE L.J. 1073–1090 (1984)

FLEMING JAMES, JR., GEOFFREY C. HAZARD, JR. & JOHN LEUBSDORF: CIVIL PROCEDURE, 5th ed., New York 2001

FOUCHARD, PHILIPPE, ED.: VERS UN PROCES CIVIL UNIVERSEL? LES RÈGLES TRANSNATIONALES DE PROCÉDURE DE L'AMERICAN LAW INSTITUTE (2001)

Frank B. Cross: *America the Adversarial*, 89 VA. L. REV. 189–237 (2003) (reviewing Robert A. Kagan, Adversarial Legalism: The American Way of Law (2001))

FRIEDENTHAL, JACK H., MARY KAY KANE & ARTHUR R. MILLER: CIVIL PROCEDURE, 4th ed., St. Paul, Minn. 2005

Friedman, Richard D.: *Anchors and Flotsam: Is Evidence Law "Adrift"?*, 107 Yale L.J. 1921–1967 (1998) (reviewing Mirjan R. Damaška, Evidence Law Adrift (1997))

Galanter, Marc: *Reading the Landscape of Disputes: What We Know and Don't Know (and Think We Know) about Our Allegedly Contentious and Litigious Society*, 31 UCLA L. REV. 4–71 (1983)

—: *The Vanishing Trial: An Examination of Trials and Related Matters in Federal and State Courts*, 1 J. EMPIRICAL LEGAL STUD. 459–570 (2004)

—: *The Hundred-year Decline of Trials and the Thirty Years War*, 2005 STAN. L. REV. 1255–1274

Gandasubrata, Purwoto: *Indonesia*, *in* ADMINISTRATION OF JUSTICE: PROCEDURAL REFORMS ON COURT CONGESTION, 1980 ASEAN COMPARATIVE LAW SERIES, VOL. 2, 1 (Purificacion Valera-Quisumbing, volume ed., Manila 1982)

Gilles, Peter: *Prozessrechtsvergleichung – Comparative Procedural Law*, *in* TRANSNATIONAL ASPECTS OF PROCEDURAL LAW 967–1091 (Int'l Ass'n of Procedural Law, ed., Milano 1998)

Goldstein, Stephen: *Contrasting Views of Adjudication: An Israeli-American Comparison*, *in* GEDÄCHTNISSCHRIFT FÜR PETER ARENS 169–186 (Dieter Leipold, Wolfgang Lüke & Shozaburo Yoshino, eds., Munich 1993)

—: *On Comparing and Unifying Civil Procedural Systems*, *in* PROCESS AND SUBSTANCE, BUTTERWORTH LECTURES 1994, 1-43 (Roger Cotterrell, ed., London 1995)

—: *The Utility of the Comparative Perspective in Understanding, Analyzing and Reforming Procedural Law*, 5 ZZPINT 375–392 (2000)

GOODMAN, CARL F.: JUSTICE AND CIVIL PROCEDURE IN JAPAN, Dobbs Ferry, NY 2004

Gottwald, Peter: *Aktive Richter – Managerial Judges*, *in* LAW IN EAST AND WEST 705–718 (Institute of Comparative Law, Waseda University, ed., Tokyo 1988)

—: *Civil Procedure in Germany after the Reform Act of 2001*, 23 C.J.Q. 338–353 (2004)

—: *Zum Stand der Zivilprozessrechtsvergleichung*, *in* FESTSCHRIFT FÜR PETER SCHLOSSER ZUM 70. GEBURTSTAG 227–245 (Birgit Bachmann, Stephan Breidenbach, Dagmar Coester-Waltjen, Burkhard Heß, Andreas Nelle & Christian Wolf, eds., 2005)

GRAF LAMBSDORFF, JOHANN: FRAMEWORK DOCUMENT. BACKGROUND PAPER TO THE 2001 CORRUPTION PERCEPTIONS INDEX (2001), <http://www.transparency.org/content/download/1936/11436/file/methodology.pdf> (last visited July 17, 2006)

Greger, Reinhard: *Die ZPO-Reform – 1000 Tage danach*, 59 JURISTENZEITUNG (JZ) 805–817 (2004)

GROSSFELD, BERNHARD: THE STRENGTH AND WEAKNESS OF COMPARATIVE LAW (Tony Weir, trans.), Oxford 1990

GUINCHARD, SERGE, MONIQUE BANDRAC, CONSTANTIN S. DÉLICOSTOPULOS, IOANNIS S. DÉLICOSTPOULOS, MÉLINA DOUCHY-OUDOT, FRÉDÉRIQUE FERRAND, XAVIER LAGARDE, VÉRONIQUE MAGNIER, HÉLÈNE RUIZ FABRI, LAURENCE SINOPOLI, JEAN-MARC SOREL: DROIT PROCESSUEL, 3rd ed., Paris 2005

GUINCHARD, SERGE & FRÉDÉRIQUE FERRAND: PROCÉDURE CIVILE, Droit interne et droit communautaire, 28th ed., Paris 2006

GWARTNEY, JAMES D., ROBERT LAWSON & WALTER BLOCK: ECONOMIC FREEDOM OF THE WORLD 1975–1995, Vancouver 1996

HABSCHEID, EDGAR, ED.: DER JUSTIZKONFLIKT MIT DEN VEREINIGTEN STAATEN VON AMERIKA/THE JURISDICTION CONFLICT WITH THE UNITED STATES OF AMERICA, Bielefeld 1986

HARTWIEG, OSKAR: DIE KUNST DES SACHVORTRAGS IM ZIVILPROZESS, Heidelberg 1988

Hasenböhler, Franz: *Beweisrecht, vorsorgliche Maßnahmen und Schutzschrift*, *in* DIE KÜNFTIGE SCHWEIZERISCHE ZIVILPROZESSORDNUNG 25–50 (Thomas Sutter-Somm & Franz Hasenböhler, eds., Zurich 2003)

HATTORI, TAKAAKI & DAN FENNO HENDERSON: CIVIL PROCEDURE IN JAPAN (2nd ed., loose-leaf, Huntington, NY, release 2, December 2004)

Hazard, Jr., Geoffrey C.: *Discovery and the Role of the Judge in Civil Law Jurisdictions*, 73 NOTRE DAME L. REV. 1017–1028 (1998)

HEATH, CHRISTOPHER & ANJA PETERSEN (EDS.): DAS JAPANISCHE ZIVILPROZESSRECHT, Tübingen 2002

Hecht, Nathan L.: *The Vanishing Civil Jury Trial: Trends in Texas Courts an and Uncertain Future*, 47 S. TEX. L. REV. 163–190 (2005)

Henckel, Wolfram: *Zur Geschichte der Zivilprozeßrechtslehrervereinigung 1920–1933*, *in* FESTSCHRIFT FÜR HANS W. FASCHING ZUM 65. GEBURTSTAG 213–226 (Richard Holzhammer, Wolfgang Jelinek & Peter Böhm, eds., Vienna 1988)

Herzog, Peter E. & Delmar Karlen: *Attacks on Judicial Decisions*, *in* INTERNATIONAL ENCYCLOPEDIA OF COMPARATIVE LAW, VOL. XVI, CIVIL PROCEDURE, CH. 8 (Mauro Cappelletti, chief ed., Tübingen 1982)

Hess, Burkhard: *Aktuelle Brennpunkte des transatlantischen Justizkonflikts*, 50 DIE AKTIENGESELLSCHAFT [AG] 897–905 (2005)

Higgins, Steve: *Eminent Group Gathers at Yale*, New Haven Register.com, September 10, 2005, <http://www.yale.edu/opa/download/newsYale/eminentGroup_nhReg_091005.pdf> (last visited July 17, 2006)

HOMMERICH, CHRISTOPH, HANNS PRÜTTING, THOMAS EBERS, SONJA LANG & LUDGER TRAUT: RECHTSTATSÄCHLICHE UNTERSUCHUNG ZU DEN AUSWIRKUNGEN DER REFORM DES ZIVILPROZESSRECHTS AUF DIE GERICHTLICHE PRAXIS – EVALUATION ZPO-REFORM (Bundesministerium der Justiz, ed., Cologne 2006)

Hong, Peder B.: *A Theory of Final Argument in Civil Trials*, 21 HAMLINE L. REV. 31–63 (1997)

Hoonaker, Philippe: *Comment introduire l'instance*, *in* DROIT ET PRATIQUE DE LA PROCÉDURE CIVILE ¶¶ 1701–1900, p. 365–411 (Serge Guinchard, ed., Paris 2002)

Horan, Dennis J., Thomas L. Browne & George W. Spellmire: *Practical Tips in Handling a Legal Malpractice Case: Complaint Through Trial*, 9 AM. J. TRIAL ADVOC. 381–409 (1986)

Hughes, James W. & Edward A. Snyder: *Litigation and Settlement under the English and American Rules: Theory and Evidence*, 38 JOURNAL OF LAW AND ECONOMICS 225–250 (1995)

Hurst, Peter: *Civil Procedure: Costs including conditional fees in England and Wales*, 10 ZZPINT 39–52 (2005)

IMF: *Guidelines on Conditionality*, September 25, 2002, <http://www.imf.org/External/np/pdr/cond/2002/eng/guid/092302.pdf> (last visited July 17, 2006)

—: *Policy Statement on IMF Technical Assistance*, April 1, 2001, <http://www.imf.org/external/pubs/ft/psta/index.htm> (last visited July 17, 2006)

Jackson, John D.: *Playing the Culture Card in Resisting Cross-Jurisdictional Transplants: A Comment on "Legal Processes and National Culture"*, 5 CARDOZO J. INT'L & COMP. L. 51–67 (1997)

Jahan, Selim: *Measuring Human Development: Evolution of the Human Development Index*, Confidential Draft, 7, 15, <http://www.undp.org.in/hdrc/APRI/Event/Colombo/resources/bgppr/Measuring%20HD-Evolution%20of%20HDI%20.pdf> (last visited July 17, 2006)

Jankowski, Janusz: *Die wesentlichen Grundsätze des Zivilverfahrens nach 40 Jahren der Geltung der polnischen Zivilprozessordnung*, 10 ZZPINT 227–241 (2005)

Jolowicz, J.A.: *Introduction. Recourse against civil judgments in the European Union: a comparative survey*, *in* RECOURSE AGAINST JUDGMENTS IN THE EUROPEAN UNION 1–23 (J.A. Jolowicz & C.H. van Rhee, eds., The Hague 1999)

—: ON CIVIL PROCEDURE, Cambridge 2000

—: *Adversarial and Inquisitorial Models of Civil Procedure*, 52 ICLQ 281–295 (2003)

Jones, Harry Leroy: *International Judicial Assistance: Procedural Chaos and a Program for Reform*, 62 YALE L.J. 515–562 (1953)

Jordan, Cally: *The Conundrum of Corporate Governance*, 30 BROOK. J. INT'L L. 983–1027 (2005)

KAGAN, ROBERT A.: ADVERSARIAL LEGALISM: THE AMERICAN WAY OF LAW, Cambridge, Mass. 2001

KASER, MAX & HACKL, KARL: DAS RÖMISCHE ZIVILPROZESSRECHT, 2nd ed., Munich 1996

Kengyel, Miklós: *Veränderungen des Inhalts der Dispositions- und Verhandlungsmaxime im ungarischen Zivilprozeßrecht*, 2 ZZPINT 273–285 (1997)

—: *Die Zukunft des ungarischen Zivilprozeßrechts nach der Zivilverfahrens-Novelle 1999*, 5 ZZPINT 361–374 (2000)

—: *Die Entstehungsgeschichte der fünfzigjährigen ungarischen Zivilprozessordnung*, *in* 1 FESTSCHRIFT FÜR KOSTAS E. BEYS ZUM 70. GEBURTSTAG 705–720 (Hideo Nakamura, Hans W. Fasching, Hans Friedhelm Gaul & Apostolos Georgiades, eds., Athens 2003)

Kerameus, Konstantinos D.: *A Civilian Lawyer Looks at Common Law Procedure*, 47 LA. L. REV. 493–509 (1987)

—: *Relevance and Computation of Time in Civil Procedure*, *in* FESTSCHRIFT FÜR FRANZ MATSCHER ZUM ZUM 65. GEBURTSTAG 241–250 (Oskar J. Ballon & Johann J. Hagen, eds., Vienna 1993)

—: *Greece*, *in* CIVIL JUSTICE IN THE COUNTRIES OF THE EUROPEAN UNION (Elio Fazzalari & Pierre Fortin, eds., Padova 1998)

KISSEL, OTTO RUDOLF & HERBERT MAYER: GVG, 4th ed., Munich 2005

Klamaris, Nikolaos K.: *Das griechische Gesetzbuch über das Civil-Verfahren (1834) und die griechische Gerichts- und Notariatsordnung (1834)*, *in* GERICHTS- UND NOTARIATSORDNUNG UND GESETZBUCH ÜBER DAS CIVIL-VERFAHREN 1834, reprint of the original edition IX–XVI (Athens 2001)

KOCH, HARALD & FRANK DIEDRICH: CIVIL PROCEDURE IN GERMANY, Munich 1998

Koch, Harald: *Neuordnung der Rechtsfamilien im Prozeßrecht. Die Lehre von den Rechtskreisen (Rechtsfamilien) und das deutsche Zivilprozessrecht – Legal families in procedural law revisited –*, *in* TRANSNATIONALES PROZESSRECHT – TRANSNATIONAL ASPECTS OF PROCEDURAL LAW, GERMAN REPORTS FOR THE WORLD CONFERENCE ON PROCEDURAL LAW IN TAORMINA, SICILY, 1995, 119 (Peter Gilles, ed., Baden-Baden 1996)

—: *Konvergenz der Rechte im Europäischen Zivilprozeß*, *in* 1 FESTSCHRIFT FÜR KOSTAS E. BEYS ZUM 70. GEBURTSTAG 733–753 (Hideo Nakamura, Hans W. Fasching, Hans Friedhelm Gaul & Apostolos Georgiades, eds., 2003)

KOHLER, MARIUS: DIE ENTWICKLUNG DES SCHWEDISCHEN ZIVILPROZESSRECHTS (2002)

Kojima, Takeshi: *Legal Families in Procedural Law Revisited*, *in* TRANS-NATIONAL ASPECTS OF PROCEDURAL LAW 1093 (Int'l Ass'n of Procedural Law, ed., Milano 1998)

—: *Japanese Civil Procedure in Comparative Law Perspective*, 46 U. KAN. L. REV. 687–726 (1998)

Kossick, Robert: *The Rule of Law and Development in Mexico*, 21 ARIZ. J. INT'L & COMP. L. 715–834 (2004)

Kritzer, Herbert M.: *American Adversarialism*, 38 LAW & SOC'Y REV. 349–383 (2004) (reviewing Robert A. Kagan, Adversarial Legalism: The American Way of Law (2001))

La Porta, Rafael, Florencio Lopez-de-Silanes & Andrei Shleifer: *What Works in Securities Laws?*, 61 THE JOURNAL OF FINANCE 1–31 (2006) (earlier draft *available at* <http://papers.nber.org/papers/w9882.pdf>; last visited July 17, 2006)

La Porta, Rafael, Florencio Lopez-de-Silanes, Andrei Shleifer & Robert Vishny: *The Quality of Government*, 15 J. OF LAW, ECONOMICS AND ORGANIZATION 222, 238 (1999)

—: *Legal Determinants of External Finance*, 52 THE JOURNAL OF FINANCE 1131–1150 (1997)

—: *Law and Finance*, 106 JOURNAL OF POLITICAL ECONOMY 1113–1155 (1998), first published as NBER Working Paper No. 5661 (1996), <http://papers.nber.org/papers/w5661.pdf> (last visited July 17, 2006)

Langbein, John H.: *Historical Foundations of the Law of Evidence: A View from the Ryder Sources*, 96 COLUM. L. REV. 1168, 1168 (1998)

—: *The Criminal Trial before the Lawyers*, 45 U. CHI. L. REV. 263–316 (1978)

—: *The German Advantage in Civil Procedure*, 52 U. CHI. L. REV. 823–866 (1985)

—: *Trashing the German Advantage*, 82 NW. U. L. REV. 763–783 (1988)

—: *The Influence of Comparative Procedure in the United States*, 43 AM. J. COMP. L. 545–554 (1993)

Laukkanen, Sakari: *Die Entwicklung des finnischen Zivilprozeßrechts und die Veränderung der Rolle des Richters*, 2 ZZPINT 227–247 (1997)

LAY, DONALD P.: LAW: A HUMAN PROCESS, St. Paul, Minn. 1996

LEIBLE, STEFAN: PROCESO CIVIL ALEMÁN, 2nd ed., Medellín 2000

Leipold, Dieter: *Prozeßförderungspflicht der Parteien und richterliche Verantwortung*, 93 ZZP 237–265 (1980)

Leubsdorf, John: *Toward a History of the American Rule on Attorney Fee Recovery*, 47 LAW & CONTEMP. PROBS. 9–36 (1984)

—: *The Myth of Civil Procedure Reform*, *in* CIVIL JUSTICE IN CRISIS 53–67 (Adrian A.S. Zuckerman, ed., Oxford 1999)

Leuenberger, Christoph: *Das ordentliche Verfahren*, *in* DIE KÜNFTIGE SCHWEIZERISCHE ZIVILPROZESSORDNUNG 51–71 (Thomas Sutter-Somm & Franz Hasenböhler, eds., Zurich 2003)

Lex Mundi: *Statement of Purpose*, <http://www.lexmundi.com/lexmundi/Statement_of_Purpose.asp?SnID=1281338160> (last visited July 17, 2006)

Licht, Amir N.: *Legal Plug-Ins: Cultural distance, Cross Listing, and Corporate Governance Reform*, 22 BERKELEY J. INT'L L. 195–239 (2004)

LINDELL, BENGT: CIVIL PROCEDURE IN SWEDEN, Uppsala 2004

Loeber, Dietrich A.: *Rechtsvergleichung zwischen Ländern mit verschiedener Wirtschaftsordnung*, 26 RABELS ZEITSCHRIFT FÜR AUSLÄNDISCHES UND INTERNATIONALES PRIVATRECHT [RABELSZ] 201–229 (1961)

Lubiński, Kazimierz: *Eigenheiten der Prozeßrechtsvergleichung*, *in* TRANS-NATIONAL ASPECTS OF PROCEDURAL LAW 1093 (Int'l Ass'n of Procedural Law, ed., Milano 1998)

Malavet, Pedro A.: *The Foreign Notarial Legal Services Monopoly: Why Should We Care?*, 31 J. MARSHALL L. REV. 945–970 (1998)

Maleshin, Dmitry Y.: *Some Cultural Characteristics of the New Russian Code of Civil Procedure of 2002*, 10 ZZPINT 385–389 (2005)

Martin, Raymond J. & Jacques M. Martin: *France*, *in* INTERNATIONAL ENCYCLOPAEDIA OF LAWS – CIVIL PROCEDURE (Roger Blanpain, gen. ed., Piet Taelman, ed., loose-leaf, 1994 version, The Hague 1994)

Mashaw, Jerry L.: *Administrative Due Process: The Quest for a Dignitary Theory*, 61 B.U. L. REV. 885–931 (1981)

Mattei, Ugo: *Three Patterns of Law: Taxonomy and Change in the World's Legal Systems*, 45 AM. J. COMP. L. 5–44 (1997)

McCabe, Neil C.: *Four Faces of State Constitutional Separation of Powers: Challenges to Speedy Trial and Speedy Dispositoin Provisions*, 62 TEMP. L. REV. 177–219 (1989)

McClintick, David: *How Harvard Lost Russia*, InstitutionalInvestor.com, January 13, 2006, <http://www.institutionalinvestor.com/default.asp?page=1&ISS=21210&SID=606917&PUB=24> (last visited April 7, 2006)

Michelsen, Hans M.: *Norwegen und das deutsche Zivilprozeßrecht*, *in* DAS DEUTSCHE ZIVILPROZESSRECHT UND SEINE AUSSTRAHLUNG AUF ANDERE RECHTSORDNUNGEN 241–245 (Walther J. Habscheid, ed., Bielefeld 1991)

Mikelėnas, Valentinas: *Reform of Civil Procedural Law in the Republic Lithuanina during 1990–1996*, 2 ZZPINT 249–258 (1997)

Möller, Gustaf: *Finnland und das deutsche Zivilprozessrecht*, *in* DAS DEUTSCHE ZIVILPROZESSRECHT UND SEINE AUSSTRAHLUNG AUF ANDERE RECHTSORDNUNGEN 246–253 (Walther J. Habscheid, ed., Bielefeld 1991)

Münch, Joachim: *Die "neue" ZPO: bedeutende Änderungen im zivilgerichtlichen Verfahrensrecht (Teil I)*, 40 DEUTSCHES STEUERRECHT (DSTR) 85–95 (2002)

Murray, Peter L. & John C. Sheldon: *Should the Rules of Evidence Be Modified for Civil Non-Jury Trials?*, 17 ME. B.J. 30–36 (2002)

MURRAY, PETER L. & ROLF STÜRNER: GERMAN CIVIL JUSTICE, Durham, N.C. 2004

Murray, Peter L.: *A Comparative Law Experiment*, 8 IND. INT'L & COMP. L. REV. 231–259 (1998)

—: *A morning at the German* Amtsgericht*: German Civil Justice in Practice*, *in* LAW AND JUSTICE IN A MULTISTATE WORLD, ESSAYS IN HONOR OF ARTHUR T. VON MEHREN 779–792 (James A.R. Nafziger & Symeon C. Symeonides, eds., 2002)

—: *The American Legal System in the Global Legal Order: The Influence of American Law and Legal Institutions in the Modern World*, 9 ZZPINT 245–265 (2004)

—: *Taking Evidence Abroad – Understanding American Exceptionalism*, 10 ZZPINT 343–357 (2005)

Németh, János: *Das deutsche Zivilprozeßrecht und seine Ausstrahlung auf die Rechtsordnungen der osteuropäischen Länder*, *in* DAS DEUTSCHE ZIVILPROZESSRECHT UND SEINE AUSSTRAHLUNG AUF ANDERE RECHTSORDNUNGEN 254–281 (Walther J. Habscheid, ed., Bielefeld 1991)

Nakamura, Hideo: *Der Einfluss des amerikanischen Rechts auf den japanischen Zivilprozess und seine Begrenzung*, *in* 2 FESTSCHRIFT FÜR KOSTAS E. BEYS ZUM 70. GEBURTSTAG 1105–1124 (Hideo Nakamura, Hans W. Fasching, Hans Friedhelm Gaul & Apostolos Georgiades, eds., Athens 2003)

Nekrošius, Vyautas: *Grundlagen der neuen litauischen ZPO (das Erkenntnisverfahren)*, 7 ZZPINT 409–427 (2002)

Nelson, Dorothy Wright: *ADR in the Federal Courts – One Judge's Perspective: Issues and Challenges Facing Judges, Lawyers, Court Administrators, and the Public*, 17 OHIO ST. J. ON DISP. RESOL. 1–17 (2001)

Nobbe, Gerd: *Scheckverkehr, in* BANKRECHTS-HANDBUCH (Herbert Schimansky, Hermann-Josef Bunte & Hans-Jürgen Lwowski, eds., 2nd ed., Munich 2001

PICARDI, NICOLA ET AL.: IL PROCESSO CIVILE CINESE (Nicola Picardi & Allesandro Giuliani, eds.) Rimini 1998

PLATTO, CHARLES (ED.): CIVIL APPEAL PROCEDURES WORLDWIDE, London 1992

POLLOCK, FREDERICK & FREDERIC WILLIAM MAITLAND: THE HISTORY OF ENGLISH LAW 2nd ed., Cambidge 1968

Posner, Daniel M.: *Measuring Ethnic Fractionalization in Africa*, 48 AMERICAN JOURNAL OF POLITICAL SCIENCE 849–863 (2004)

Posner, Richard A.: *A Theory of Negligence*, 1 JOURNAL OF LEGAL STUDIES 29–96 (1972)

Pringsheim, Fritz: *The Inner Relationship between English and Roman Law*, 5 CAMBRIDGE L.J. 347–365 (1935)

PRS Group: About ICRG, <http://www.icrgonline.com/page.aspx?page=icrgmethods> (last visited July 17, 2006)

—: International Country Risk Guide, <http://www.prsgroup.com/icrg/icrg.html> (last visited July 17, 2006)

Prütting, Hanns: *Ein neues Kapitel im Justizkonflikt USA – Deutschland, in* 1 FESTSCHRIFT FÜR ERIK JAYME 709–718 (Heinz-Peter Mansel, Thomas Pfeiffer, Herbert Kronke, Christian Kohler & Rainer Hausmann, eds., Munich 2003)

Rajan, Raghuram G. & Luigi Zingales: *The Great Reversals: The Politics of Financial Development in the 20th Century*, NBER Working Paper No. 8178 (2002), <http://papers.nber.org/papers/w8178.pdf> (last visited July 17, 2006)

Rammos, A.: *Der Gang des Erkenntnisverfahrens nach dem Entwurf der neuen griechischen ZPO*, 78 ZEITSCHRIFT FÜR ZIVILPROZESS [ZZP] 241–264 (1965)

RECHBERGER, WALTER H. & DAPHNE-ARIANE SIMOTTA: ZIVILPROZESSRECHT. ERKENNTNISVERFAHREN, 6th ed., Vienna 2003

Reitz, John C.: *Grundlegende Unterschiede zwischen dem deutschen und dem U.S.-amerikanischen Zivilprozeßrecht: Vorzüge, die sich ausschließen?*, 104 ZZP 381–396 (1991)

Resnik, Judith: *Managerial Judges*, 96 HARV. L. REV. 374–448 (1982)

RHEINSTEIN, MAX: EINFÜHRUNG IN DIE RECHTSVERGLEICHUNG (Reimer von Borries, ed.), 2nd ed., Munich 1987

RÖHL, KLAUS F. & MATTHIAS WEIß: DIE OBLIGATORISCHE STREITSCHLICHTUNG IN DER PRAXIS, Münster 2005

ROSENBERG, LEO: LEHRBUCH DES DEUTSCHEN ZIVILPROZESSRECHTS, 2nd ed., Berlin 1929

Roth, Herbert: *Grundfreiheiten des EG-Vertrages und nationales Zivilprozeßrecht, in* RECHT UND RECHTSWISSENSCHAFT 351–370 (Peter-Christian Müller-Graff & Herbert Roth, eds., Heidelberg 2000)

Sawczuk, Mieczysław: *Das deutsche und das polnische Zivilprozeßrecht in der Zeit von der ersten polnischen ZPO bis zur Gegenwart, in* DAS DEUTSCHE ZIVILPROZESSRECHT UND SEINE AUSSTRAHLUNG AUF ANDERE RECHTSORDNUNGEN 282–292 (Walther J. Habscheid, ed., 1991)

SCHACK, HAIMO: EINFÜHRUNG IN DAS US-AMERIKANISCHE ZIVILPROZESSRECHT, 3rd ed., Munich 2003

—: *Wechselwirkungen zwischen europäischem und nationalem Zivilprozessrecht*, 107 ZZP 279–300 (1994)

Schafer, Burkhard & Olav K. Wiegand: *Incompetent, Prejudiced and Lawless? A Gestalt-Psychological Perspective on Fact Finding in Law as Learning*, 3 LAW, PROBABILITY AND RISK 93–108 (2004)

SCHLESINGER, RUDOLPH B., HANS W. BAADE, PETER E. HERZOG: COMPARATIVE LAW, 6th ed., New York 1998

SCHLOSSER, PETER: DER JUSTIZKONFLIKT ZWISCHEN DEN USA UND EUROPA, Berlin 1985

SCHULZ, FRITZ: CLASSICAL ROMAN LAW, Oxford 1951

Schütze, Rolf A.: *Conceptual Differences and Areas of Potential Collision between United States and "Civil Law" Procedure from the German Perspective, in* LITIGATION OF BUSINESS MATTERS IN THE UNITED STATES AND INTERNATIONAL LEGAL ASSISTANCE 21–41 (Roger Zäch, ed., Bern 1984)

—: *Zum Stand des deutsch-amerikanischen Justizkonfliktes*, 50 Recht der Internationalen Wirtschaft [RIW] 162–167 (2004)

Scott, Robert E. & Paul B. Stephan: *Self-Enforcing International Agreements and the Limits of Coercion*, 2004 WISCONSIN L. REV. 551–629

SHAPIRO, MARTIN: COURTS: A COMPARATIVE AND POLITICAL ANALYSIS, Chicago 1981

—: *The Logic of the Triad*, *in* THE STRUCTURE OF PROCEDURE 284–290 (Robert M. Cover & Owen M. Fiss, eds., Mineola N.Y. 1979)

SHAVELL, STEVEN: FOUNDATIONS OF ECONOMIC ANALYSIS OF LAW, Cambridge, Mass. 2004

Siems, Mathias M.: *Legal Origins – Reconciling Law & Finance and Comparative Law*, Heinrich-Heine-University Düsseldorf Center for Business and Corporate Law Research Center Paper Series no. 0023 (01/2006), *available at* <http://papers.ssrn.com/sol3/papers.cfm?abstract_id=879720> (last visited July 17, 2006)

—: *Numerical Comparative Law: Do We Need Statistical Evidence in Law in Order to Reduce Complexity?*, 13 CARDOZO J. INT'L & COMP. L. 521–540 (2005)

Smith, Eva: *Dänemark und das deutsche Zivilprozessrecht*, *in* DAS DEUTSCHE ZIVILPROZESSRECHT UND SEINE AUSSTRAHLUNG AUF ANDERE RECHTSORDNUNGEN 219–229 (Walther J. Habscheid, ed., Bielefeld 1991)

Snyder, Edward A. & James W. Hughes: *The English Rule for Allocating Costs: Evidence Confronts Theory*, 6 JOURNAL OF LAW, ECONOMICS & ORGANIZATION 345–380 (1990)

Spamann, Holger: *On the Insignificance and/or Endogeneity of La Porta et al.'s 'Anti-Director Rights Index' under Consistent Coding*, HLS John M. Olin Center for Law, Economics, and Business Discussion Paper No. 7, 3/2006, *available at* <http://papers.ssrn.com/sol3/papers.cfm?abstract_id=894301> (last visited July 17, 2006)

Stadler, Astrid: *The Multiple Roles of Judges and Attorneys in Modern Civil Litigation*, 27 HASTINGS INT'L & COMP. L. REV. 55–76 (2003)

STAEHELIN, ADRIAN & THOMAS SUTTER: ZIVILPROZESSRECHT, Zurich 1992

Stefánsson, Stefán Már: *Überblick über das isländische Zivilprozessrecht unter dem Aspekt des deutschen Zivilprozessrechts und deutscher Rechtsvorstellungen*, *in* DAS DEUTSCHE ZIVILPROZESSRECHT UND SEINE AUSSTRAHLUNG AUF ANDERE RECHTSORDNUNGEN 230–240 (Walther J. Habscheid, ed., Bielefeld 1991)

Stürner, Rolf & Astrid Stadler: *Eigenarten der Prozeßrechtsvergleichung – Special features of comparative procedural law –*, *in* TRANSNATIONALES PROZESSRECHT – TRANSNATIONAL ASPECTS OF PROCEDURAL LAW, GERMAN REPORTS FOR THE WORLD CONFERENCE ON PROCEDURAL LAW IN TAORMINA, SICILY, 1995, 263–292 (Peter Gilles, ed., Baden-Baden 1996)

Stürner, Rolf: *U.S.-amerikanisches und europäisches Verfahrensverständnis*, *in* FESTSCHRIFT FÜR ERNST C. STIEFEL ZUM 80. GEBURTSTAG 763–784 (Marcus Lutter, ed., Munich 1987)

—: *Gründe und Ursachen des Problems der Ineffizienz von Verfahren – ein historischer Überblick, German National Report for the VIIIth World Conference on Procedural Law in Utrecht 1987*, *in* EFFIZIENTE RECHTSVERFOLGUNG/EFFICIENCY IN THE PURSUIT OF JUSTICE 1–31 (Peter Gilles, ed., Heidelberg 1987)

—: *Das deutsche Zivilprozeßrecht und seine Ausstrahlung auf andere Rechtsordnungen – von Deutschland aus gesehen*, *in* DAS DEUTSCHE ZIVILPROZESSRECHT UND SEINE AUSSTRAHLUNG AUF ANDERE RECHTSORDNUNGEN 3–40 (Walther J. Habscheid, ed., Bielefeld 1991)

—: *Gegenstand und Formen der Rezeption im neueren Prozeßrecht*, *in* LAW IN EAST AND WEST 287–298 (Institute of Comparative Law, Waseda University, ed., Tokyo 1988)

—: *Der deutsche Prozeßrechtslehrer am Ende des 20. Jahrhunderts*, *in* FESTSCHRIFT FÜR GERHRAD LÜKE ZUM 70. GEBURTSTAG 829–844 (Hanns Prütting & Helmut Rüssmann, eds., Munich 1997)

—: *Some European Remarks on a New Joint Project of the American Law Institute and UNIDROIT*, 34 INT. LAW. 1071–1086 (2000)

—: *Discorvery and Sanctions Against Non-Compliance*, VI UNIF. L. REV. NS 871–886 (2001-4)

—: *Die Partei als Beweismittel im europäischen Zivilprozeß*, *in* FESTSCHRIFT FÜR AKIRA ISHIKAWA ZUM 70. GEBURTSTAG 529–539 (Gerhard Lüke, Takehiko Mikami & Hanns Prütting, eds., Berlin & New York 2001)

—: *Why Are Europeans Afraid to Litigate in the United States*? 45 REVIEW OF THE CENTRO DI STUDI E RICERCHE DI DIRITTO COMPARATO E STRANIERO 1–23 (2001), *available at* <http://w3.uniroma1.it/idc/centro/publications/45sturner.pdf> (last visited July 17, 2006)

—: *Schlussbetrachtung und Ausblick*, *in* 41 JAHRBUCH BITBURGER GESPRÄCHE 143–150 (2003)

—: *Parteidisposition über Tatsachen und Beweismittel im Prozess ausgewählter europäischer Staaten*, *in* RECHT UND RISIKO. FESTSCHRIFT FÜR HELMUT KOLLHOSSER ZUM 70. GEBURTSTAG 727–740 (Reinhard Bork, Thomas Hoeren & Petra Pohlmann, eds., Karlsruhe 2004)

—: *Procedural Law and Legal Cultures*, *in* PROZESSRECHT UND RECHTSKULTUREN/ PROCEDURAL LAW AND LEGAL CULTURES 9–52 (Peter Gilles & Thomas Pfeiffer, eds., Baden-Baden 2004)

—: *The Principles of Transnational Civil Procedure. An Introduction to Their Basic Conceptions*, 69 RABELSZ 201–254, 341–350 (2005)

—: *Quelques remarques sur l'image actuelle de la procédure allemande et sa relation avec la procédure française et les tendances internationales*, *in* DE LA COMMÉMORATION D'UN CODE À L'AUTRE: 200 ANS DE PROCÉDURE CIVILE EN FRANCE 329–337 (Loïc Cadiet & Guy Canivet, eds., Paris 2006)

Subrin, Stephen N.: *David Dudley Field and the Field Code: A Historical Analysis of an Earlier Procedural Vision*, 6 LAW & HIST. REV. 311–373 (1988)

—: *Discovery in Global Perspective: Are We Nuts?*, 52 DEPAUL L. REV. 299–318 (2002)

Summers, Robert S.: *Evaluating and Improving Legal Processes: A Plea for "Process Values"*, 60 CORNELL L. REV. 1–52 (1974)

Sutter-Somm, Thomas: *Schwerpunkte und Leitlinien des Vorentwurfs zur Schweizerischen Zivilprozessordnung*, *in* DIE KÜNFTIGE SCHWEIZERISCHE ZIVILPROZESSORDNUNG 11–23 (Thomas Sutter-Somm & Franz Hasenböhler, eds., Zurich 2003)

Taniguchi, Yasuhei: *The 1996 Code of Civil Procedure of Japan – A Procedure for the Coming Century?*, 45 AM. J. COMP. L. 767–791 (1997)

Taruffo, Michele: *Legal Cultures and Models of Civil Justice*, *in* FESTSCHRIFT FÜR HIDEO NAKAMURA ZUM 70. GEBURTSTAG 621–637 (Tokyo 1996)

Transparency International: Annual Report 2001, <http://www.transparency.org/content/download/2282/14290/file/TI%20Annual%20Report%202001.pdf> (last visited July 17, 2006)

—: Corruption Perceptions Index 2001, <http://www.transparency.org/policy_and_research/surveys_indices/cpi/2001#source> (last visited July 17, 2006)

United Nations Development Programme (UNDP): Human Development Report 1994, New Dimensions of Human Security (1994), English version only without dataset *available at* <http://hdr.undp.org/reports/global/1994/en/>. French and Spanish version fully *available at* <http://hdr.undp.org/reports/global/1994/fr/hdr_fr_1994.pdf>

and <http://hdr.undp.org/reports/global/1994/sp/hdr_sp_1994.pdf> (last visited July 17, 2006)

Vagts, Detlev: *Comparative Company Law – The New Wave*, *in* FESTSCHRIFT FÜR JEAN NICOLAS DRUEY 595–605 (Rainer J. Schweizer, Herbert Burkert & Urs Grasser, eds., Zurich 2002)

Varano, Vincenzo: *Civil Procedure Reform in Italy*, 45 AM. J. COMP. L. 657–674 (1997)

VOLLKOMMER, MAX: FORMENSTRENGE UND PROZESSUALE BILLIGKEIT, Munich 1973

VON JHERING, RUDOLF: GEIST DES RÖMISCHEN RECHTS AUF DEN VERSCHIEDENEN STUFEN SEINER ENTWICKLUNG Vol. 2/2, 5th ed., Leipzig 1898

WACH, ADOLF: VORTRÄGE ÜBER DIE REICHS-CIVILPROCESSORDNUNG, 2nd ed., Bonn 1896

Wahi, Namita: *Human Rights Accountability of the IMF and the World Bank: A Critique of Existing Mechanisms and Articulation of a Theory of Horizontal Accountability*, 12 U.C. DAVIS J. INT'L L. & POL'Y 331–407 (2006)

Warshawsky, Laura Margolis: *Objectivity and Accountability: Limits on Judicial Involvement in Settlement*, 1987 U. CHI. LEGAL F. 369–387

World Bank: The BEEPS II Interactive Dataset: Enterprise Survey in Transition, <http://info.worldbank.org/governance/beeps2002/> (last visited July 17, 2006)

—: The BEEPS Interactive Dataset, <http://info.worldbank.org/governance/beeps/> (last visited July 17, 2006)

—: World Business Environment Survey (WBES) 2000 Webtool Interactive, <http://info.worldbank.org/governance/wbes/> (last visited July 17, 2006)

—: World Business Environment Survey, "Measuring Conditions for Business Operation and Growth, Private Enterprise Questionnaire, <http://www.ifc.org/ifcext/economics.nsf/AttachmentsByTitle/IC-WBESCoreQuestionnaire/$FILE/wbescore1.pdf> (last visited July 17, 2006)

—: World Development Indicators 2001, Washington, D.C. 2001

—: *OP 8.60 – Development Policy Lending*, THE WORLD BANK OPERATIONAL MANUAL, August 2004, <http://web.worldbank.org/WBSITE/EXTERNAL/PROJECTS/EXTPOLICIES/EXTOPMANUAL/0,,contentMDK:20240031~pagePK:64141683~piPK:64141620~theSitePK:502184,00.html> (last visited July 17, 2006)

—: *Judicial Independence: What It Is, How It Can Be Measured, Why It Occurs*, <http://www1.worldbank.org/publicsector/legal/judicialindependence.htm> (last visited November 27, 2006)

Yarkov, Vladimir: *Contemporary Problems of Russian Civil Procedure*, 10 ZZPINT 371–383 (2005)

Zimbalist, Andrew: *The State of the Art of Comparative Economics*, 31 COMPARATIVE ECONOMIC STUDIES 6–15 (1989)

Zimmerman, Tina Drake: *Representation in ADR and Access To Justice for Legal Services Clients*, 10 GEO. J. ON POVERTY L. & POL'Y 181–203 (2003)

Zuckerman, Adrian A.S.: *Justice in Crisis: Comparative Dimensions of Civil Procedure*, *in* CIVIL JUSTICE IN CRISIS 3–52 (Adrian A.S. Zuckerman, ed., Oxford 1999)

ZWEIGERT, KONRAD & HEIN KÖTZ: INTRODUCTION TO COMPARATIVE LAW (Tony Weir, trans.), 2nd ed., Oxford 1992

ZWEIGERT, KONRAD & HEIN KÖTZ: INTRODUCTION TO COMPARATIVE LAW (Tony Weir, trans.), 3rd ed., Oxford 1998

Index

Veröffentlichungen zum Verfahrensrecht

Herausgegeben von Rolf Stürner und Gerhard Walter

Alphabetische Übersicht

Atteslander-Dürrenmatt, Agnes H.: Der Prozessvergleich im internationalen Verhältnis. 2006. *Band 41.*

Baumgärtner, Samuel P.: The Proposed Hague Convention on Jurisdiction and Foreign Judgments. 2003. *Band 32.*

Bender, Hans-Udo: Merkmalskombinationen in Aussagen. 1987. *Band 2.*

Bertele, Joachim: Souveränität und Verfahrensrecht. 1998. *Band 20.*

Bohnert, Joachim: Ordnungswidrigkeiten und Jugendrecht. 1989. *Band 4.*

Bosch, Wolfgang: Rechtskraft und Rechtshängigkeit im Schiedsverfahren. 1991. *Band 5.*

Brenner, Harald: Die strafprozessuale Überwachung des Fernmeldeverkehrs mit Verteidigern. 1994. *Band 11.*

Breyer, Michael: Kostenorientierte Steuerung des Zivilprozesses. 2006. *Band 42.*

Bruns, Alexander: Informationsansprüche gegen Medien. 1997. *Band 16.*

Gärditz, Klaus: Strafprozeß und Prävention. 2003. *Band 31.*

Görtz-Leible, Monika: Die Beschlagnahmeverbote des § 97 Abs. 1 StPO im Lichte der Zeugnisverweigerungsrechte. 2000. *Band 24.*

Hager, Guenter: Konflikt und Konsens. 2001. *Band 26.*

Hauck, Gerswith: 'Schiedshängigkeit' und Verjährungsunterbrechung nach § 220 BGB. 1996. *Band 15.*

Jacoby, Florian: Der Musterprozeßvertrag. 2000. *Band 22.*

Kern, Christoph: Justice between Simplification and Formalism. 2007. *Band 45.*

Kleinheisterkamp, Thomas: Prozessführung über gepfändete Geldforderungen. 2001. *Band 25.*

Koch, Birgit: Rechtsschutz durch Gegendarstellung in Frankreich und Deutschland. 1995. *Band 13.*

Kofmel Ehrenzeller, Sabine: Der vorläufige Rechtsschutz im internationalen Verhältnis. 2005. *Band 39.*

Kohler, Marius: Die Entwicklung des schwedischen Zivilprozeßrechts. 2002. *Band 29.*

Koshiyama, Kazuhiro: Rechtskraftwirkungen und Urteilsanerkennung nach amerikanischem, deutschem und japanischem Recht. 1996. *Band 14.*

Krause, Rainer: Urteilswirkung gegenüber Dritten im US-amerikanischen Zivilprozeßrecht. 1994. *Band 10.*

Kwaschik, Annett: Die Parteivernehmung und der Grundsatz der Waffengleichheit im Zivilprozeß. 2004. *Band 35.*

Lames, Peter: Rechtsfortbildung als Prozeßzweck. 1993. *Band 9.*
Lüke, Wolfgang: Die Beteiligung Dritter im Zivilprozeß. 1993. *Band 8.*
Marotzke, Wolfgang: Von der schutzgesetzlichen Unterlassungsklage zur Verbandsklage. 1992. *Band 6.*
McGuire, Mary-Rose: Verfahrenskoordination und Verjährungsunterbrechung im Europäischen Prozessrecht. 2004. *Band 34.*
Miras, Antonio: Die Entwicklung des spanischen Zivilprozeßrechts. 1994. *Band 12.*
Mossler, Sven F. : Beschleunigter Rechtsschutz für Zahlungsgläubiger in Europa. 2004. *Band 38.*
Müller, Henning Ernst: Behördliche Geheimhaltung und Entlastungsvorbringen des Angeklagten. 1992. *Band 7.*
Oepen, Klaus: Massefremde Masse. 1999. *Band 21.*
Otte, Karsten: Umfassende Streitentscheidung durch Beachtung von Sachzusammenhängen. 1998. *Band 19.*
Reichenbach, Sandy B.: § 1004 BGB als Grundlage von Beweisverboten. 2004. *Band 37.*
Reischl, Klaus: Die objektiven Grenzen der Rechtskraft im Zivilprozeß. 2002. *Band 28.*
Riepl, Frank: Informationelle Selbstbestimmung im Strafverfahren. 1998. *Band 17.*
Rink, Florian: Die Sicherheit von Grundpfandrechten in Deutschland und England. 2006. *Band 43.*
Rott, Thilo: Vereinheitlichung des Rechts der Mobiliarsicherheit. 2000. *Band 23.*
Schafft, Thomas: Selektion von Rechtsmittelverfahren durch gesetzliche Zugangsbeschränkungen. 2005. *Band 40.*
Scheuermann, Isabel: Internationales Zivilverfahrensrecht bei Verträgen im Internet. 2004. *Band 36.*
Schnabl, Daniel: Die Anhörungsrüge nach § 321a ZPO. 2007. *Band 44.*
Stadler, Astrid: Der Schutz des Unternehmensgeheimnisses im deutschen und U.S.-amerikanischen Zivilprozeß und im Rechtshilfeverfahren. 1989. *Band 3.*
Städtler, Hans Jörg: Grundpfandrechte in der Insolvenz. 1998. *Band 18.*
Stürner, Rolf: Die richterliche Aufklärung im Zivilprozeß. 1982. *Band 1.*
Timmerbeil, Sven: Witness Coaching und Adversary System. 2004. *Band 33.*
Toepel, Friedrich: Grundstrukturen des Sachverständigenbeweises im Strafprozeßrecht. 2002. *Band 27.*
Ziegert, Kathrin: Die Interventionswirkung. 2003. *Band 30.*